Y0-EHY-215

Volume 33

ADVANCES IN LIBRARIANSHIP

Advances in
Librarianship

Volume 33

ADVANCES IN LIBRARIANSHIP

Advances in
Librarianship

Edited by
Anne Woodsworth

New York, USA

Emerald

United Kingdom • North America • Japan
India • Malaysia • China

Emerald Group Publishing Limited
Howard House, Wagon Lane, Bingley BD16 1WA, UK

First edition 2011

British Library Cataloguing in Publication Data
A catalogue record for this book is available from the British Library

ISBN: 978-0-85724-755-1
ISSN: 0065-2830

Emerald Group Publishing
Limited, Howard House,
Environmental Management
System has been certified by
ISOQAR to ISO 14001:2004
standards

Awarded in recognition of
Emerald's production
department's adherence to
quality systems and processes
when preparing scholarly
journals for print

INVESTOR IN PEOPLE

Contents

Trends, Issues, and Lessons Learned

Contributors

Numbers in parentheses indicate the pages on which the author's contributions begin.

Jonathan Warwick (3), Faculty of Business, London South Bank University, London, UK

Petros A. Kostagiolas (31), Department of Archive and Library Science, Ionian University, Corfu, Greece

Stefanos Asonitis (31), Department of Archive and Library Science, Ionian University, Corfu, Greece

Maureen L. Mackenzie (51), Townsend School of Business, Dowling College, Oakdale, NY, USA

James P. Smith (51), Library, St. Francis College, Brooklyn, NY, USA

Elisabeth Newbold (75), San Diego County Library, San Diego, CA, USA

Mary Carroll (105), Faculty of Workforce Development, Victoria University, Melbourne, Australia

Suzana Sukovic (131), School of Philosophical and Historical Inquiry, Faculty of Arts, University of Sydney, Australia

Preface

The first half of this volume is on the theme of library operations and management. The second half covers three different topics which point toward trends and implications for libraries, education, and the use of electronic texts by humanities researchers.

The first chapter is by Professor Jonathan Warwick in the Faculty of Business at London South Bank University, UK. He reviews the growth and decline of Operations Research (OR) in general and in academic libraries in particular. Since OR has been reevaluated and shifted its focus to modeling activities that involve problem structuring. It is argued that with this shift academic libraries should adopt the new OR paradigms in order to face the unprecedented changes and challenges they face. They need to manage both strategies and change and a new paradigm of library OR will enable this.

Flowing nicely from this is a chapter about managing intellectual capital in libraries, one of only a few such studies in the field. Petros A. Kostagiolas and Stefanos Asonitis are both with the Department of Archive and Library Science at Ionian University, in Corfu, Greece. A thorough literature review is followed by an analysis is undertaken that relates library management to intellectual capital. They provide extensive classification systems as well as economic valuation methods of intellectual capital. The chapter concludes with the effect of spatial factors and cooperation and competition upon intellectual capital utilization in libraries and information services.

Taking a more research-based approach to the library's intellectual capital, Associate Professor Maureen L. Mackenzie (Townsend School of Business at Dowling College, Oakdale, NY) and Library Director James P. Smith (St. Francis College, Brooklyn, NY) analyze the results of a survey of library directors to find out how they were prepared to assume roles as managers and directors. Their major findings were that half of the respondents indicated that their formal library and information science education had not prepared them for their roles. Half reported that they had taken advantages of other venues for developing leadership and management skills. Although the authors assert that there is a direct relationship between leadership skills and organization results, they stressed the need for further discussions by the field (both educators and practitioners) about both formal

LIS education programs and other professional development opportunities to "grow" the leaders and managers needed for libraries.

Fourth chapter provides one of only a handful of studies about Native American tribal libraries. Author Elisabeth Newbold took a handful of cases and analyzed their operations from the perspective of staffing, funding, technology, and administrative support over a year. With initial interviews in the spring of 2009, and follow up interviews a year later, she identified key factors for success: having a designated librarian; support from tribal governments; plans or a vision for the future; and last but not least, partnerships and connections with other libraries or organizations. In her conclusion she notes that these case studies can apply in any country with far flung and ethnically or culturally isolated libraries.

In Chapter five, Mary Carroll on the Faculty for Workforce Development at Victoria University in Melbourne Australia, provides historical analysis of the two streams of library education in Australia over 40 years. The two streams are (1) university-based degree programs, or higher education and (2) vocational education library technician programs. As she explains the nuances and tensions between the two it becomes clear that library technician educational preparation and its curricula are based on tasks done in the workplace and library technicians' places in a library's hierarchy. University degree programs on the other hand are based on theoretical and conceptual structures.

The last chapter is by Dr. Suzana Sukovic, a Research and Policy Officer at the University of Technology in Sydney, Australia and a Research Associate at the University of Sydney. She studied a part of the digital frontier that few have explored to date, namely the nature and extent of humanities scholars engagement with electronic texts. Her discoveries found a distinctive pattern of information seeking by humanities scholars which she dubbed *netchaining*. Not only did Sucovic identify how researchers in the humanities seek information but also how they organize it and store it in personal collections for subsequent use. Her seminal results will inform development of digital collections by individual scholars as well as etext collections in digital and traditional libraries. It will also help to shape information services and educational programs or training needs in environments where e-research is conducted.

Thanks are due to these authors for their promptness and responsiveness to editorial suggestions. Without their willing help, this volume would have been impossible to produce. Thanks are also due to members of the Editorial Advisory Board for their helpful feedback and review of submissions, namely Barbara A. Genco, Editor of Collection Management, *Library Journal*; New York, Tula Giannini, Dean of the School of Information and Library

Science, at Pratt Institute, Brooklyn, NY; Kenneth Haycock, Follett Chair in Library and Information Science at Dominican University, River Forest, IL; Maureen L. Mackenzie, Associate Professor of Management and Leadership at Dowling College, Oakdale, NY; Pat Molholt, Columbia University (Retired), New York; W. David Penniman, Executive Director of Nylink, Albany, NY; Marie L. Radford, Associate Professor, Rutgers University, Newark, NJ; and Robert A. Seal, Dean of Libraries at Loyola University Chicago, IL. Also much appreciated is the support and guidance provided by Diane Heath, Publisher, at the Emerald Group.

Anne Woodsworth
Editor

Library Operations and Management

Library Operational Research: Time for a New Paradigm?

Jonathan Warwick

Faculty of Business, London South Bank University, London, UK

Abstract

This chapter describes the growth and decline of Library Operational Research (Library OR) since the first descriptions of such activity appeared in the 1960s. The changing nature of OR and of the academic library is discussed and a case is made for recognition of a new paradigm in Library OR. First explored are the origins of OR and its application to academic libraries, summarizing some of the critical assessments of Library OR from those active in the field, and exploring some of the literature that relates to the development of OR itself, the academic library as an entity, and the modeler/library–practitioner interaction. Each indicates that a new way of working in Library OR is required if it is to deliver the results that OR has delivered in other contexts. The growth and decline of Library OR has been very marked. The decline has coincided with a reevaluation of the nature and contribution of OR itself, particularly in relation to modeling activities. New modeling approaches have evolved involving problem structuring, and these new paradigms extend naturally to Library OR and would help ease a number of concerns raised against the use of traditional OR models. Practical implications of this chapter are that academic libraries are facing an era of unprecedented change and some of the issues to be addressed relate to identifying and managing strategy and managing change. The adoption of new paradigms could enliven the practice and contribution of Library OR.

I. Introduction

As we move into the second decade of the 21st century, higher education (HE) in the United Kingdom is facing a period of unprecedented change as restrictions on the public finances seem set to demand greater efficiencies from HE institutions. At the same time, the quality of provision must be maintained and because students are expected to be contributing more and more to the financial cost of their education, the "student experience" is becoming more central to our ideas of educational quality.

ADVANCES IN LIBRARIANSHIP, VOL. 33
© 2011 by Emerald Group Publishing Limited
ISSN: 0065-2830
DOI: 10.1108/S0065-2830(2011)0000033004

The notion of the academic library is also going through a period of unprecedented change, not only because of the library's position as a fundamental part of any university but also because of the ongoing revolution in digital technology and the effects this has had on collections along with modes of learning activities adopted by students.

It might be thought that in such times Operational Research (OR) would become a central pillar of library management decision-making because OR has built a reputation as an analytical toolbox for optimizing the use of limited resources and has been highly successful when applied in a number of organizations and industries. However, the reality in the context of academic libraries (so-called Library OR) is somewhat different and although the emergence of Library OR saw a great deal of published work from the 1960s through to the 1980s, there has, since then, been a marked decline in such work so that Library OR now seems to feature quite rarely in the published literature.

This chapter explores some of the reasons behind this rise and fall and discusses how Library OR could be reconceptualized so as to realize some of the benefits to the academic library that OR has offered and continues to offer in other disciplines. We shall first consider the origins of OR and then explore some of the early work conducted in connection with academic libraries. Some criticisms of this early work are then offered as well as a description of the schism in OR that provoked the development of new OR paradigms. Finally, we conclude with a personal view as to how Library OR might offer, through these new paradigms, real value and support for those involved in the management of academic libraries.

II. The Origins of Operational Research

The UK OR Society defines OR as "the discipline of applying advanced analytical methods to help make better decisions." Furthermore, the society describes the problem context within which OR workers operate as "messy and complex, often entailing considerable uncertainty" and that their mode of working involves the use of "advanced quantitative methods, modelling, problem structuring, simulation and other analytical techniques to examine assumptions, facilitate an in-depth understanding and decide on practical action" (UK ORSOC, 2010). This definition encompasses the full range of activities that currently fall within the scope of OR and embraces problems that span the tactical, operational, and strategic dimensions of management and planning.

The original conceptualization of OR though was far more modest and with the discipline rooted in military projects undertaken just before, and during, World War II, the first use of the term Operational Research was in 1936 (Gass, 2002). The war itself provided an acid test for effectiveness of the mathematical methods being applied to military planning and there were some notable successes. For example, a key to the defensive successes of the Royal Air Force was the development of radar technology, and it has been estimated that while the advent of new technologies had improved the likelihood of enemy aircraft detection by a factor of 10, the work of OR workers, in developing the man-machine system, had further increased this by a factor of two (Kirby, 1999). Such operational successes certainly had a profound impact in establishing OR as an area of activity of importance, even though it was essentially conducted by civilian rather than military scientists. Other important areas of wartime application included the scheduling of aircraft maintenance and inspection and enhancing the effectiveness of aircraft attack strategies on enemy submarines (Beasley, n.d.).

In the immediate postwar years, restrictions on the availability of resources (manpower, time, and physical resources) meant that it became imperative that maximum benefit should be derived from these resources. The transition of OR from a military discipline to one that had applications to business and management within the United Kingdom was initially rather slow, with adoption of the modeling methods developed being primarily limited to two major industries—the coal industry and iron and steel. Kirby (1999) argues that the real golden age of OR began in the 1960s and was essentially the result of a "modernization" of British industry in which companies moved from being predominantly family owned and controlled to having US-style multidivisional structures importing science-based managerial approaches, again originating mainly from the United States. Serious UK government interest in OR only became apparent in the later 1960s with the election of a Labor government that was committed to further industrial modernization and economic planning.

Thus, interest in OR grew rapidly in both the public and the private sectors, and as organizations grew and international competition increased, OR practitioners could offer support to managers through new computer technologies and mathematical methods that offered a degree of detailed planning and control that earlier generations of managers could never have had.

With the UK OR Society (founded in 1953) providing a focus for the development and practice of OR, the education of new generations of OR specialists came to the fore in the mid-1960s with the creation of new universities and business and management schools. These were keen to embrace the new business approaches and methods already being offered by their

American counterparts and, therefore, university courses in OR and Management Science began to appear. The expansion of OR as an academic and professional discipline continued through the late 1960s and into the 1970s.

But what was the nature of this discipline that was emerging? At that time, it was certainly well rooted in scientific method and took as its core the development and analysis of mainly mathematical models with the intention of finding (in the majority of cases) optimal solutions to a range of business problems. This particular approach (we will call this the "traditional" paradigm of OR) constrained the type of problems that OR was capable of tackling. Rosenhead and Mingers (2001) provide an excellent discussion of the traditional OR paradigm and describe six characteristics that the paradigm exhibits:

1. Problem formulation in terms of a single objective and optimization. This simplification of the problem domain only allows for multiobjective decision-making if objectives can be traded against each other on a common scale so that the notion of a single best solution is still achievable;
2. Overwhelming data demands. Mathematical and statistical models are at their best in data-rich environments, but of course, this assumes that the data are both available and accurate;
3. Assumed consensus. This can be problematic as it is a view of organizational decision-making that ignores the influence of the individual's politics, prejudice, bias, judgment, and experience—in other words, the human aspects of organizational life;
4. People treated as passive objects. Reinforcing the previous characteristic, the traditional paradigm is one that focuses on logical processes and a scientific method and eschews human behavioral considerations as too complex to model;
5. An assumed single decision-maker and clear hierarchical organizational structure. Here we are assuming a certain organizational transparency and an ability to implement whichever "solution" is suggested by the modeling activity; and
6. The abolition of future uncertainty. Although many models will include aspects of risk with the inclusion of probability distributions and expected outcomes, genuine uncertainty about possible futures tends to be ignored with, instead, assumptions made that current trends are likely to continue into the future.

Having described the early development of OR methods and the characteristics of this traditional OR paradigm, it is now appropriate to consider how these early modeling developments contributed to the analysis of academic library systems during the early days of expansion in Library OR. For the purposes of this exposition, we shall consider as "early" those examples of Library OR that appeared in print during the first 25 years of activity, that is, from 1968 (when Phillip Morse published *Library Effectiveness*) up to about 1993. In only citing a few examples, the range of applications of OR to libraries is by no means fully represented, but any of the review articles cited in the following will give a much more complete picture.

III. Early Application of Operational Research to Libraries

When conducting even a brief review of the early published literature in Library OR, it is difficult to decide how to categorize the vast amount of such literature. A number of authors have undertaken such reviews including Slamecka (1972), Kantor (1979), Rowley and Rowley (1981), Kraft and Boyce (1991), and Reisman and Xu (1994). Each adopted a different scheme for organizing the literature. One of the common ways of classifying Library OR models is based on the technique adopted, for example, queuing theory, simulation, and inventory control theory. This method is appropriate perhaps to those who are familiar with the meaning of these terms, but it would mean little to others. Some authors have been dismissive of classification schemes based just on techniques (Rivett, 1980) as these only consider the end product of the modeling process and tell us little about, for example, the nature of the problem being solved. Others have used schemes that have more of a problem focus (Hamburg et al., 1974) and consider models relating to, say, space utilization, weeding, classification, and cataloguing, whereas others have grouped models according to the purpose of the research (Kantor, 1979), considering categories such as system description, modeling the system, and application.

In this section, just a few examples of Library OR work are considered, which illustrate a spectrum of model use with categories as suggested by Pidd (2010a). This scheme will be helpful in highlighting problems and issues relating to the early Library OR models. Pidd proposes a simple descriptor that relates (at the extremes) to the extent to which model use is expected to be regular and routine, as opposed to infrequent or "one-off." The scheme defines four archetypes:

1. Decision automation: These are models that may be used routinely and frequently with little requirement to set the model up for each use other than to enter appropriate data as the basis for the decision;

2. Routine decision support: These models assist (but do not replace) those who are making routine decisions so that the model provides some but not all of the input required for a decision to be made;

3. Investigation and improvement: These models are used on an irregular basis and their usage is tailored to system design, improvement or just exploring, and understanding the system better; and

4. Providing insights: These models are to help explore complex and messy problems that may have many stakeholders, viewpoints, interpretations, and so on.

This scheme was published in an attempt to categorize the variety of OR models used currently, not just in the library context but across all areas of application. It is useful to look back at the early modeling work in light of this categorization scheme. Therefore, our first task is to see the extent to which examples from the literature of early Library OR models fit each of the aforementioned categories.

A. Decision Automation

Modeling in this category represents attempts to try and find algorithms and automatic processes that will essentially replace human decision-making, insomuch as the decisions to be made are not usually complex or of fundamental importance. Thus, if the model produces a poor decision, then the consequences for the organization are not disastrous. Within the library context, it is difficult to find examples in this category because few OR models have found their way into such a day-to-day routine decision-making role. Thinking might be extended, however, to models that suggest operational rules-of-thumb that can generate such routine decisions. An example would be providing one copy of a title per x users or to weed out texts which have not circulated for y years. Some researchers have conducted work aimed at these types of analyses with one such example being that of Buckland (1975) in relation to loan and duplication policy. Buckland's work suggested a number of simple relationships between the loan period, duplication policy, book popularity, and satisfaction levels (as measured by the probability of finding a required book on the shelf). This resulted in the implementation of a variable loan and duplication policy so that both of these last two parameters could be related to book demand. Results of the study were implemented in the University of Lancaster library (United Kingdom) with the outcome of an increase in the satisfaction level measured some 6 months later. Changes in demand patterns for books, as library performance improved, were automatically accommodated by changes to loan policy and duplication levels.

Although decision automation has now become more commonplace as computers have become more and more prevalent (automatic credit scoring being a current example), in the early days of Library OR, examples of fully automated decision processes were rare. This is not surprising because it was the commonly held view around that time that no OR model (or indeed any computer-based system) should take the place of a manager's judgment in running a department or organization (De Gennaro, 1978). Thus, this category of model is sparsely populated.

B. Routine Decision Support

In this category, there might be models that provide us with some support for decision-making, and therefore, the decision-maker might explore relationships and better understand the interrelationships between various parameters as part of the decision-making process. An example here would be the work of Leimkuhler (Leimkuhler, 1966; Leimkuhler and Cooper, 1971), who was interested in explaining the long-term interactions between acquisition, circulation, storage, loan period, and duplication policy. The work of another early pioneer Trueswell (1965, 1966) developed the idea that within a collection, 80% of usage comes from about 20% of holdings, and he was able to identify the subset of a collection that would satisfy any given level of user requirement. Stochastic models of varying complexity have been developed by a number of researchers such as Goyal (1970) who explored the effect of the loan period on the waiting time for customers and the utilization of library staff. However, much pioneering work in the mathematical analysis of library systems was conducted in the 1960s by Morse (1968) who made extensive use of Markov and of queuing models to examine and predict the circulation rates of books. This was achieved by relating the average circulation of a book in any year, to the average circulation in previous years. Morse suggested a procedure for deciding when duplicate copies are necessary (perhaps an early candidate for decision automation?) based on circulation rates and also noted other dynamic characteristics such as doubling the number of copies will not double circulation. These models provide support and guidance for those seeking to make library decisions but do not recommend decisions automatically.

A further example here makes the analogy between the network of library operations and information flows and a system of queues. Specifically, one can undertake the analysis of customer or information flows around the various facilities that make up a library (or indeed study message and document transfers within library networks) by the application of queuing theory. The work of William Rouse is relevant here relating to, for example, the performance of library networks (Rouse, 1976), assessing the impact of technology on inter-library loan systems (Rouse and Rouse, 1977) and resource allocation within libraries (Smith and Rouse, 1979). In their 1980 paper, Rouse and Rouse commented that, in relation at least to the analysis of library networks, "we can perhaps conclude that those investigators working in the area of analysis of library networks have been successful in applying operations research methodologies to library problems" (p. 148).

Although there is far greater modeling activity that can be attributed to this category, it is still difficult to find examples of Library OR work that have been truly integrated with the routine decision-making frameworks of library practitioners. Much of the work reported in the literature is in the nature of stand-alone OR projects and one-time modeling investigations, and these belong within the next category.

C. Investigation and Improvement

Much of the Library OR work reported in the literature relates to the investigation and improvement of library systems and therefore belongs in this category. Perhaps, the best examples of models in this area are the simulation models that have been developed to explore system behavior and to experiment with changes to library policy and policy parameters. More than 40 years ago, Leimkuhler (1968) doubted the advisability of attempting purely analytic descriptions of complex systems involving random or semi-random processes and concluded that it might be better in such cases to develop a computer-based simulation model. Despite the fact that simulation is one of the most frequently used decision support techniques within the management science area, it remained (in the early days of Library OR) an underutilized approach to the modeling of library systems (Main, 1987). There are, however, examples of simulation use since 1970 and these have included applications by Baker and Nance (1970), Arms and Walter (1974), and Thomas and Wight (1976). These types of investigation allowed a rather more integrated view of library systems to be explored. Baker and Nance, for example, tried to relate library activities to user needs in terms of lending books, providing service personnel, and providing storage and study space. Circulation analysis was undertaken by Shaw (1976), but the most comprehensive simulation work in this area has probably been that of Buckland (1975) mentioned earlier.

D. Providing Insights

There is some overlap between this final category of modeling and the previous ones in that any model that helps to uncover new relationships, unexpected results, or enhance practitioner understanding can be thought of as providing insights. However, in this category are models that help with the exploration of complex, "wicked" problems, that is to say problems situated rather more at the strategic level of organizational management than at the operational level. This category takes a step back and considers the act of modeling itself as a process that adds value to decision-making activities, rather than the use of a final model or solution. Certainly there are examples of Library OR which have contributed to strategic decision–making, and Reisman and Xu (1994) provide a number of early examples of this. In these cases, it is the completed models that have been primarily used to suggest or evaluate strategic alternatives, and we have not seen the modeling process itself used as an aid to exploring and learning about the complexity of the system. This is where more recent developments in the field of OR have been concentrated.

Two other authors can be cited here as having recognized this deficiency. In 1978, Michael Buckland published a paper surveying 10 years of Library OR and identifying areas of library activity where there seemed to be gaps in the literature. He identified the need to explore a number of factors: users and user behavior (paying particular attention to information gathering behaviors); analytical cost models (particularly in times of economic hardship); and what he terms library "goodness" in which he distinguishes between the capability of a service and the value of a service and how each might be measured (Buckland, 1978). Furthermore, he suggests that Library OR studies tended to be narrowly focused, perhaps exploring only one part of library activity, and comments that greater value would be derived by linking the parts together.

A little later, in 1984, Edward O'Neill published an overview of operations research and made some interesting observations about the impact that Library OR has had on the practice of librarianship and the operation of libraries. Generally, he was able to conclude that in answer to the question of whether Library OR has changed the way we understand libraries and the way they are operated, he could respond only with a qualified "yes." What he saw as the key deficiency of Library OR he described as follows: "It is an effective methodology for determining *how* to do something; however, operations research cannot determine *what* should be done" (O'Neill, 1984, p. 518). In other words, he was emphasizing the fact that there was very little in the OR modelers toolbox that has enabled the "provision of insights" into complex library issues.

IV. The Decline of Library OR

As we have seen, the application of OR modeling techniques to the study of academic libraries produced a burst of activity, exploring a range of library problems through the use of mathematical and statistical models. Figure 1 illustrates the rise in library OR publications as listed in Slamecka's (1972) selective bibliography of library OR.

But as we moved through the 1970s, the momentum seemed to be lost so that in the early 1980s, there seemed to be significantly less Library OR appearing in the literature than had hitherto been the case. In fact a simple tabulation of the work cited in the review of Library OR by Reisman and Xu (1994) indicates that approximately 20% of the work they referenced dated from the 1960s, with 54% from the 1970s and just 19% from the 1980s.

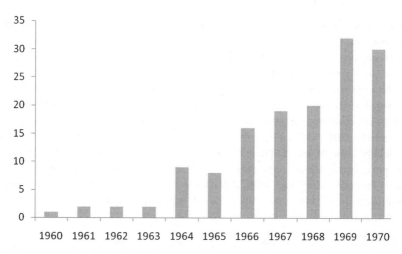

Fig. 1   Number of publications cited by year (from 1960–1970) by Slamecka (1972).

In 1975, Michael Bommer published an opinion paper in the *Journal of the American Society for Information Science* in which he gave a personal critical assessment of OR in libraries (Bommer, 1975). In the article, Bommer discusses why he feels that OR had failed to meet the expectations of its proponents within the field of librarianship. He cites four general reasons for such impediment to achievement and these related to the following:

1. The extent to which the OR models rely on quite complex mathematical formulations so that they are too sophisticated to be readily applicable in supporting management decision-making and often make assumptions that render them unrealistic and therefore unusable;
2. The lack of model implementation stemming from a failure of the modeler to recognize the nonquantifiable elements of management that, although difficult to model, must be part of the dialog between the modeler and the manager;
3. The failure to appreciate that OR is an organic process of enquiry involving more than just the development and analysis of a model; and
4. The failure of OR models to make a significant contribution to some of the crucial strategic decisions faced by library managers.

Expanding this last point a little further, Leimkuhler (1977) reinforced the limitations of the traditional OR models by commenting that attempts to build analytical models of library systems, which specifically try to incorporate human and social factors, have been virtually nonexistent. That these issues were being raised as early as 1975 is interesting as the real debate about the future of OR within the OR community itself did not really ignite for another 5 years or so. Certainly, the warning that Bommer issued, that OR was not achieving its potential in library contexts as it certainly had in other contexts, went unheeded and the decline in Library OR activity seemed to continue through the next two decades.

In other articles, I have suggested reasons for this (Warwick, 2009a, b) and some of these arguments are summarized and expanded later. Although I agree with the observations made by Bommer, my view is that in looking for the causes of this decline in activity, we should really consider three specific clusters of issues: First, the nature and practice of OR itself and the emerging new paradigms; second, the nature of the relationship between modeler and library practitioner; and third, the changing nature of the 21st century academic library. We now consider each of these in turn.

A. New Paradigms in OR

In the early 1980s, serious debate began within the OR community as to the future of OR and whether the narrow problem focus of traditional OR was too restrictive and prevented practitioners from having an impact in decision arenas that might be described as more strategic in nature rather than at the purely operational and tactical levels. As we have noted, similar issues were being raised within the confines of Library OR also, with the suggestion that OR models were seen as having a very narrow focus of application and were not necessarily seen as relevant to helping with any of the "bigger" problems of library management (Dahlin, 1991). Similarly, there were questions being raised relating to the utility of the published models within the library context. Rouse commented back in 1980 that it seemed as though real applications of models and their value to library practitioners was seldom reported in the literature and instead "one reads of the derivation or development of the model and is left to wonder about how the model was actually used to aid decision making" (Rouse and Rouse, 1980, p. 145).

As a reaction to the debate on the future of OR, a growing number of OR modelers became interested in exploring ways of applying OR to the really tough, complex, and messy problems that managers often face in reality. Unfortunately, these problems have characteristics that are not consistent with those listed earlier and that define the locus of traditional OR. Murmurings of discontent were being heard from a number of quarters. Ackoff wrote that,

> Managers are not confronted with problems that are independent of each other, but with dynamic situations that consist of complex systems of changing problems that interact with each other. I call such situations messes ... Managers do not solve problems: they manage messes. (1979, p. 99)

Messes are often characterized by a lack of consensus, multiple (often conflicting) objectives to be met simultaneously, a paucity of reliable data, and politics and prejudices expressed by the people involved in defining, understanding, and ultimately resolving a problem.

Two excellent discussions in this regard are those by Dando and Bennett (1981) and Habermas (1984). The former argues that although traditional OR had been largely successful within the limits defined by its scientific and depoliticized view of the world, it was time to explore new alternative paradigms for decision support so that OR might evolve and be useful in supporting decision-makers right across an organization and at all levels. They draw on the ideas of Thomas Kuhn (1962) in describing OR has having been through a period of "normal" development but that now a paradigm shift, a new way of thinking, was needed to allow OR to engage with the full range of organizational issues. In a paper published just a little later, Habermas (1984) makes a distinction between three environments within the problem space: The objective environment around us that we all observe; the social environment within which we interact with others and which helps to define behavior; and our own internal, personal environment through which we experience everything and try to make sense of it. Habermas makes the point that each of these environments is different and argues that while traditional OR has been successfully used to understand the objective environment (while largely ignoring aspects of the social and personal environments), any further broadening of the application domain of OR would require definition of an epistemology that could open up the social and personal worlds to scrutiny as well.

The expansion of OR to include paradigms that allow opening up the social and personal worlds gave birth to what was originally termed "soft" OR. Initially, there were a number of sharp exchanges between the proponents of the "traditional" and "soft" paradigms, with the former regarding the latter as completely unscientific and lacking in rigor, and the latter regarding the former as irrelevant to the needs of modern management professionals (Mingers, 2007). The passing years have largely moderated the tone of the debate, and there is now a consensus view that both sets of techniques have a place within OR, and the techniques in the new paradigms have been more accurately re-titled as problem structuring methods (PSMs). The defining characteristic of PSMs is that they are tools and techniques through which a client group can structure and learn about a complex problem, and through that learning process arrive at a suitable course of action. In situations of high complexity, rapid change, and uncertainty, the most challenging aspect of the manager's craft is in the framing and definition of the critical issues that constitute the problem and in understanding the systematic relationships between these issues. PSMs themselves are not solution techniques. Rather, they are modeling methods that "foster dialogue, reflection and learning about the critical issues, in order to reach a shared understanding and joint agreements regarding these key issues" (Shaw *et al.*, 2006, p. 757). The focus of the modeling is to explore questions relating to the "why," "when," and "what" of an issue rather than the "how." Daellenbach (2001) describes this nicely by asking questions such as what is the nature of the issue; what are appropriate objectives; what is the appropriate definition of the system for the issue considered; and which changes are systemically desirable and culturally feasible. Only when these questions are answered can a start be made to consider how these changes are best brought about.

The modeling process now concentrates on the resolution of the problem through debate and negotiation between the stakeholders, rather than from the development of analytical models, and the role of the OR specialist changes from being one of "problem analyst" to one of becoming a facilitator and resource person who relies on the technical subject expertise of the stakeholders. The process is one of mediating the exchanges between different interested parties, of making explicit what perhaps has been hidden (assumptions, politics, and personal views) and enabling a learning process that will lead to the generation of agreed actions. Of course, "how" type questions, when they are addressed, may generate the need for modeling activities of a more traditional nature, but these would be set within the problem structuring framework.

As such, PSMs are representative of the new paradigms of OR and the extent to which PSMs have been developed and used is testament to the value that they add in the exploration of complex problems.

B. The Practitioner/Modeler Interaction

The traditional model-building approach to OR work has had the effect of entrusting the model building process to an OR specialist who is most likely to have some form of engineering or mathematical training. The model building process as described in a number of standard OR texts (see, e.g., Edwards and Hamson, 2001; Lawrence and Pasternack, 2002) will usually require the modeler (usually not a specialist in the application area) to extract specifications from the problem owner so that the process of model building, testing, and validation can be undertaken. Thus, the locus of control of the problem solution process passes from the problem owner (problem identification and specification) to the modeler (model building, testing and validation, and solution generation) and back to the problem owner (for solution implementation). The mathematical nature of much of traditional OR makes a close interaction between problem owner and modeler difficult. Within the field of Library OR, this gap was quite noticeable particularly in the early days. Then library practitioners were not operating within an environment which encouraged regular debate with those undertaking research, and practitioners certainly were not trained in the art of modeling from an OR perspective. Thus, the divide between practitioners (problem owners) and OR modelers (problem solvers) effectively opened a gap between researchers and practitioners.

The existence of this gap has been acknowledged for many years. In their review of Library OR literature dating from 1977, Kraft and McDonald (1977, p. 4) state that "More cooperation and communication is required, however, if library operations research is to have more of a significant impact on the literature." This gap between modeler (or more generally researcher) and practitioner has been more recently studied by Haddow and Klobas (2004), and their analysis of the Library Information Systems (LIS) literature identifies 11 criteria that have contributed to this gap. These include criteria relating to culture (researchers and practitioners effectively speak different languages, have differing sources of knowledge, and there is a lack of mutual understanding), relevance (what constitutes problems worthy of investigation differs between the two groups and practitioners view research as not relevant or practical enough), and terminology (the terminology of each group is not necessarily understood by the other).

It is interesting to note that although the fields of librarianship and informatics have grown considerably in recent years, so that more mathematical aspects of information collection and analysis are now well represented, few of the criteria identified by Haddow and Klobas have been explicitly addressed and the gap still remains—although it may have narrowed just a little.

C. The Changing 21st-Century Academic Library

In March 2007, the Association of College and Research Libraries, a division of the American Library Association, made public its Top Ten Assumptions for the future of academic and research libraries. The assumptions (Mullins et al., 2007) covered a range of aspects of library activity but, taken as a whole, emphasized the role that technological development and the changing attributes and expectations of the typical library customer will play in shaping future academic libraries. The assumptions listed included that students will demand faster and greater access to materials and increasingly see themselves as customers/consumers thus expecting high quality services;

that the growth in demand for technology-related services would continue (and would require funding); and that HE institutions will increasingly view themselves as businesses. Now, just 3 years later, these assumptions are still valid and the pace of change brought about by developments in information technology shows no sign of abating. In fact so all embracing has been the growth and influence of the internet that university students no longer regard the academic library as their key information source (Wells, 2007).

The debate about the future of the academic library in the information age has been evolving for many years. Bazillion (2001) expected that libraries would become "a value-added component of the educational process ..." (p. 54) contributing in ways that would include providing access through special facilities and equipment to a variety of electronic information sources both providing a source of expertise in evolving information systems, web surfing, and electronic search method and helping to integrate technology into teaching and research programs. This evolutionary process has not necessarily taken us in the right direction, and some have argued that what we currently have are simply digitized versions of the old-style library or, in some cases, where new media and new technologies have made an impact, a kind of hybrid library (Watson, 2010). Neither of these configurations really address the changing nature of the library customer or the emerging distinctions between place as library or library as place (Davenport, 2006). Lucas (2006) summarizes the literature exploring the developing notion of the library as that it

> reveals that long-standing hallmarks of the undergraduate library are experimentation, innovation, willingness to change service configurations, flexibility, and dealing with a large population of students with limited resources (pp. 304–305)

A relevant question to ask here is what are the characteristics of this large population of under-resourced students with whom academic libraries are expected to deal? One response is given by Law (2009) who reports on the abilities and expectations of today's digital natives (CIBER, 2007) noting that they

- expect research to be easy and feel that they can be independent in the process;
- do not seek help from librarians and only occasionally from professors or peers;
- when they cannot find what they need, give up and assume that the information cannot be found. Students often stop after their initial searches thinking that they have completed the research process;
- have, through access to full text articles, seemed to have changed their cognitive behavior. Instead of having to read through material at the library, they can now download material at their desks.

They do not feel the need to take notes or read through them to develop themes and ideas, an activity usually considered central to a focused research project;
- have failed to read through material, which is possible because electronic articles enable cutting and pasting. This, in turn, almost certainly leads to increased plagiarism—although the suspicion must be that this is done through ignorance more often than malice; and
- use a model of collecting information of browsing and grazing (pp. 56–57).

A slightly different view is proposed by Lucas (2006) who comments, "We see a confident, driven achiever; a sophisticated consumer; and a demanding user of technology who is accustomed to lots of attention and being able to purchase and use the latest technology in the marketplace" (p. 316). The literature is very clear that clinging to the status quo is not a realistic option and that library managers need to be able to embrace change and to be able to respond to the changing environment and to the demands of learners (Walton, 2007a). Wells (2007) makes the suggestion that flexibility needs to be addressed through three central themes and these are described in Table 1.

Clearly, many words have already been printed on the need for academic libraries to change and to redefine themselves within the context of education in the digital age.

The pace of change is likely to remain fast and may even get faster to the extent that the operation of the academic library as it is currently defined no longer becomes fit for the purpose. Similarly the learning behavior of students is also changing rapidly as social technologies advance and formal learning is augmented by informal learning processes. Indeed, Watson states that "In my view, facing up to this means not just harnessing it to do what we do but rethinking our purpose. This is a new paradigm and not just 'normal' change" (2010, p. 47).

Traditional Library OR has not been able to meet these challenges, and, as we have seen, from both the OR standpoint and the academic library standpoint we have had calls for a paradigm shift in the way that we conceptualize and explore these domains. We now consider what the future of Library OR might be able to offer in a world of technological and educational change.

V. The Future of Library OR: A New Paradigm?

So far, the early applications of Library OR have been reviewed and some reasons have been suggested about why OR has not been able to benefit academic libraries as much as it has in other areas. The arguments proposed are summarized in Table 2 where they have been set against the defining

Table 1
Library Change and Flexibility

Locus of change	Description
Flexibility and knowing the library user	The context here is one that represents good practice in any business situation, which is to know your customer. The library should strive to establish data collection processes that allow an accurate picture of users' needs, and such "evidence-based librarianship" serves to inform managers on the services required by users and the levels of demand for those services, which services are redundant and likely developments for the future (Walton, 2007b)
Flexibility and library human resources	Any system operating in an uncertain and rapidly changing environment places requirements on staff to be rapidly adaptable. Furthermore, the requirement for staff to develop is constant and it has been suggested that the requirement for staff flexibility is a stimulant for staff development (Johnston, 1999)
Flexibility and library management	Wells (2007) makes the point here that flexibility has to be balanced with the provision of some stability so that processes and procedures that guarantee the quality of service to customers are not eroded. The difficulty here is that the management of flexibility requires management processes that are inclusive of all levels of staff and are information rich. Note that we use the term information rather than data as the information may be in the form of perceptions, views, gut feelings, anecdotal stories, or any of the rich variety of information sources on which experience and judgment are based

Source: Adapted from Wells (2007).

characteristics of the traditional OR model as defined by Rosenhead and Mingers (2001) and described earlier.

Before beginning to explore what the future of Library OR might look like, it is perhaps worth taking a step back and considering the value that models actual add to the decision-making process, because without models and modeling, OR would have very little to offer in any context. I have so far been very critical of the application of OR to academic libraries, so what does OR itself say about the benefits of modeling?

Table 2
Critique Summary of Traditional OR Models

Classic OR model characteristics	Commentary in relation to Library OR	Reference
Problem formulation in terms of a single objective and optimization	Models tend to be "one-off" projects and do not address broader, linked problem domains. Emphasis is on the "how" rather than the "what." Often quite complex mathematical techniques adopted. Real problems are complex messes	Buckland (1978), O'Neill (1984), Bommer (1975), and Ackoff (1979)
Overwhelming data demands	Quantitative models require data. Academic libraries are not research focused and do not routinely collect the data that models require. Assumptions made by modelers about data are sometimes unrealistic and misunderstood by practitioners	Bommer (1975) and Haddow and Klobas, (2004)
Assumed consensus	OR is an organic process that should not assume consensus. Greater communication among modeler and library practitioner required to explore areas where consensus is lacking. There are differences in what is taken as "relevant" for investigation between modeler and library practitioner	Bommer (1975), Kraft and McDonald, (1977), and Haddow and Klobas, (2004)
People treated as passive objects	Models have tended to ignore the nonquantifiable elements of management, which hinders implementation. Also the view is depoliticized and ignores the personal. OR must be inclusive of the personal and social worlds	Bommer (1975), Dando and Bennett (1981), Habermas (1984)
An assumed single decision-maker	OR has not contributed to strategic planning that assumes multiple views and voices for decision-making in most organizations	Bommer (1975) and Dahlin (1991)

Table 2. (*Continued*)

Classic OR model characteristics	Commentary in relation to Library OR	Reference
The abolition of future uncertainty	Uncertainty in the academic library domain cannot be ignored and the future direction that libraries take will require considerable debate and engagement with learners. Libraries must be able to be flexible and fleet of foot	Walton (2007a), Wells (2007), and Watson (2010)

Pidd (2010b) defines a model as "an external and explicit representation of part of reality as seen by the people who wish to use that model to understand, to change, to manage and to control that part of reality" (p. 10). This definition is highly relevant to the new paradigm of OR in that it does not conceptualize a model as just an abstract representation of reality but links the model firmly with practitioners and the need to use models as part of a change and control process.

Some 20 years ago, Williams (1990) gave five reasons why he believed models are important to OR and highlighted the need to explain to non-OR practitioners the reasoning behind the use of (often mathematical) models. The reasons are cited as follows:

1. As models make relationships explicit, modeling often leads to a greater understanding of the situation under study;
2. An understanding of the factors and parameters appearing in the model helps to distinguish between the subjective elements of decision and the objective ones. Specific techniques can then be employed to deal with the subjective elements;
3. Models are flexible and allow for experimentation, far more than would be possible with a real system;
4. Once constructed, models can be subjected to analysis that may yield ideas and courses of action that may not have been apparent before the modeling was undertaken; and
5. Many of the standard models that are regularly used in OR applications are well understood, have assumptions that have been made explicit over the years of use, and are amenable to solution by computer algorithms.

There is little doubt that the reasons aforementioned for the use of models are all very valid reasons why we should be undertaking modeling. What seems to be the primary issue is not the generation of models per se, but the way in which the modeling is undertaken and here I believe is the key to the future development of Library OR. I would further suggest that we need to integrate Library OR very firmly within the library management process so that it can provide a medium through which library evolutionary processes can be explored and controlled.

To explain this further, the earlier discussion of the decline in Library OR highlighted the limiting nature of traditional OR models, the modeler/ practitioner gap, and the changing nature of the academic library as groups of issues that have impacted negatively on Library OR. I am convinced that for Library OR to maintain its identity and the utility of its contribution to library management, it needs to be focused within the fourth of Pidd's modeling categories relating to the provision of insights. The new paradigms of OR have identified PSMs as tools for assisting managers in exploring problem situations, understanding, and making explicit the views and assumptions of those engaged with the problem and assisting them in moving toward an agreed course of action, strategic plan, and so forth.

The use of PSMs immediately removes the modeler/practitioner gap because problem ownership always remains with the library practitioners. The limitations of traditional modeling techniques are removed as PSMs open a window into the social and personal worlds of those involved, and yet, these traditional approaches are still available if such modeling is felt to be beneficial. PSMs also allow practitioners to gain traction on the key issue of flexibility in being able to respond to the changing environment and to the demands of learners.

As examples, let us consider three areas that emerge from the literature as important to the future running, and purpose, of academic libraries. These relate to the organization and management of information sources and of library operations; the development of the library as an integrated part of the student learning experience; and understanding the HE environment and defining strategic direction for an institution's library provision. In a broad sense, these three views of the library are nested in that they form a hierarchical structure in which library operational management (the lowest level) is conceptualized within the context of the wider student environment (the middle level), which in turn is set within the national and international contexts of HE so that we can move up and down the levels in a systematic way. Let us consider each of these perspectives in turn.

A. Organization and Management of Information Sources and Libraries

At this level, the library is concerned with making the most efficient use of its resources and it is here that traditional OR models have seemed an attractive proposition and have, in the past, made a contribution to our understanding of resource allocation. Of course, library collections are going through a process of change as they are now a mixture of what might be termed legacy sources (traditional printed materials), materials converted into digital forms, and material which is digital at source. Law (2009) has considered how the library's role might need redefinition to accommodate the digital age and has defined an agenda that encompasses five principle, core activities that may be summarized as follows:

1. Building e-research collections and contributing to a virtual research environment;
2. Providing a system of information assurance by means of kite-marking, trust metrics, relevance ranking, and so on;
3. Effective management of digital (and other) assets and ensuring appropriate access mechanisms are in place;
4. Providing support and training in information literacy; and
5. Providing advice on policy and standards to the institution at large.

These core activities represent the academic library as both a core resource for students and staff and also as an agent for change within the institution's strategic management processes, and traditional OR modeling has so far been able to make very little impact here. Also included here is consideration of the way in which library operational procedures should attempt to remain agile and responsive. Walton (2007b) emphasizes the need for flexibility in terms of library services, structure, and staff. Flexibility of service and structure is governed by a requirement for "evidence-based librarianship" through which the needs of users can be ascertained and accommodated but balanced with some stability, so that quality of service can be assured. PSMs have a clear role to play here perhaps supported by more traditional modeling projects.

B. The Library and the Student Learning Experience

For Watson (2010), the emerging role of academic libraries needs to switch from being a passive provider of resources to "being about people and making a real contribution to the learning landscape" (p. 51). But what might this contribution be and how can OR modeling assist in making this contribution?

I feel that there are four main areas to be explored here and these are described briefly below:

1. One of the major areas of growth in academic research over the past decade has been that of pedagogic research. Certainly within the United Kingdom HE environment, the Government

has placed great weight on teaching scholarship and the student experience is taken as one of the measures in deciding whether a university is fit-for-purpose. The enormous amount of pedagogic research now conducted across virtually all universities has transformed the classroom experience of many students; yet, it is unclear whether there has been much engagement with this pedagogic literature within academic libraries. OR techniques (including statistical methods) have contributed much to this research agenda and it is incumbent on those who undertake this research to ensure dissemination of results at a local (institutional) level (published papers are not frequently read) and this leads to our second consideration.

2. We need to foster a better interaction between modeler, library practitioner, and academic lecturer to understand more clearly the expectations of students and the expectations of lecturers. This involves processes that can facilitate dialog between these parties but also between these staff and students so that their expectations might be better understood and, where these are thought to be unreasonable, challenged.

3. Better linking of research and the academic curriculum is needed. Conventionally, the academic library has been required to respond to new course developments insofar as providing the appropriate and needed learning resources. Library practitioners can also contribute to the design of curricula, particularly in areas related to the skills of lifelong learning and the use of information as a strategic resource for students.

4. The library has a role to play in personal development. Here, library practitioners can contribute to the delivery of research and information acquisition/management skills that will be part of the personal development of all students.

All of those university members engaged in defining and delivering the student experience can best serve the student by coordinating their various areas of expertise, but traditional OR provides very little modeling assistance here. PSMs on the contrary allow a structured analysis of these complex interactions so that systems can be put in place, which will allow the necessary information flows and enable decision frameworks.

C. Defining a Strategic Direction

Traditional management approaches to HE planning have been under scrutiny for a number of years and many have argued (including this author) that HE planning at the strategic level is not something that is amenable to traditional modeling approaches but rather what is required is a more systems-based enquiry process (Bell *et al.*, 2005; Galbraith, 1998).

The new paradigms of OR have a direct translation to the world of the academic library. Library OR should embrace PSMs with fervor because, as has already been stated, they allow the exploration of the complex, multifaceted problems associated with strategic planning and yet do not require the locus of problem ownership to shift away from the library practitioner. Figure 2 gives an indication of the interactions that can be mediated by PSMs and I would expect that traditional modeling (where it still takes place) would be in the form of smaller scale projects aimed at

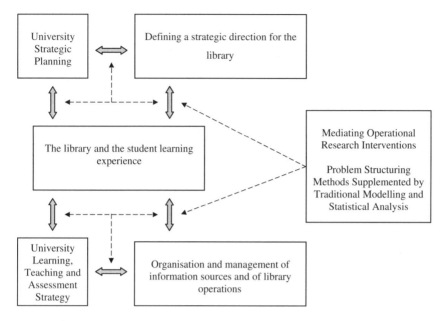

Fig. 2 A new locus of Library OR in mediating change interactions.

supporting and informing practitioners by providing structured data, forecasts, and so on and perhaps helping to understand the possible consequences of actions.

Just as each of the three perspectives described earlier are interconnected, there is also a need for the library to reflect, and be able to influence, the strategic direction of the university. In many institutions, this will involve engagement with the strategic planning process and also with the learning, teaching, and assessment policy (or the academic strategy as some institutions have adopted). Such engagement and discussion can also, of course, be facilitated using PSMs.

Thus, Library OR can be conceptualized as a unifying process that oils the wheels of interaction between practitioner groups, between the library and its users, and the library and its host organization, the university. Its focus is on structuring, learning, understanding, and the provision of insights. Modeling is not seen as a divisive activity delineating the boundary between modeler and practitioner but instead is a way of asking questions relating to the "what?", "when?", and "why?" of issues rather than just "how?". After all, how we achieve an outcome is only relevant after we have decided what outcome is to be achieved, by when, and for what reason.

VI. Conclusion

Academic libraries are going through a process of unprecedented change as they respond to technological change and the changing needs of learners while adapting to operate in a world of limited resources. Lucas (2006) testifies to the durability of the academic library:

> The persistence of the undergraduate library indicates that it provides a unique environment for the incubation and implementation of new services, programs, and functions to meet challenges posed by advances in technology, changing undergraduate student learning preferences, and evolving faculty teaching methods. (p. 318)

Traditional Library OR has historically failed to establish itself as a routine part of library management, and these new conditions are generating managerial problems with which the traditional tools of the OR modeler are not able to assist. If Library OR is to make a contribution, then it must adopt the new paradigms of OR and use them to help library practitioners explore possible future directions and manage the change processes that are inevitably taking place.

References

Ackoff, R. L. (1979). The future of operations research is past. *Journal of the Operations Research Society* 30, 93–104.

Arms, W. Y., and Walter, T. P. (1974). A simulation model for purchasing duplicate models in a library. *Journal of Library Automation* 7, 73–82.

Baker, N. R., and Nance, R. E. (1970). Organisational analyses and simulation studies of university libraries: A methodological overview. *Information Storage and Retrieval* 5(4), 153–168.

Bazillion, R. J. (2001). Academic libraries in the digital revolution. *EDUCAUSE Quarterly* 1, 51–55.

Beasley, J. E. (n.d.). *OR-Notes*. Retrieved from http://people.brunel.ac.uk/~mastjjb/jeb/or/intro.html

Bell, G. A., Cooper, M. A., Kennedy, M., and Warwick, J. (2005). The Holon framework: Process improvement and control for higher education. In *On Becoming a Productive University* (J. E. Groccia and J. E. Miller, eds.), pp. 23–33, Ankar Publishing, Bolton, MA.

Bommer, M. (1975). Operations research in libraries: A critical assessment. *Journal of the American Society for Information Science* 26, 137–139.

Buckland, M. K. (1975). *Book Availability and the Library User*. Pergamon Press, London, England.

Buckland, M. (1978). Ten years progress in quantitative research in libraries. *Socio-Economic Planning Science* 12, 333–339.

CIBER (2007). *Information Behaviour of the Researcher of the Future*. Retrieved from http://www.bl.uk/news/pdf/googlegen.pdf

Daellenbach, H. G. (2001, November). Hard OR, soft OR, problem structuring methods, critical systems thinking: A primer. *ORSNZ Conference Twenty Naught One*, University of Canterbury, Christchurch, New Zealand.

Dahlin, T. C. (1991). Operations research and organisational decision-making in academic libraries. *Collection Management* 14(3/4), 49–60.

Dando, M. R., and Bennett, P. G. (1981). A Kuhnian crisis in management science? *Journal of the Operational Research Society* 32, 91–104.

Davenport, N. (2006). Place as library. *EDUCAUSE Review* 41, 12–13.

De Gennaro, R. (1978). Library administration & new management system. *Library Journal* 103, 2477–2482.

Edwards, D., and Hamson, M. (2001). *Guide to Mathematical Modelling*. Palgrave Macmillan, Basingstoke, UK.

Galbraith, P. L. (1998). When strategic plans are not enough. *System Dynamics: An International Journal of Policy Modelling* 10(1/2), 55–84.

Gass, S. (2002). Great moments in histORy. *OR/MS Today* 29(5). Retrieved from http://www.lionhrtpub.com/orms/orms-10-02/frhistorysb1.html

Goyal, S. K. (1970). Application of operational research to problems of determining appropriate loan periods for periodicals. *Libri* 20(1), 94–99.

Habermas, J. (1984). *The Theory of Communicative Action, vol. 1: Reason and the Rationalization of Society*. Heinemann, London, England.

Haddow, G., and Klobas, J. E. (2004). Communication of research to practice in library and information science: Closing the gap. *Library & Information Science Research* 26, 29–43.

Hamburg, M., Clelland, R. C., Bommer, M., Ramist, L., and Whitfield, R. (1974). *Library Planning and Decision Making Systems*. MIT Press, Cambridge, MA.

Johnston, R. (1999). Beyond flexibility: Issues and implications for higher education. *Higher Education Review* 32(1), 55–67.

Kantor, P. B. (1979). A review of library operations research. *Library Research* 1, 295–345.

Kirby, M. (1999). Operations research trajectories: The Anglo-American experience from the 1940s to the 1990s. *Operations Research* 48(5), 661–670.

Kraft, D. H., and Boyce, B. R. (1991). *Operations Research for Libraries and Information Agencies*. Academic Press, San Diego, CA.

Kraft, D. H., and McDonald, D. (1977). Library operations research: A bibliography and commentary on the literature. *Information Reports and Bibliographies* 6, 2–10.

Kuhn, T. (1962). *The Structure of Scientific Revolutions*. University of Chicago Press, Chicago, IL.

Law, D. (2009). Academic digital libraries of the future: An environmental scan. *New Review of Academic Librarianship* 15, 53–67.

Lawrence, J. A., and Pasternack, B. A. (2002). *Applied Management Science*. Wiley, New York.

Leimkuhler, F. F. (1966). Systems analysis in university libraries. *College and Research Libraries* 27, 64–71.

Leimkuhler, F. F. (1968). Mathematical models for library systems analysis. *Drexel Library Quarterly* 4, 185–196.

Leimkuhler, F. F. (1977). Operations research and systems analysis. In *Evaluation and Scientific Management of Libraries and Information Centres* (F. W. Lancaster and C. W. Cleverdon, eds.). Noordhoff, Leyden, Netherlands.

Leimkuhler, F. F., & Cooper, M. D. (1971, November–December). Analytic models for library planning. *Journal of the American Society of Information Science* 22(6), 390–398.

Lucas, K. (2006). The undergraduate library and its librarians in the large research university: Responding to change to remain vital and relevant. *Advances in Librarianship* 30, 299–323.

Main, L. (1987). Computer simulation and library management. *Journal of Information Science* 13, 285–296.

Mingers, J. (2007). Operational research: The science of better? *Journal of the Operational Research Society* 58, 683.

Morse, P. M. (1968). *Library Effectiveness—A Systems Approach.* MIT Press, Cambridge, MA.

Mullins, J. L., Allen, F. R., and Hufford, J. R. (2007). Top ten assumptions for the future of academic libraries and librarians: A report from the ACRL research committee. *College &.Research Library News,* 68, 240–246.

O'Neill, E. (1984). Operations research. *Library Trends* 32(4), 509–520.

Pidd, M. (2010a). Why modelling and model use matter. *Journal of the Operational Research Society* 61(1), 14–24.

Pidd, M. (2010b). *Tools for Thinking: Modelling in Management Science.* Wiley, Chichester, England.

Reisman, A., and Xu, X. (1994). Operations research in libraries: A review of 25 years of activity. *Operations Research* 42(1), 34–40.

Rivett, P. (1980). *Model Building for Decision Analysis.* Wiley, New York.

Rosenhead, J., and Mingers, J. (2001). *Rational Analysis for a Problematic World Revisited.* Wiley, Chichester, England.

Rouse, W. B. (1976). A library network model. *Journal of the American Society for Information Science* 27, 88–99.

Rouse, W. B., and Rouse, S. H. (1977). Assessing the impact of computer technology on the performance of inter-library loan networks. *Journal of the American Society for Information Science* 28, 79–88.

Rouse, W. B., and Rouse, S. H. (1980). Analysis of library networks. *Collection Management* 3(2/3), 139–150.

Rowley, J. E., and Rowley, P. J. (1981). *Operations Research: A Tool for Library Management.* American Library Association, Chicago, IL.

Shaw, D., Franco, A., and Westcombe, M. (2006). Problem structuring methods: New directions in a problematic world. *Journal of the Operational Research Society* 57, 757–758.

Shaw, W. M. (1976). Library user interface: A simulation of the circulation subsystem. *Journal of Information Processing and Management* 12(1), 77–91.

Slamecka, V. (1972). A selective bibliography on library operations research. *Library Quarterly* 42(1), 152–158.

Smith, J. M., and Rouse, W. B. (1979). Application of queuing network models to optimization or resource allocation within libraries. *Journal of the American Society for Information Science* 30(5), 250–263.

Thomas, P. A., and Wight, T. (1976). Computer simulation and library management. *EURIM II, A European Conference on the Application of Research in Information Services and Libraries.* Aslib, London, UK.

Trueswell, R. W. (1965). A quantitative measure of user circulation requirements and possible effects on stack thinning and multiple copy determination. *American Documentation* 16, 20–25.

Trueswell, R. W. (1966). Determining the optimal number of volumes for a library's core collection. *Libri* **16**, 49–60.

UK ORSOC (2010). *What Operational Research Is*. Retrieved from http://www.orsoc. org.uk/orshop/(m1vwwpmqryhyxfjizuxcaa55)/orcontent.aspx?inc=about.htm

Walton, G. (2007a). Theory, research and practice in library management: New column for library management. *Library Management* **28**(3), 163–164.

Walton, G. (2007b). Theory, research and practice in library management 1: Flexibility. *Library Management* **28**(3), 165–171.

Warwick, J. (2009a). On the future of library operations research. *Library Management* **30**(3), 176–184.

Warwick, J. (2009b). On 40 years of queuing in libraries. *Library Review* **58**(1), 44–55.

Watson, L. (2010). The future of the library as a place of learning: A personal perspective. *New Review of Academic Librarianship* **16**, 45–56.

Wells, A. (2007). A prototype twenty-first century university library. *Library Management* **28**(8/9), 450–459.

Williams, H. P. (1990). How important are models to operational research? *IMA Journal of Mathematics Applied in Business and Industry* **2**, 189–195.

Managing Intellectual Capital in Libraries and Information Services

Petros A. Kostagiolas and Stefanos Asonitis
Department of Archive and Library Science, Ionian University, Corfu, Greece

Abstract

Intellectual capital is the set of all intangible assets, that is, invisible, non-monetary assets held by a library, which can be identified as separate assets. Intellectual capital has become the buzzword of a knowledge-based economy and is the ultimate source of competitive advantage. In this work, we review the literature to analyse the effect of intellectual capital utilisation in the overall library management, to identify and classify intellectual capital and to provide some guidelines for researchers and practitioners. A literature review for the intellectual capital in libraries is conducted, and a qualitative analysis is undertaken, which interrelates library management to intellectual capital is taking place. The review leads to identification and classification of intellectual capital as well as to a number of quite innovative and interesting issues for the interrelation of intellectual capital to the management of libraries. The issues studied include intellectual capital economic valuation methods, the effect of the locality (spatial factor) to intellectual capital utilisation and the analysis of co-opetition (cooperation and competition) for intellectual capital utilisation. This is one of only a few studies about the management of intellectual capital in libraries and information services (LIS)—an innovative and challenging area of research in library management.

I. Introduction

In the second decade of the new century, libraries operate within an exciting world, the world of intellectual capital utilisation. Libraries and information services (LIS) all over the world strive to redefine their role and to develop novel systems and services. Even if we do not immediately realise it, when we use a library as part of our daily practice, we rely heavily on non-tangible assets. Library administration and management, now more than ever, embrace decisions about investments in technological/structural, organisational and human capital. These assets need to be properly identified and measured to better understand their possible usages, structure, production

ADVANCES IN LIBRARIANSHIP, VOL. 33
© 2011 by Emerald Group Publishing Limited
ISSN: 0065-2830
DOI: 10.1108/S0065-2830(2011)0000033005

and value. Intellectual capital is gradually becoming a crucial factor fostering innovation that genuinely improves a library's operations and services.

A. Definitions

Intellectual capital is assumed to be the set of all intangible assets, that is to say, the invisible, non-monetary assets held by a library, which can be identified as separate assets. This work is explained by the following interrelated postulates:

  I.   Intellectual capital is a crucial factor fostering innovation, which brings about genuine improvements in library's operations & services;
  II.   The library environment is becoming more and more complicated and knowledge-based, hence conventional instruments are no longer directly appropriate for decision-making; and
  III. Expenditures and investments in intellectual capital are either mis-measured or not measured at all.

A potential venue for discussion is whether the notion of library management should be reconsidered when we move from the world of the tangible to the world of the intangible (Vasconcelos, 2008) where libraries are beginning to develop and deploy new methods that aim at managing its intellectual capital. Indeed, research and guidance is a prerequisite for library management to fully utilise intellectual capital.

A definition for the intellectual capital management is provided by Roos *et al.* (2005) as follows: "Intellectual capital management is the deployment and management of intellectual capital resources & their transformations (into intellectual capital resources or into traditional capital resources) to maximize the present value of the organization's value creation in the eyes of its stakeholders" (p. 42). It is rather obvious, however, that not all the different intangible assets are of the same importance to value creation. A first step towards managing intellectual capital is identification of the intangible assets that have a positive effect on library stakeholders' viewpoints. For instance, in the case of a corporate library, its main concern is to maximise financial returns of the company. This however might not be to the case in non-profit libraries such as academic and public libraries. An important underlying research issue is the fact that intellectual capital plays an important role in determining the overall value of a library.

In this chapter, literature is reviewed to qualitatively analyse the added value of intellectual capital utilisation in library services. The review leads to identification and classification of the intangible assets as well as to the identification of a number of innovative and interesting issues for management of intellectual capital in libraries. Considering the three aforementioned postulates, we focus on metrics and valuation, the effect of the locality (spatial factor) to intellectual capital utilisation and on an analysis of cooperation and competition for intangible assets utilisation. Throughout the analysis, a number of practical directions for library administration and management are provided. Intellectual capital is an innovative and promising area of research, which may provide competitive advantages as well as the foundation for a novel management paradigm.

II. Libraries within the New Economic Environment

Over the past two decades, intellectual capital has gradually become the buzzword of a novel knowledge-based global economy. Starting in the mid-1970s, the current globalisation process was supported by a status quo of the three worldwide dominant currencies (dollar, euro and yen) and the liberation of capital movements (OECD, 2005).

Globalisation according to the OECD (2003) is "the increasing internationalization of markets for goods and services, the means of production, financial systems, competition, corporations, technology and industries" (p. 334). Intense competition requires utilisation of intellectual capital, accumulating capital through the cooperation among organisations as well as cooperation with users, suppliers or even competitors. Competition also requires creativity and innovation through the utilisation of human resources and new management techniques. Globalisation and the advances in information technologies are the main causes for the enormous increase of the utilisation of intangible assets over the past decades.

The new economic environment is unfolding and evolving thereby delivering changes to libraries. Understanding intellectual capital management and the management of libraries within a novel economic environment is essential to working effectively in the field. Literature suggests that monetary capital and working capital are not themselves a sufficient condition for success in the current era. According to Andriessen (2004), innovation plays a significant role in value creation when combined with capital and labour. Knowledge is indeed considered as the essential wealth-producing factor in our era. Ark (2002) comments on the significant role that intangible assets play in productivity nowadays, stating that "productivity measures the effectiveness with which inputs (materials, capital and labor) are transformed into output" (p. 69). This transformation process is complemented by continuous improvements in the quality of inputs such as a rise in skill levels of workers, the creation of knowledge, organisational changes within firms or setting up professional networks. Libraries have the opportunity, if not the responsibility, of actively participating in the establishment of a new economic reality that is heavily reliant on information and knowledge. Indeed, the new economy is the economy driven by information and communication technologies (OECD, 2003).

A. Library Settings

LIS in both their tangible form (e.g., infrastructure, equipment and traditional collections) and their intangible form (e.g., digital collections, automation systems and networking synergies) are becoming very important to businesses and enterprises. Harris (2002) recognises that the globalisation process requires the utilisation of innovation capacity, entrepreneurship, synergies among employees, customers, suppliers or even competitors, the utilisation of physical and human resources as well as novel marketing techniques. With the exception of physical resources, all other factors identified by Harris (2002) are intangibles by nature. Hand and Lev (2003) ascertain that during the 1990s investments in tangible assets in the United States remained stable (as a percentage of the gross domestic product (GDP)) to the respective percentage pertain to 1950s and 1960s. To the contrary, investments in intangible assets during the past 20 years have seen impressive growth.

Intellectual capital has been identified in all human activities from the origins of civilisation (Lev, 2001). Changes in the utilisation of intellectual capital have been also studied by Kostagiolas and Asonitis (2008) using the *Worlds of Production* framework provided by Storper and Salais (1997). The aim is to explain the diversity and complexity of economic life by identifying four possible worlds of production as follows: the industrial world, market world, interpersonal world and the world of intellectual resources. Each "world" is a conventional world, appearing as a set of rules, coordination practices, conventions and norms among the persons who develop the product. Storper and Salais also introduced a "model of production" for each world. A model of production is "the set of routines, organizational structures and operational principles which guide the firm from day to day and year to year" (p. 44). Through evolvement of the economy, and indeed in intellectual world, where the core product is knowledge itself, intellectual capital needs more than ever to be fully utilised in the production process. This capital may, for example, include the creation of a valuable network of suppliers/distributors, the development of computer software, databases, patents, copyrights and so forth.

However, we should not generalise so readily and a single world of production model cannot be appropriate for all types of libraries. This may be justified because the libraries are rather unique as organisations, in view of the fact that they are both tangible and intangible in nature. Hence, for a traditional library, its fixed investments in real assets, particularly in buildings, are absolutely essential. Tangible investments in furniture (e.g., workstations, seats and study carrels) and in office equipment (e.g., photocopiers) are important for a conventional library. Childs (2006) presents many examples proving that tangible investments in refurbishment, location and new building projects are an effective way to attract new library users. In these cases, investments in intangible assets may indicate a need to include recruitment of specialised personnel, small-scale training programs, the acquisition of special software in support of library services. In other cases, however, library operations demand substantial investments to any of the three categories of intellectual capital: human, organisational (structural) and relational. Such cases include, for example, digital libraries and research/academic libraries (Kostagiolas and Asonitis, 2009) where the quality of library's staff, team development, copyrights, computer software and data bases, participation in information networks and the like are absolutely essential.

In the near past, intellectual capital has not been totally ignored and was estimated as the difference between the book value of an organisation and its real value assigned by the market (Vasconcelos, 2008). This difference may be explained by the presence of intangible assets belonging to all three categories. This was assumed to be subjective, representing the value or potential value in the eyes of the buyer, not the company value, and this is referred to as "goodwill" by Vasconcelos (2008). Goodwill incorporates resources with long-term benefits to a library that have not been identified as separate assets. Thus, the overall value of a group of assets is not simply a collection their separate values. Investments have to utilise both tangible and intangibles resources. Beyond doubt, however, intellectual capital in LIS go beyond a financial dimension. Issues related to the identification, classification, assessment and management of intangible assets, as well metrics for their contribution to the overall library performance, should be faced up by any library management team.

III. Review and Analysis of Intellectual Capital in Libraries

A. Definition and Classifications

1. Tangible and Intangible Assets

Intellectual capital is the set of all intangible assets, that is, invisible, non-monetary assets held by an organisation, which are amassed over time and can be identified as separate assets. The term "intangible asset" has several interpretations (Kaufmann and Schneider, 2004). In economics, the term "knowledge asset" is commonly used as an equivalent to "intangible asset," whereas in management, the term "intellectual capital" is commonly used (Lev, 2001). Definitions assigned to the term intangible asset, and its equivalents, may be conceptual or descriptive (a list of assets considered to be intangibles are recorded). Examples of conceptual definitions are Lev's "an intangible asset is a claim to future benefit that does not have a physical or financial (a stock or a bond) embodiment" (p. 5) and the definition given by Bouteiller (2000) that an intangible asset is a result of "past events" with no physical nature, legally protected and capable of producing future economic benefits. An example of a descriptive definition recording an indicative list of intangibles is given by Reilly and Schweihs (1998), namely computer software and databases, patents, copyrights, trademarks, customer lists, applied marketing techniques, contracts with suppliers and so on. The set of intangible assets held by a firm or an organisation constitute the intellectual capital of a firm or organisation.

The literature shows that quite a few efforts have been made to develop a classification of intangible assets or intellectual capital (Choong, 2008; Grasenick and Low, 2004). A classification usually sets out a number of categories into which intangibles are listed. A classification may serve various research needs. For example, a classification serving an assessment analysis is proposed by Reilly and Schweihs (1998). According to their classification, intangibles are embodied into 10 categories: marketing, technology, art, data processing, engineering science, customers, obligation derived from contracts, human capital, locality and trademark. Lev (2001) proposed a classification based on the creator of the intangible asset. Other classification approaches may be industry- or firm-specific, thus serving bounded or internal analysis needs. For example, Porta and Oliver (2006) classify intangibles in cluster of enterprises. Other classifications serve accounting purposes or are based on the economic performance of intangibles.

Intellectual capital falls into three distinct categories: (1) human capital, (2) organisational (or structural) capital and (3) relational capital, originating from the works of Edvinsson and Malone (1997), Roos et al. (1997); Sveiby (1997) and Grasenick and Low (2004). Recently, through an extensive analysis of the literature, Choong (2008) recommended the classification of intellectual capital as introduced in the work of Sveiby (1997), MERITUM (2002) and Bontis (2002) as the prevalent. *Human capital* is the knowledge, the experiences, the competencies and the creativity the staff of a firm or an organisation has (Edvinsson and Malone, 1997). Resources related to human capital are assigned to individuals and cannot be replaced by machines (Roos *et al.*, 2005). *Organisational or structural capital* is according to Edvinsson and Malone (1997), "all those things that remain in the organization when the employees have left the building but that you cannot find in the balance sheet" (p. 19). Examples of these are the organisational structure, the management system, the information systems (computer software and databases), the patents and the copyrights owning to a firm or an organisation. *Relational capital* (Grasenick and Low, 2004) is the value raised through relationships that a firm or organisation deploys with its external environment (i.e., providers, customers, potential customers, users, sellers, other firms and organisations). Relational capital also includes the value derived from relationships the firm or organisation has with its stakeholders, investors and creditors as well as the value of its brand name.

B. Intellectual Capital in Libraries

In a pioneering work, Koenig (1997) argued that intellectual capital should be turned into a comparative advantage by librarians. The author recognised the importance of measuring intellectual capital in the library context. An annual report presenting the current status of intellectual capital utilisation was considered to be equally important as any other library report. Such a report should be composed from a list of indicators reflecting the library's resources and investments in intellectual capital. For instance, within the relational capital category, an intangible asset is the loyalty of the library users, which can be expressed by an indicator for a percentage of the active library users. Another intangible asset of the same category is the relations built with publishers expressed by an indicator of active printed and digital library subscriptions. Proper management decisions could be based on annual reports for the intangible assets indicators. Not so long ago, White (2007a) stated that the identification of intangible assets in a library provides three advantages to the management team: (a) the ability to present to the stakeholders a report illustrating library's effectiveness; (b) to unify library's tangible and intangible resources to meet the stakeholders requirements and (c) to utilise the library's intangibles to achieve the strategic objectives. For that purpose, he classified intellectual capital into customer (or relationship capital), human capital and structural capital. Moreover, human capital was identified by White (2007b) as a core element in assessing library's performance. An effective human capital assessment could become a tool to use in making decisions about budget allocation, recruitment, staff training and library service improvements.

In the same way, Livonen and Huotari (2007) analysed the three categories of intellectual capital (human, structural and relational) in the context of an academic library. Intangible assets in human capital are the knowledge, experience, capabilities, skills and competencies of the staff. Staff's knowledge, skills and competences are further analysed and explained through various paradigms. Intangible assets that have been identified as being embodied in structural capital are the organisational structure, the library's systems, databases, content description, metadata and access to information resources. For the relational capital category, the authors identified library's information literacy training programs, relationships between the academic library and the academy (e.g., students, researchers and teachers) as well as others such as cooperation with publishers.

More recently, Kostagiolas and Asonitis (2009) discussed the practical and theoretical significance of intangible assets management in academic libraries. The authors studied indicative intangible assets through the same classifications, that is, human, organisational (or structural) and relational capital. With regard to human capital, they studied staff training, team development, experience and flexibility. For organisational capital, they studied library automation, innovation, patents and management systems (business plans and quality certification). Finally, considering the relational capital category, the authors discussed intangibles such as the lists of users, user training and the participation in information networks. In a more recent work, Asonitis and Kostagiolas (2010) proposed a methodological framework, based on analytic hierarchy process (AHP) method, for determining a hierarchy among the three categories of intellectual capital (human, organisational and relational) in libraries. Criterion for the hierarchy is the contribution of each of the intellectual capital category to the objective of improving library's performance. Hierarchy arises from the calculation of the corresponding weights of each of the intellectual capital categories. A case study, implementing the framework, was produced for the Greece's central public libraries.

Although the literature directly related to intangible assets in libraries is quite limited, a significant amount of work with indirect references to intellectual capital may deserve further mention. This extensive literature is indirectly related in a sense that the term intangible asset/knowledge asset or intellectual capital may not be referred to directly at all, although interesting research for specific intangibles is presented. This vast amount of loosely interconnected work may reveal the actual underlying importance of specific intangible assets in libraries. Table 1 provides examples that are indicative of this nature. The classification of intangible assets into human, organisational/ structural and relational is presented with indicative intangible assets for each category. Furthermore, in the following subsections, an analysis for the management of these specific intangible assets is provided.

Table 1
Indicative Intangible Assets for Libraries and Information Services

Intellectual capital category	Indicative intangible assets
Human capital (HC)	Personal networks Staff training/education Staff quality/competence Attributes
Organisational/structural capital (OC/SC)	Contracts Intellectual property/copyrights Digitised collections Access view policies Quality and safety assurance/certifications Branding Knowledge-based teams Learning culture Human resource management Remote information services Systems for accessing databases Systems for network development User surveys
Relational capital (RC)	Customer relationship management Networking and cooperation among libraries Participation in innovation networks Cooperation Trust loyalty User training

1. Human Capital

Human capital is the library staff. Training of library's staff and in general the quality of the staff are important intangible assets embodied in library's human capital. Continuous training of library staff is a significant factor in encouraging innovation and creativity and ensuring the library is the information starting point for its community of users (Broady-Preston and Felice, 2006). Staff training may cover topics such as advanced searching techniques on databases, the use of the OPAC, development of information literacy programs, resource evaluation, the use of e-journals and e-books and research methods. The perspective of Bond University library's scorecard (Cribb, 2005) provides specific characteristics for the quality of library staff.

These characteristics include flexibility, user-focus, motivation, pro-activeness, innovation and team-oriented.

2. Organisational/Structural Capital

Organisational/structural capital includes organisational structure, the management system, the collection (both digital and conventional), automation systems, the patents and the copyrights of a library. Zhang (2006) argues that contracts and copyrights, the digitised collection as well as the access policies should be accounted for in a digital library valuation. Indeed, information dissemination is a significant quality of a digital library contributing to its overall structural quality. Organisational capital includes team organisation and library's learning culture. Sheng and Sun (2007) state that hierarchical organisational structures (pyramid structures) have disadvantages such as poor communication, bureaucracy, conflicts among the departments and a general lack of coordination in day-to-day business operations. They suggest that knowledge-based, self-managed teams should be able to overcome bureaucratised structures in libraries in the 21st century. Knowledge-based team organisation structure may enable a library's staff opportunities to use their skills and competences, to take risks on developing innovative services and to implement pioneering activities and services. A learning culture environment is suitable for any library because it focuses on good communication, trust and continuous improvement. Mullins (2001) also suggested that the classical organisation hierarchy needs to be replaced by team-centred management.

A library's organisational assets include databases and digitised information content as well as the infrastructure developed to connect library users to other authorities such as a local, public library. Anttiroiko and Savolainen (2007) discuss the role of a public library as being "to serve as mediating and filtering mechanisms in local-global interactions" (p. 61) between the local community and the global community. In that respect, intellectual capital includes remote services that a public library can develop for connecting its users with local authorities and public administration services. Moreover, the presence of digitised content on the Internet is increasing rapidly. A library can be the intermediate node collecting this information from heterogeneous networks, assessing its accuracy, organising it and then providing this information to their primary constituents. User surveys are intangible assets subsumed to the organisational/structural capital. Research on library strategic planning (Pacios, 2007) showed that user surveys identified important objectives that are needed in public library planning and developing library collections.

Brand names are valuable intangible assets. Anfruns (2009) identifies the brand name, the know-how and the assets embodied in human capital, as vital intangible assets of a museum. Important museum assets may also be derived from franchise agreements such as licenses for using brand name, trademarks, lending exhibits, transferring of know-how in building or managing a museum. Consider for example the significance of the brand name of a museum (Anfruns, 2009) such as the following: Guggenheim, Louvre and Hermitage. The valuation of such intangible assets is quite high. Guggenheim Bilbao, Spain museum, created in 1997 paid a franchise fee of €18 million (around $21.5 million, which is about 15% of the total investment) to the Guggenheim in Manhattan, New York. The Louvre Abu Dhabi Museum in the United Arab Republic which is to be opened in 2012 has to pay €300 million (around $358 million) over a period of 30 years to the famous Musée du Louvre of Paris, France, to get the license to use the brand name Louvre. Hermitage Amsterdam in the Netherlands gives 1% of its annual income to the Hermitage museum in Saint Petersburg in Russia. Branding is embodied into a library's structural capital. According to Hood and Henderson (2005), branding is an important asset for reversing potential negative perceptions towards public libraries. This may be achieved by improving public awareness about library services and activities, thus building user loyalty, and enhancing the library's reputation.

3. Relational Capital

Relational capital is the capital included in the relationships a library sets up with its external environment, that is, providers, customers, potential customers, other libraries and organisations, and investors. Hence, a library's relational capital includes the participation in library networks, participation in innovation networks and digital content network development, professional networks and so forth. Indeed, strategies such as customer relationship management (CRM), virtual help desks (VHD) as well as a community of practice approach (i.e., groups of people interested on a specific knowledge area—CoP) are building relational capital. According to Anttiroiko and Savolainen (2007) to increase its value, a public library should participate in information networks with other libraries and build link with publishers and other information distribution and innovation networks. Partnerships developed in this way may take the form of contracts, agreements and synergies through common activities. These are library's intangible assets embodied into library's relational capital.

Libraries are the organisations that can guarantee the provision of reliable and qualitative educational, cultural, entertainment and government material to the public. Furthermore, the proliferation of digital scholarly material may lead libraries to create the synergies for getting access rights to a document instead of acquiring document. Hence, libraries should take part in collaborative networks. Collaboration (Sheng and Sun, 2007) is based on mutual trust and libraries of all kinds need to invest in "trust development." Examples of cooperative services undertaken by library networks are catalogue sharing, inter-library loans and document delivery, technology and know-how sharing. Train and Elkin (2001) argue that user training programs are important to develop a sustainable and trustworthy relationship between staff and users. Such a library initiative may include literacy and reader development programs. A reader development project could be structured through workgroup sessions or events such as Book of the Month club readings or "Book Forager" game for children. These actions not only enhance reading pleasure and enable shared reading experiences within group, but it also highlights and promotes the library. Research on library strategic planning by Pacios (2007) indicates that the design of summer reading programs, the cooperation with teachers in organising reading events and implementation of reading activities focusing on the elderly or children are key features to promote a library.

IV. Issues for Managing Intellectual Capital in Libraries

Roos *et al.* (2005) suggest that management should make judgements based on the following three dimensions for the intellectual capital resources: (a) How influential is a given intangible asset on the organisation's ability to create value? (b) What level of quality does the intangible asset holds when compared to the ideal? and (c) What quantity of the intangible asset should the organisation acquire, when compared to the ideal situation? The identification and valuation of intellectual capital, together with the pre-mentioned questions, construct a rather challenging environment for management of intellectual capital in LIS. Vasconcelos (2008) recommended that one should focus on the library's unique features, wherein lays most of the library's value. Roos *et al.* (2005) suggest a set of five requirements for utilising intangible assets:

I.   To be valuable, in a sense that could support the library's strategic goals.
II.   To be durable, in a sense that should hold its attributes over time.
III.   To be scarce, in a sense that should not be easily accessible by potential competitors.
IV.   To be inimitable, in a sense that a potential imitator should experience significant costs for its duplication.
V.   To be unsubstitutable, in a sense that a substitute is difficult if not impossible to be developed.

Although the significance of intellectual capital in value creation in libraries is rather obvious, the real issue to be addressed is which is the best approach for measuring and valuing intangible assets. Management of intellectual capital is based on the fact that an organisation's real value is not the one presented in the balance sheet of assets and liabilities. Indeed, an organisation's total value is expressed as the sum of its financial position that is described in a balance sheet and the value of its intellectual capital. For evaluating intellectual capital in an organisation, Vasconcelos *et al.* (2001) proposed a so-called *relationship to product versus content dilemma*. They expressed uncertainty estimation of intellectual capital value because it cannot be precise. Often the value of the intangible assets is dependent on the context of its deployment and often "lies in the eye of the beholder" (Vasconcelos, 2008). The authors also suggested that one should concentrate on a specific point in time or should concentrate in the future based on the library's strategic goals.

Valuation of intellectual capital is not straightforward. The first step of any valuation method is to define the objective to be valued (Andriessen, 2004). Hence, a library has to identify its intangible assets before proceeding to their valuation. Identification of intangibles requires an introspection of library's resources, activities, structure and day-to-day operation features, from the point of view of intangibles. Valuation of quality and quantity of intangibles also helps the management team to assess the performance and effectiveness of its services, better allocate its resources and investments on new innovated information services and report its intellectual capital status to the stakeholders. One of the advantages of intellectual capital reporting is that it gives transparency to the use of funds (Roos *et al.*, 2005), which is often required in library areas.

While intellectual capital valuation is a complex problem, libraries fortunately do not have to grapple with solving the problem. Despite the uniqueness of the libraries, some valuing methods and techniques are available. Valuation of intellectual capital or of a specific intangible asset may take the form of a financial measurement or of a performance valuation. Financial measurement ascribes a monetary value to the intangible assets. Performance valuation is based on key performance indicators and on the assessment of stakeholders' perception about the examined intellectual capital/intangible asset. Three approaches are available for financial valuation of a specific intangible asset (Reilly and Schweihs, 1998): cost, market and income. The cost approach estimates the cost of recreating the utility of the intangible asset. The market approach estimates the equilibrium price of the intangible, which is the market price at which the supply of an item equals the quantity demanded. The income approach estimates the future income expected from the possession or the usage of the intangible asset and then calculates the present value of the estimated cash flow using an appropriate discount rate.

The market-to-book-ratio method takes a holistic approach to give a monetary value to the intellectual capital of a firm. According to this method, monetary value is calculated by comparing the library's market value against its book value. The Value-Added Intellectual Coefficient (VAIC™), proposed by Pulic (2004), also assigns monetary value to a firms' human and structural capital. According to this method, the value added is defined as the difference between the output (total sales) and the input (cost of material and services). Human capital is not assigned in inputs, but instead is considered as an investment. Human capital, structural capital and intellectual capital efficiency are calculated by VAIC™ methodology. All data required by VAIC™ can be found in library's financial statements.

Andriessen (2004) provides more methods for valuing and measuring intangibles in businesses. In his work, methods are described, categorised under various criteria and advantages and disadvantages, appropriateness of usage, are evaluated. Performance valuation of intellectual capital (Roos and Roos, 1997) may include qualitative research, quantitative research, empirical research and interviews based on structured questionnaires. It may also include the usage of key performance indicators, statistical methods or, to the extent of a desired situation, a metric measuring the importance or the increment or decline of intellectual capital in a library. Measurement under a mathematical measurement theory is a type of mapping between a set of elements containing the object to be measured and a subset of numbers (Hubbard, 2007). Yes or no questions, nominal and ordinal scales, that may be used in semi-structured questionnaires, have all been studied as measuring tools. In a statistical method, a value for a statistical metric (e.g., mean value and unbiased estimator) is accompanied by the corresponding statistical error. For example, Asonitis and Kostagiolas (2010) used a structured questionnaire to capture stakeholders' perceptions about the importance of each of the three categories of intellectual capital (human, structural and relational) in public libraries. Importance was assessed through the contribution of each of the intellectual capital categories to the objective of improving library's services and effectiveness. Furthermore, they employed the AHP, which is a rigorous mathematical model to establish a metric, prioritising the importance of intellectual capital categories. The AHP process comes from the field of operational research.

The libraries around the world operate in distinctive environments. The intangible nature of the intellectual capital may erroneously imply that the allocation of intangible assets over space as well as the location of a specific library is irrelevant. In other words, one may suggest that an investment in intangible assets may have the same return, irrespective of the location factor. The location consideration of intellectual capital utilisation goes beyond the choice of a library's location. Indeed, the library's systems and services should be defined by all of their characteristics, including the location of the library. In fact, although the tangible assets of a library can be transferred and largely remain unchanged, intangible assets embrace human experiences and interactions and therefore are rather difficult to transfer. Hence, the same services, which may be provided by different libraries, should be treated as a different service. In Vasconcelos (2008), it is also argued that the exchange value of information services, channels and systems should be studied using "classical" economic and accountancy methods, but the utilisation of information should be studied using a user-centric cognitive approach that includes the user, the use and the contributions of the information.

It is assumed that libraries produce services that become intellectual capital for the individuals and organisations they serve. Value-in-use of information is described by Repo (1986). The value of the information services and intellectual capital produced by the libraries is determined by market forces through their exchange value as well as their expected and perceived value-in-use. Nevertheless, it would be rather unrealistic to consider what would be the utilisation of intellectual capital for the pro-vision of the same services, without some consideration of a library's location. For example, the utilisation of human capital may be significantly influenced from cultural characteristics, active social networks and different higher educational systems. Moreover, neighbouring scientific and academic insti-tutions as well as an urban or a rural environment may influence the quality of staff and the availability of training programs. Organisational and relational capital may be significantly influenced by regulations and laws that are specific to a given country and therefore may or may not foster exploitation of the relevant intangible assets. The spatial dimension may play a significant role, but its importance remains to be determined for managing intellectual capital in libraries.

Over the past decades, competition for libraries has become more and more intense. In a Porterian approach, new rivals intensify competition due to an upsurge of services (for free or not) on the Internet, which are competitive to services traditionally supplied by a library. For example, "Google Scholar" is a free search engine specialising in academic publications. Therefore, members of the academic community could use "Google Scholar" as a starting point for scholarly searches rather than their academic library. On the other hand, publishers often have contractual agreements with institutions (e.g., universities) and/or networks of libraries.

Hence, individual libraries act as the proxy of the agreement between the publisher and the institution or the network. In this case, free information on the Internet is a competitive service to that given by a library. Google's ambitious project called "Google Books Library Project" may also evolve to be an information service competitive to the services provided by the public libraries. According to Google (2010), the aim of the project is to "make it easier for people to find relevant books – specifically, books they wouldn't find any other way such as those that are out of print – while carefully respecting authors' and publishers' copyrights. Our ultimate goal is to work with publishers and libraries to create a comprehensive, searchable, virtual card catalogue of all books in all languages that helps users discover new books and publishers discover new readers." To survive in the long run, libraries need to utilise intellectual capital such as that provided by the library staff.

V. Conclusion

A significant number of issues related to the management of intellectual capital within the libraries have been identified as well as the role that the libraries play within the new knowledge-based economic environment. Andriessen (2004) identifies the globalisation of the markets, the lower of the barriers in international transactions (i.e., of goods and services and investments) and the growth of information and communication technology as key drivers for the new economy. If this is true, LIS potentially have a significant role to play within the new economy. Libraries through their services and systems can distribute a core segment of all necessary knowledge and information required by the global competitive economic environment. On the contrary, libraries all over the world face the pressure of competition and are pushed to modernise their management and other systems.

The libraries do not remain unaffected by the ever-changing environment, and for many, the reductions in funding is a harsh reality to face while other libraries are facing similar problems ahead. Like in every innovative concept, such as the concept of intellectual capital, dilemmas arise because we can only approximate the degree to which we are benefiting from any intellectual capital management actions. The extent and the spread of this threat however may push libraries further to take action immediately. In addition, increased competition and pressures from global economic threats may also force libraries to redefine their strategies in relation to intellectual capital.

Indeed, a way forward is utilisation of intangible assets. Small-scale investments in library's intangible assets (compared with those made in tangible ones) may yield benefits well beyond the amount of money invested. The ability to motivate library management teams to participate in professional networks is an example of such an action. Participation of libraries in collaborative networks adds significantly to the intellectual capital of the library by:

- enabling broader access to the available information material (e.g., databases and documents);
- improving the human capital (e.g., skills, competences, experience and teamwork capacity of staff);
- sharing experiences or actions aiming at structural capital assets (e.g., management techniques and practices, user surveys, software platforms access to heterogeneous data stores and retrieval environments); and
- improving relational capital (e.g., relationship marketing, trust development, user training programs in information literacy and lifelong learning).

All of the above can lead to the development of new innovative LIS. An innovative service is difficult for competitors to imitate. Invisible and unsurpassed quality within an integrated system of components designed to serve individualized needs is difficult to imitate. Whatever their form or shape, libraries can accumulate clear-cut benefits from services with longer life cycle expectancy giving sustainable cash flow.

Management of intangibles may aid library administration and management to identify its core intangible assets and to evaluate the effectiveness of investments made on these assets. Results of intellectual capital management should be illustrated in reports and complement to annual financial reports. This would give library stakeholders all of the required information to keep track of steps being taken to achieve an appropriate role in forthcoming economic and social realities. The management of the distinct categories of intellectual capital may require different approaches based on conceptual frameworks from different disciplines. For instance, for relational capital, one may valuate intellectual capital in a market sense, but not for human capital. This would involve a disciplinary shift, from an accounting model to a non-accounting one. Resolution of different viewpoints for management of intellectual capital cannot take place within the conceptual framework of a single discipline.

References

Andriessen, D. (2004). *Making Sense of Intellectual Capital: Designing a Method for the Valuation of Intangibles*. Elsevier Butterworth-Heinemann, Oxford, England.

Anfruns, J. (2009, May). The role of International Council of Museums for the safeguarding of intangible heritage and museums development of intangible assets. *World Conference on Intellectual Capital for Communities in the Knowledge Economy (IC5)*, Paris, France. Retrieved from http://info.worldbank.org/etools/docs/library/251715/Anfruns%20Intangible%20heritage%20Final.pdf

Anttiroiko, A-V., and Savolainen, R. (2007). New premises of public library strategies in the age of globalization. *Advances in Library Administration and Organization* 25, 61–81.

Ark, B. (2002). *Understanding Productivity and Income Differentials among OECD Countries: A Survey*. The Review of Economics Performance and Social Progress, pp. 69–72. Retrieved from http://www.csls.ca/repsp/2/bartvanark.pdf

Asonitis, St., and Kostagiolas, P. (2010). An analytic hierarchy approach for intellectual capital: Evidence for the Greek central public libraries. *Library Management* 31(3), 145–161.

Bontis, N. (2002). *World Congress on Intellectual Capital Reading*. Butterworth-Heinemann, Boston, MA.

Bouteiller, C. (2000, August). *The Evaluation of Intangibles: Advocating of an Option Based Approach*. Paper presented at Alternative Perspectives of Finance & Accounting Conference, Hamburg, Germany.

Broady-Preston, J., and Felice, J. (2006). Customers, relationships and libraries: University of Malta–a case study. *Aslib Proceedings: New Information Perspectives* 58(6), 525–536.

Childs, P. (2006). Sssh! The quiet revolution. *New Library World* 107(1222/1223), 149–156.

Choong, K. K. (2008). Intellectual capital: Definitions, categorization and reporting models. *Journal of Intellectual Capital* 9(4), 609–638.

Cribb, G. (2005, August). Human resource development: Impacting on all four perspectives of the balanced scoreboard. *World Library and Information Congress: 71th IFLA General Conference and Council,* Oslo, Norway. Retrieved from http://docs.google.com/viewer?a=v&q=cache:yB2n2jUNPKoJ:archive.ifla.org/IV/ifla71/papers/075e-Cribb.pdf

Edvinsson, L., and Malone, M. S. (1997). *Intellectual Capital*. Harper Collins, New York.

Google (2010). *Google Books Library Project [Internet]*. Retrieved from: http://books.google.com/googlebooks/library.html

Grasenick, K., and Low, J. (2004). Shaken, not stirred: Defining and connecting indicators for the measurement & valuation of intangibles. *Journal of Intellectual Capital* 5(2), 268–281.

Hand, J., and Lev, B. (2003). *Intangible Assets*. Oxford University Press, New York.

Harris, P. (2002). European challenge: Developing global organizations. *European Business Review* 4(6), 416–425.

Hood, D., and Henderson, K. (2005). Branding in the United Kingdom public library service. *New Library World* 106(1208/1209), 16–28.

Hubbard, D. (2007). *How to Measure Anything: Finding the Value of "Intangibles" in Business*. Wiley, Hoboken, NJ.

Kaufmann, L., and Schneider, Y. (2004). Intangibles a synthesis of current research. *Journal of Intellectual Capital* 5(3), 366–388.

Koenig, M. (1997). Intellectual capital and how to leverage it. *The Bottom Line: Managing Library Finances* 10(3), 112–118.

Kostagiolas, P., and Asonitis, St. (2008). Utilizing intangible assets in the worlds of production. *The International Journal of Knowledge, Culture & Change Management* 8(2), 1–8.

Kostagiolas, P., and Asonitis, St. (2009). Intangible assets for academic libraries. *Library Management* 30(6/7), 419–429.

Lev, B. (2001). *Intangibles: Measurement, Management and Reporting*. Brookings Institution Press, Washington, DC.

Livonen, M., and Huotari, M. (2007). The university library's intellectual capital. *Advances in Library Administration and Organization* 25, 83–96.

MERITUM (2002). *MERITUM* guidelines for managing & reporting on intangibles, measuring intangibles to understand and improve innovation management–MERITUM. Madrid, Spain.

Mullins, J. (2001). People-centered management in a library context. *Library Review* 50(6), 305–309.

OECD (2003). *Glossary of Statistical Terms* [*Internet*]. Retrieved from http://stats .oecd.org/glossary/detail.asp?ID=1121

OECD (2005). *OECD Handbook on Economic Globalisation Indicators*. OECD, Paris, France.

Pacios, A. (2007). The priorities of public libraries at the onset of the third millennium. *Library Management* 28(6/7), 416–427.

Porta, J. I. D., and Oliver, J. L. H. (2006). How to measure IC in clusters: Empirical evidence. *Journal of Intellectual Capital* 7(3), 354–380.

Pulic, A. (2004). *Basic Information on VAIC™*. Retrieved from http://www.vaic-on .net

Reilly, R. F., and Schweihs, R. P. (1998). *Valuing Intangible Assets*. McGraw-Hill, New York.

Repo, A. (1986). The dual approach to the value of information. *Information Processing and Management* 13(5), 373–383.

Roos, G., Pike, S., and Fernström, L. (2005). *Managing Intellectual Capital in Practice*. Elsevier Butterworth-Heinemann, Oxford, England.

Roos, G., and Roos, J. (1997). Measuring your company's intellectual performance. *Long Range Planning: Special Issue on Intellectual Capital* 30(3), 413–426.

Roos, J., Roos, G., Edvinsson, L., and Dragonetti, N. C. (1997). *Intellectual Capital: Navigating in the New Business Landscape*. Macmillan, London, England.

Sheng, X., and Sun, L. (2007). Developing knowledge innovation culture of libraries. *Library Management* 28(1/2), 36–52.

Storper, M., and Salais, R. (1997). *Worlds of Production*. Harvard University Press, London, England.

Sveiby, K. E. (1997). *The New Organizational Wealth: Managing and Measuring Knowledge-Based Assets*. Berret Koehler, San Francisco, CA.

Train, B., and Elkin, J. (2001). Measuring the unmeasurable: Reader development and its impact on performance measurement of the public sector. *Library Review* 50(6), 295–404.

Vasconcelos, A., Ellis, D., Pieter, L., and Chavda, A. (2001). Problems in the Measurement of Intellectual Assets. In *Proceedings of the Second European Conference on Knowledge Management* (pp. 705–720). Bled School of Management, Bled, Slovenia.

Vasconcelos, A. C. (2008). Dilemmas in knowledge management. *Library Management* **29**(4/5), 422–443.

White, L. N. (2007a). Unseen measures: the need to account for intangibles. *The Bottom Line: Managing Library Finances* **20**(2), 77–84.

White, L. N. (2007b). A kaleidoscope of possibilities: Strategies for assessing human capital in libraries. *The Bottom Line: Managing Library Finances* **20**(3), 109–115.

Zhang, W. (2006). Digital library intellectual property right evaluation and method. *The Electronic Library* **25**(3), 267–273.

How Does the Library Profession Grow Managers? It Doesn't—They Grow Themselves

Maureen L. Mackenzie[a] and James P. Smith[b]
[a]Townsend School of Business, Dowling College, Oakdale, New York, USA
[b]Library, St. Francis College, Brooklyn, New York, USA

Abstract

This chapter explores the question of where and how leaders in the library field gain the knowledge, skills, and ability to lead and manage people. The authors report empirical evidence to answer this question based on the results of the third stage of an ongoing study—a study which examines the academic preparation of professional librarians who have become directors of libraries. The results of a survey inquiring into the formal training received by practicing library directors are detailed. Among other findings, 55.1% of the library directors surveyed and observed that graduate library school did not prepare them to become library directors. There is some evidence that a shift of perception regarding the need for traditional management training has begun to occur in library schools. The authors contend that this trend needs to accelerate if the information profession intends to prepare library directors to assume leadership roles in the future. This chapter briefly reviews the research findings from stage one and two research, which provided the foundation for the current study. As a result of this research a fourth stage of research is planned which will use in person in-depth interviews of library directors. The influence of leadership on organizational results has been explored within the broader management literature. There is clearly a relationship between leadership and results. What is unclear is how and where these leaders gain the knowledge, skills, and ability to lead and manage.

I. Introduction

A. Line-Management in Nontraditional Businesses

This study evolved from a broader research agenda of defining and understanding the process of educating the individuals who hold management positions in non-traditional businesses. Examples of such non-traditional business managers, and the graduate degrees they hold, include: Library

ADVANCES IN LIBRARIANSHIP, VOL. 33
© 2011 by Emerald Group Publishing Limited
ISSN: 0065-2830
DOI: 10.1108/S0065-2830(2011)0000033006

Directors: MLS, Primary and Secondary School Principals: Ed.D; Museum Directors: MFA, College Provosts and Presidents: Ph.D.; and Physicians: M.D. These individuals have achieved management positions as a result of their expertise in a defined field. For example, college provosts often emerge from the faculty of a discipline-specific department. However, the Doctorate of Philosophy Degree (Ph.D.), which certifies the individual as academically qualified (AQ), may not have provided the needed management and leadership training.

The route to management outlined above is fundamentally different from that taken by the individual who has sought an advanced degree in management with the intention of assuming a management and leadership role within *any* industry. The Master of Business Administration (MBA) degree is the terminal degree that prepares an individual to be a manager regardless of discipline. The pedagogical goal of faculty members who teach in an MBA degree program is to create an in-depth learning experience in order to prepare their students to navigate the complexity of any workplace environment. Specialized accrediting organizations for business school programs focus on the graduates' ethical and creative ability to face critical issues in the ever-changing global business environment (International Assembly for Collegiate Business Education 2009).

B. The World of Library Administrators

Librarianship can be found at the heart of the taxonomy involving the many facets of information storage and retrieval. It is a well-established profession. Librarianship evolved to meet the need to organize an ever-growing collection of tangible knowledge artifacts (Battles, 2003). The American Library Association (ALA) is the major organization for librarianship in the United States and Canada, and exerts influence throughout the world. Founded in 1876, the ALA's mission is "to provide leadership for the development, promotion, and improvement of library and information services and the profession of librarianship in order to enhance learning and ensure access to information for all" (American Library Association, 2010).

The terminal degree for librarians has evolved over time and is represented by many names. In this chapter, the authors will broadly refer to the ALA-accredited terminal degree as the Master of Library Science (MLS), although this traditional name has been replaced by more current terminology. This research revealed a lack of consensus about the name of the degree and its content (Mackenzie and Smith, 2007). What is agreed within the library field is that the desired outcome for individuals earning this degree, is the preparation needed to assume a role in the multifaceted field of librarianship (Gorman, 2006).

The Library Director position is the prevalent managerial position within the profession. Librarians work in a broad range of institutions and perform a broad range of functions including management. Library directors, most explicitly, must deal with the same personnel decisions that more traditional managers must face. Library directors must be cognizant of various human resource-related topics, such as reasonable accommodation, sexual harassment, fair labor standards, equal employment opportunity provisions, and the like. As a part of their duties, library directors must appraise performance, set standards, motivate and manage change, as well as select and release individuals from the employment relationship (Mackenzie and Smith, 2007, 2009).

The specific focus of this series of articles is on the academic preparation of individuals who chose to enter the information field as librarians and who subsequently assume a director and other leadership positions. Although the question of library director leadership and management education has been debated for many years (Woodsworth and von Wahlde, 1988), this study captures the insights of practicing library directors.

The central question remains: Do accredited library education programs properly prepare library students to enter management level positions within the library profession? The research presented herein used multiple methodologies in order to attempt to answer this question.

C. Literature Review

A review of the professional literature suggests that the library profession is not alone when considering management training in its master-level programs. Stakeholders of the Master of Fine Arts (MFA) programs, Master of Social Work (MSW) programs, and wildlife student programs, have all shared a common concern; that newly educated professionals lack adequate training in crucial management skills (Kroll, 2007; Nesoff, 2007; Rhine 2007).

In the field of social work, Nesoff (2007, p. 284) wrote about the "ten competencies that the National Network of Social Work Managers have proposed be added to MSW programs. Doing so would counter the perceived need to overcome the lack of management training their master level social work graduates receive. The ten competencies include "advocacy, public/community relations and marketing . . . planning . . . human resource management and staff development." Nesoff states that "Schools of social work need to pay particular attention to the 'competition' that their MSW graduates are facing from managers who have learned on-the-job and through continuing education, and from graduates of MBA, MPA, or nonprofit management degree programs" (Nesoff, p. 283).

Kroll (2007) wrote about his concern for wildlife students' "lack of adequate training. In his opinion they should receive training in "planning, consensus-building, and communication..." Without it they were unable to "bridge the science-management gap..." Kroll further suggested that professional internships and training in "communication, economics and political science" should be included in wildlife students' education in order to close the gap" (p. 226).

Rhine (2007) wrote about the results of a study he conducted of the perceptions of decision-making authorities in theaters regarding the "practical preparation" of recent MFA graduates. He found there was a need to place more emphasis on "management training, management experience and internship."

However, some still hold the view that specialized degrees should not surrender their professional ideals. Jerry Saltz (2007) in his article titled, *Has Money Ruined Art?*, thought that the MFA is becoming the new MBA.

Although it has been suggested that there are drastic differences among other such environments (e.g., political, military, and business) when compared to the library environment, Lowry (1988) suggested that there *are* common characteristics that can define effective leadership within all of these environments. Unfortunately, library literature is characterized by a dearth of studies in leadership. Riggs (1985, p. 9) further suggested that librarians should "take their cue from the business community."

Gapen (1988) proposed that the interest in the professional development of the library director is but one puzzle piece in the larger landscape of higher education. She articulated the challenges, or more appropriately, the differences of managing in an academic venue, versus to managing in a for-profit mainstream business. She stated that the environment "is a looser context where personal idiosyncrasy and individual behavior are not readily susceptible to direction or control" (p. 48). Yet, library directors must be managers. The faculty may expect directors to be their advocate, but clearly the director is an administrator and therefore the administration expects them to act as such.

Professional experiences and research have suggested that library leadership can, at times, be accidental (Hoffmann, 1988) rather than intentional. She asserts that career management for library directors and leaders requires mentors, a good fit in the job, and networking.

Lynch (1988) discussed how libraries, though the product is nontraditional compared to a for-profit business, seek to improve and lean on the innovations emerging from the broader field of management and innovations. Even cataloging, a fundamental skill in the library discipline, leans on innovations in emerging technologies and new systems. At the same time, civil rights requirements, union agreements, and the profession's own attitudes about the role of library employees create management conflict. The idea of tenure when related to a job creates dysfunction in the management of those improvements. Therefore, she states that "such dysfunctions are not easy to manage organizationally or humanly. They require great talent and skill on the part of librarians and library managers at all levels" (Lynch, 1988, p. 76).

Just as persuasive is Creth's (1988) position that the relationship of the library to industry is intimately intertwined She suggested that ". . . as the economic base of society emerges more strongly as an information one, libraries and the industrial sector will become more closely intertwined. As this occurs, librarians need to be in a position to exercise strong leadership and play a central role in defining the information society" (p. 79).

The attributes for library directors are no different than what is required and desired in industry leaders. These attributes include but are not limited to energy, creativity, and commitment to their organizations, strong communication skills, acknowledging and rewarding staff, the ability to energize others and create new direction. Creth stated that "Leadership requires more than being articulate and persuasive; the individual must have credibility in order to instill the confidence in those who are needed to make the revision for the future occur" (p. 83). The traditional management role must be demonstrated in staffing, contingency plans for moving and promoting staff, creating a healthy and open environment where staff can share ideas, and processes for resolving conflict between organizational stakeholders.

Williams (1988) suggested that the "performance for research libraries is therefore directly related to the leadership and management skills of their directors, middle managers, and prospective managers; managers who must be able to plan with effect, organize services and resources for ready/ maximum accessibility, attract, motivate and lead staff, evaluate and utilize new information control technologies for library operations, and evaluate organizational performance on an ongoing, formal basis" (p. 100). He said that as a result, "the availability of competent managers is directly proportional to the kind and content of leadership training in research librarianship. Training, whether through a library school, workshops, institutes, internships, fellowships, or in-house programs, must be designed to provide the framework for continued leadership development, and thus organizational effectiveness" (p. 100). He further asserted that directors' skills, knowledge, and ability should include creative and analytic thought, data gathering and analysis, decision making, group leadership, identification of goals and objectives, interpersonal relations, managerial competencies, managerial roles, organizational diagnosis, performance, and planning. The knowledge content that library leaders require is traditionally integrated in an MBA program.

The levels of graduate education for librarianship focus on different target audiences. The master's level curriculum develops fledgling library and information professionals according to Lester (1988). It appears that most management skills are offered at the post graduate level through various continuing education venues. At the doctoral level there is an opportunity for leadership training or development, but Lester points out that generally, it is not the primary focus. She stated that "the degree to which the library and information science education community as a whole has given conscious attention to the need to educate for leadership, especially within the parameters of the master's level program, is almost imperceptible..." (p. 131). She adds that library schools tend to focus on competencies and have therefore not been concerned with laying the foundation for long-term leadership development and specifically cites the need for leadership education as well as internships and mentoring.

The literature suggests that library directors *are* traditional managers who require specialized management skill development (Giesecke, 2001; Montgomery and Cook, 2005; Weingand, 2001). Koenig's (2007) viewpoint is similar in that the information field has been dissatisfied with the education and competencies taught in library and information science programs. His review of key articles published in Education for Information points to the debate between an education focused on theory versus application and suggests that the tension between the practitioner and the theorist continues to grow. Koenig also points to the insights in both Cronin's and Line's articles that emphasized the need for marketing, financial management, and administrative training for librarians (Koenig, 2007).

II. The Research Framework

The overall design of this study is exploratory in nature (Morse and Richards, 2002), which is an appropriate approach when specific areas of knowledge are being probed with the intent of drawing meaning from the data collected (Kidder, 1981). The research design is also iterative. The results from *stage one* and *stage two* of the previous studies (Mackenzie and Smith, 2007, 2009) were used to inform the research focus of *stage three*, the results of which are presented here. Each stage of the study built upon and extended the results of the prior stage. For the benefit of the reader, and for the sake of clarity, insights from the first two stages of research will be briefly reviewed herein. For more in-depth details see Mackenzie and Smith (2007, 2009).

A. Insights from Stages One and Two

Stage one of the research offered evidence that the library profession has not yet agreed upon the curriculum requirements for preparing future librarians for managerial positions. The study was based on an analysis of *t* 48 ALA fully accredited, English language, programs in the United States and Canada. Schools with conditional accreditation at the time of the study were excluded. Results found 13 different degree titles, many with overlapping terms. (Mackenzie and Smith, 2007). It also revealed that 43.8% of the ALA-accredited library school programs required *no* management courses. Therefore students who anticipate a career path into leadership must somehow construct a curriculum or continuing education program that will prepare them to assume a management positions. For those programs that *did* require a management course (56.2%), most required only one course (54.2%) for completion of the graduate library degree. The requirement of a professional internship is another indicator as to intent to prepare an individual for a future management role is. At the time of the study 81.3% of the 48 reviewed programs did *not* explicitly require a professional internship (Mackenzie and Smith, 2007, 2009).

The data resulting from stage one also suggested that some library schools have a clear vision that management training *is* needed and they provide a range of management courses to meet that need. Other library school programs offered little choice of coursework to those students interested in traditional management preparation. Sixteen of the 48 programs required only one traditional management-related course. Five of the programs offered neither required nor elective management courses.

Stage two more closely examined the management-related curriculum and focused on the coursework level rather than at the program level (stage one). This was done to provide insight into what was perceived as the knowledge and skills required to manage employees and processes. The analysis of 24 syllabi drawn from the ALA accredited programs focused on *managing people* within an organizational environment. Syllabi were obtained from two sources: a scan of Websites; and direct email to faculty to ask for copies of their syllabi. Of the syllabi analyzed, 58.3% included human resource management and 54.2% included strategy, planning, and process. The consensus, as to what should be included, begins to weaken with only 37.5% of the 24 courses covering management of effective teams and leadership theories. The role of management was explicitly taught in only 33.3% of the management-related courses reviewed.

A total of 30 management topics were found within the 24 syllabi reviewed. All 30 of these topics were represented in the management course(s) that were *required* by their degree programs. The evidence of frequency in the *required* courses versus the *lack* of frequency in the *elective* courses was evident. The topic of human resource management was included in 75% of the required courses, yet only 41.7% of the elective management courses. The topics of leadership and leadership theories were included in 58% of the required management courses, yet in only 16.7% of the elective management courses.

In addition, the review of the 24 syllabi found that 75% of the courses reviewed were 100% dedicated to management topics. A comparison of *required* courses to *elective* courses revealed that the required courses were more focused, with 83.3% of the required courses focusing 100% of their content on management-related topics. Only 66.7% of the elective courses were focused solely on management-related content.

Stage two results suggested that there is a mismatch between what is proscribed for management curriculum in business schools and that which passes for management coursework in library school curricula. It appears that library schools have made an effort to include in their curriculum topics such as marketing, public relations, the pursuit of outside funding, and management of external relationships. However, at the present time, it seems that focus on the management of internal relationships with *employee* stakeholders is a lost opportunity.

III. The Current Research: Stage Three

In stage three, the authors expanded the scope of their research to include practicing library directors. The resulting empirical evidence permits triangulation, which improves the research rigor within the qualitative paradigm. The prior two stages focused on what coursework content was offered to students as they earned their graduate library degrees. *Stage three* turned its focus on the individuals who work as managers in the library profession in order to gain insight into the outcomes of the educational processes.

A. Methodology

Stage three utilized a questionnaire to be sent to library directors which was approved by Dowling College's Institutional Review Board. The questionnaire was designed to probe their experiences as practicing librarians who have assumed management positions. The method for *stage three* emerged from both the quantitative and qualitative paradigms. Probability theory suggests that a random sample of the population would provide results that can be cautiously projected to the larger population. As a result, the authors used the personnel index of the 2007–2008 American Library Directory (McDonough, 2007) to identify 100% of the ALA-member libraries and their directors in the United States and Canada. This directory formed the sampling frame for stage three (Salant and Dillman, 1994). With a 5% desired error rate, a 95% confidence rate, and a population of 30,416 libraries, the appropriate sample size was determined to be 380.

A random sample of 380 was drawn from the sampling frame and the questionnaires were mailed twice to them. Follow-up questionnaires also were mailed to improve the response rate. This resulted in a total of 59 responses with 49 surveys deemed usable for the study. The final response rate for stage three was an acceptable 2.9%.

The questionnaire included seven broad questions with multiple sub-sections. The questionnaire consisted of both closed and open-ended questions in order to draw out the experiences from the sample of library directors. Where appropriate, content analysis and open coding (Berg, 1998) were used to analyze the answers provided in response to the open-ended questions.

B. Results

Survey Question: Did you graduate from an ALA-accredited graduate library program? What year did you graduate?

The results provided good coverage for the intent of this study. Of the 49 respondents, 43 (87.8%) reported that they had graduated from an ALA-accredited library school program. Forty-two of the respondents provided their graduation years which *n* ranged from 1967 to 2005.

The 43 respondents who graduated from ALA-accredited programs represented a wide range of institutions. In total, 28 library science programs were represented. Adding to the strength of the results is that no one institution was found to be over-represented. There were no more than three respondents who graduated from the same institution. Two of the 28 institutions were Canadian. The remaining respondents graduated from institutions located in the United States.

Survey Question: What was Name of the Degree. If no library degree, describe college level experience.

Thirty-eight respondents provided the name of the library degree they had earned. The result was a list of eight degree titles with some overlapping terminology. The most prevalent degree title was the "Master of Library Science" degree with 22 respondents (44.9% of all responses). The remainder affirmed the diversity of degree names which had been previously found in stage one of the 2007 study (Mackenzie and Smith, 2007). The details uncovered in *stage three* are presented in Table 1.

Six library directors reported that they had *not* graduated from an ALA-accredited library school. As a follow-up question, they were asked to indicate their educational experience. Three of the six directors had earned graduate degrees in other fields (Master degree or Ph.D.). One director had earned a four-year degree, and two directors held two-year degrees.

Survey Question: Did your library school curriculum include traditional management courses? Please name.

Of the 41 library directors who responded to this question, 32 reported that their library school curriculum did include one or more traditional management course(s). The results are presented in Table 2.

As indicated in Table 3, 36 of the respondents (73.5%) could not recall or did not provide a name of the management courses in their library programs. Thirteen of the 49 library directors (26.5%) did provide some

Table 1
Name of Graduate Library Degree

Name of ALA-approved degree earned	Number of library directors	Percent of total
MLS	22	44.9
MLIS	5	10.2
MSLIS	3	6.2
MSLS	3	6.2
MALS	2	4.1
ME (LS)	1	2.0
ML	1	2.0
MSIN	1	2.0
No answer or no ALA degree	11	22.4
	49	100

Table 2
Respondents' Graduate Library School Curriculum

Did your library school curriculum include traditional management courses?	Number of library directors	Percent of total
Yes, my library curriculum did include traditional management courses	32	65.3
No, my library curriculum did not include traditional management courses	9	18.4
No answer or did not earn a library degree	8	16.3
	49	100

Table 3
Respondents' Graduate Library School Management Curriculum

Name/content of traditional management course	Number of library directors responding	Percent of total
Knowledge of specific type of library (e.g., law, academic, special, public)	6	12.2
Library management or library administration	5	10.2
Combination of courses including both categories mentioned earlier	2	4.1
Can't remember or did not answer	36	73.5
	49	100

indication of the content of the management course(s) included in their programs. The results are presented in Table 3.

Owing to the small number of responses to this question, more pertinent data may be derived from the following question.

Survey Question: **What was the focus of the traditional management course(s)?**

The results from *stage one* and *stage two* of the prior studies (Mackenzie and Smith, 2007, 2009) revealed that many library programs considered collection development, managing the computer networks, and managing a variety of library resources, to be traditional management coursework. Combination courses provided *some* instruction on managing people, but the results indicated that courses with a primary focus on *people* management were infrequent.

The current study (*stage three*) sought to follow-up on these preliminary findings, culled from a review of program course syllabi. The practicing library directors were asked to describe the *focus* of the management courses that they had taken while in library school. Only 65.3% of 49 respondents indicated that their library school curriculum *did* include traditional management courses (Table 2).

The 59.2% of the respondents answered the question regarding the focus of the management courses but only one director stated that the management course focused primarily on managing people. Directors recalling that their courses solely focused on managing the collection accounted for 8.2%, and an additional 2% recalled the focus to be on external management factors such as fundraising. Forty-seven percent of the directors indicated that the traditional management courses were combination courses covering a range of topics, such as managing the physical plant, managing patrons, managing the collection, and managing the employees. The results of this question are presented in Table 4.

In addition, the results indicated that less than half of the management courses were offered in the library school (42.9%) and less than half of the management courses (42.9%) were required courses. Of those courses not offered in the library schools, the rest were provided by the same institution's business or management schools.

Table 4
Focus of Management Courses

What was the focus of the traditional management course you took while in library school	Number of library directors	Percent of total
Courses combined general management, collection management, plant management, patron management, people management	23	47.0
Courses focused primarily on managing the collection	4	8.2
Courses focused on external factors	1	2.0
Courses focused primarily on managing people	1	2.0
No answer	20	40.8
	49	100

Survey Question: Did your library school education prepare you to manage a library?

The responses to this question revealed that only 6.1% of the practicing library directors answered with an unconditional "yes." Most of the respondents (55.1%) replied "no," indicating that library school had not prepared them to manage a library. In addition, 20.4% of the respondents stated that they had received an introductory education, or were partially prepared to be managers of libraries. The results are presented in Table 5.

An additional question asked whether the respondents gained their current knowledge, skill, and ability (KSA) to manage a library from library school. Only one respondent (2%) replied "yes."

The next question was designed as a follow-up of the previous question probing the assumption that if library school did *not* prepare the director to manage a library, what steps he or she had taken to become prepared. Because the subjects were practicing library directors, the responses provided real-world insight into what these individuals had done to gain the knowledge, skills, and abilities (KSA) to prepare them to be library directors.

Forty-six of the 49 (93.9%) library directors responded that they used one or more techniques or strategies beyond their library school education to gain the needed knowledge, skills, and ability (KSA) to manage a library. Only one director (2%) replied that library school had contributed to his or her ability to manage.

The responses to this open-ended question were condensed to reveal seven categories of skills or knowledge building techniques. The results are represented in Table 6.

Additional coursework included such topics as recruiting, hiring, compliance with labor laws, performance standards, motivating staff, appraising performance, establishing performance standards, sexual harassment, and more. The preponderance of their preparation was heavily focused on managing the library's human resources.

One library director's verbatim comment to the contrary suggested, "no classroom can truly prepare you for some experiences—particularly personnel work."

Survey Question: In your opinion as a practicing library director, what areas should be offered or required in a library school program?

Nearly 80% of the responding library directors shared details as to what should be offered to help prepare future library school graduates to successfully assume leadership roles. Using content analysis, the answers

Table 5
Library School Prepared Managers of Libraries

Did your library school education prepare you to manage a library	Number of library directors	Percent of total
No	27	55.1
Partially prepared, introductory	10	20.4
Yes	3	6.1
No answer	9	18.4
	49	100

Table 6
Responses to Question about Management Skill Preparation

What did you do to prepare yourself to manage a library	Number of library directors responding that they used this strategy to gain needed KSA	Percent of 46 responding directors using this technique
Self-taught	29	59.2
Attended conferences, seminars, and/or workshops	19	38.8
Mentors provided direction and training	13	26.5
Additional coursework	11	22.4
Used experiences gained from other positions in other fields	9	18.4
On-the-job-training after graduation	9	18.4

from 39 respondents were condensed into seven categories. Those categories are indicated in Table 7.

The question was intentionally open-ended to encourage the directors to provide detailed answers. Selected verbatim comments provide additional insight to the categories outlined in Table 7. When considering the concept of management, topics such as organizational behavior, leadership, change management, strategic leadership, human resource policy, human resource

Table 7
Response to Question about Courses that should be Offered

Management related coursework	Number of library directors that suggested this category of coursework be offered in the graduate library program	Percent of 39 responding library directors included this topic
Management	34	87.2
Marketing and public relations	17	43.6
Accounting and finance	17	43.6
Interpersonal skills	5	12.8
Information technology and information literacy	4	10.3
Collection management	3	7.7
Grant writing	2	5.1

management, and more, were all noted as desirable subject matter. The words of the respondents express it best:

> In 2001 I hired an individual who possesses a business degree; although ... she will this fall begin a degree in MSLIS, her business background proved to be an invaluable asset ...

> Personnel management—people are the most important aspect and the least time is spent on that ...

> Working within a union environment ...

> I believe there should be more education in areas of personnel management and working with the legal issues of regulations, boards, union, and bidding practices ...

> Problem employees—how to handle, document, terminate, motivate ...

> Political side of managing; working with critics, library boards, friends groups, and other landmines.

> Hot button legal issues—ADA, sexual harassment ...

> Every potential librarian should have at least one management course—particularly dealing with interpersonal relationships.

> More courses involving management of staff—I've found the trickiest part of managing to be the staff.

> I think a solid management course should be required including as many possible elements.

The comments above demonstrate that problems related to people management are often found to be the most difficult for library directors to manage. They reported being least prepared for this facet of their jobs. In addition, several directors' comments suggested that it may be a challenge to properly prepare a library director within the scope of the library school curriculum. Again, verbatim comments from the subjects express this best:

> I think that it is unrealistic to expect persons to graduate from library school with adequate management skills; I think it would be more realistic to offer courses on such topics as continuing education topics.

> Professional training needs to focus on the profession; many of the managerial practices come from training and experience in specific work places ... collection management and for that matter, cataloguing rules!

The library directors also expressed a desire for increased preparation in areas such as accounting, finance, budgeting, and marketing. "How to manage a budget," "strategic and long range planning," understanding "how libraries are funded," were among the comments provided by the directors.

Directors' comments related to improving interpersonal skills and relationship skills were explicitly expressed. Topics such as conflict resolution, managing difficult staff members, coaching skills, and public speaking, were all mentioned as desirable skills for managers of libraries.

C. Analysis

Several key factors were revealed by comparing the library directors who graduated before 1983 to those who graduated after 1983. First, the most noticeable difference is the title of the graduate degree. Nearly 70% of the more senior library directors earned what could be referred to as the traditional Master of Library Science degree (MLS). A diversity of degree titles was more evident for those library directors who graduated *after* 1983. For example, 26.3% of those library directors responded that they earned an MLS, 21.1% reported that they earned an MLIS, 10.5% earned an MALS, 10.5% earned an MSLIS, and 10.5% earned an MSLS.

Another result that indicated that there was a shift in the focus of library school curricula over time was whether the few management courses were offered within the library school program, and whether these management courses were required or elective. For library directors graduating before 1983 there was a higher incidence reported of *elective* courses, whereas the majority graduating after 1983 reported that the management course(s) was *required*.

Similarly noted was the shift in schools offering the management courses to their students. A minority of the library directors graduating before 1983 (39.1%) reported that the management course(s) offered in their program was taught by the library school faculty. Although on the other hand, a *majority* of directors (57.9%) graduating after 1983 reported that the management course(s) was offered within the library school. Courses not taught within the library school were taught in schools of management or business within the same institution.

A slight shift was noted in responses to the question, "Did your library school education prepare you to manage a library?" 69.6% of the library directors graduating before 1983 answered this question with an unconditional "no," whereas only 52.6% of the library directors graduating after 1983 answered "no." The one library director, who stated that his library education did contribute to his ability to manage, graduated after 1983.

Although these differences appear inconclusive they may serve as an indicator that a shift of perception regarding the need for traditional management training has begun to occur. Innovative programs to provide management training to information professionals in leadership positions are emerging. A program like the Public Library Administrators' Certificate Program is an example of growing interest in closing the management education gap for library directors (Nichols and Koenig, 2005). It is their view that this trend needs to be accelerated if the profession desires to prepare library directors properly to assume leadership roles in the future.

IV. Discussion and Conclusion

Where then do library directors get prepared to become such? There is limited evidence that the ALA expects library directors to emerge as a direct result of ALA-accredited MLS programs. The ALA refers to its accreditation standards as "indicative, not prescriptive" (ALA, 1992). The term *management* can be found sprinkled throughout the language of the accreditation standards. Most often, however, the concept of management is associated with the management of library services and information technologies. No clear direction is offered by the Standards for Accreditation about the desired preparation of future library managers.

Library directors rely upon library schools to teach their librarians the knowledge and skills required to function successfully in their careers in the early years. Library schools have successfully covered the various components of *knowledge*: its creation, selection, acquisition, organization, description, storage, retrieval, preservation, analysis, evaluation, and management (ALA, 1992). However the management of *people and processes* appears to be lacking. To a great extent, most MLS training has ignored the human resource management aspect of librarianship. A library director's management concerns are similar to those of other managers. Yet, a resounding 55.1% of the directors who participated in this study reported that library school did not prepare them to manage the human resource aspects of their positions. Clearly, additional preparation is required by librarians who aim their career ladders at management positions in their later career stages.

Cataloging and classification, and reference policies and services, are traditional library subjects that are well represented in the MLS curriculum. This study has demonstrated there is a well documented *lack* in human resource management training. There is little explicit guidance from ALA as to how the master's level curriculum should be developed to cover management skills, knowledge, and abilities. This means that schools which do offer such courses develop and offer them using different parameters. Hence they can have varying outcomes. This means that there is little to ensure that graduating MLS students leave with specific people-management learning outcomes. The implication is that librarians whose jobs include managing people are at a severe disadvantage, particularly beginning librarians who are increasingly pushed into management, or at least supervisory roles, early in their careers. On the contrary, if library managers come to their jobs with management experience in another field, this obviates the need for it to be in the library school curricula.

Library work involves much human interaction. Traditionally this has been recognized as interaction through serving the public. There has been a lack of recognition, attention, and commitment to the interaction with and among coworkers and the subordinate personnel. Ignoring this is to the detriment of the members of the profession and their library employee partners. By extension this also exerts a detrimental effect on the individuals who avail themselves of the valuable information services and resources libraries provide.

To their credit, the library directors who responded to this study have recognized that they lack management skills and have used their information location skills to find programs, materials, and mentors to give them the information and training they lack. Various professional library organizations have also recognized a need for additional management training and offered continuing education programs and workshops involving management skills. In larger library systems internal programs are mounted for librarians and others being promoted to supervisory and management positions. For libraries within companies, colleges and universities, and public libraries that are part of a city or county government, the human resources units for the parent organization often provide management and leadership building programs.

Much of this independent work would not be necessary if library school curriculum better met the real world management needs of librarians—perhaps through continuing education program if not their formal curricula. With many schools offering the MLS with only 36 credits, they may be hard-pressed to focus more on management in the face of a rapidly changing information world. Meanwhile, it is entirely possible that libraries are not being managed as effectively as they should be.

If a library school student is provided with only one opportunity to learn the broad spectrum of management concepts before earning his or her terminal degree, there should be consensus as to the minimum content and topics required. The ALA Standards for Accreditation should probably be a little less "indicative" and more "prescriptive" about this. Human resource management, strategy, planning, leadership, managing teams, managing change and conflict, communications, and decision-making, should all be universally accepted as part of the requirements for the MLS degree, if not as separate courses, then across the curriculum.

A. Future Research

The research agenda summarized in this chapter continues to evolve. Plans are underway to take this study to its natural next step. Stage four of this research will build on the results of stages one, two, and three by employing in-person in-depth interviews of library directors (Richards, 2005). Content analysis will be used to analyze and synthesize the data and draw out themes in order to tenuously offer results and build a body of theory. More research will be required before definitive recommendations can be made. The preliminary conclusion offered here to the library community is that discipline-wide discussions are needed. These should be in partnership with management faculty and practicing library directors. There is need to determine what curriculum revisions if any are needed to prepare individuals better for a management career in the information professions and develop alternate paths through professional development programs.

References

American Library Association. (1992). *Standards for accreditation of master's programs in library and information studies 1992*. Retrieved from http://www.ala.org/ala/accreditation/accredstandards/standards.cfm

American Library Association. (2010). *Mission and Priorities*. Retrieved from http://www.ala.org/ala/aboutala/missionhistory/mission/index.cfm

Battles, M. (2003). *Library: An unquiet history*. W.W. Norton, New York.

Berg, B. L. (1998). *Qualitative research methods for the social sciences*. Allyn and Bacon, Boston, MA.

Creth, S. D. (1988). Organizational leadership: Challenges within the library. In *Leadership for Research Libraries* (A. Woodsworth and B. A. von Wahlde, eds.), pp. 79–99, Scarecrow, Metuchen, NJ.

Gapen, K. (1988). The campus context. In *Leadership for Research Libraries* (A. Woodsworth and B. Von Wahlde, eds.), pp. 41–66, Scarecrow, Metuchen, NJ.

Giesecke, J. (2001). *Practical Strategies for Library Managers*. American Library Association, Chicago, IL.

Gorman, M. (2006). *Comments on "Updating the 1992 [ALA] Standards for accreditation of master's programs in library and information studies overview and comments"/Standards Review Subcommittee [of the COA]*. Retrieved from http://www.ala.org/ala/hrdr/abouthrdr/hrdrliaisoncomm/committeeoned/Gorman_ALA accreditationstandards.pdf

Hoffmann, E. J. (1988). Career management for leaders. In *Leadership for Research Libraries* (A. Woodsworth and B. Von Wahlde, eds.), pp. 166–187, Scarecrow, Metuchen, NJ.

International Assembly for Collegiate Business Education. (2009, April). *Accreditation manual. Chapter 1 – Introduction, excellence in business education*. Retrieved from http://www.iacbe.org/Accreditation_Manual_-_April_2009.pdf

Kidder, L. H. (1981). *Research methods in social relations*, 4th ed. Holt, Rinehart & Winston, New York.

Koenig, M. E. D. (2007). Looking back: A review of four key articles from volume one. *Education for Information*, 25, 57–61.

Kroll, A. J. (2007). Integrating professional skills in wildlife student education. *Journal of Wildlife Management* 71(1), 226–230.

Lester, J. (1988). Roles of schools of library and information science. In *Leadership for Research Libraries* (A. Woodsworth and B. Von Wahlde, eds.), pp. 126–188, Scarecrow, Metuchen, NJ.

Lowry, C. B. (1988). Reexamining the literature: A Babel of research and theory. In *Leadership for Research Libraries* (A. Woodsworth and B. Von Wahlde, eds.), pp. 1–40, Scarecrow, Metuchen, NJ.

Lynch, B. P. (1988). Changes in library organization. In *Leadership for Research Libraries* (A. Woodsworth and B. Von Wahlde, eds.), pp. 67–78, Scarecrow, Metuchen, NJ.

Mackenzie, M. L., and Smith, J. P. (2007, October). An exploratory study of libraries and their managers: Management education for leaders of non-traditional businesses. *Proceedings of the 70th Annual Meeting of the American Society for Information Science and Technology*, 44, 960–975.

Mackenzie, M. L., and Smith, J. P. (2009). Management education for library directors: Are graduate library programs providing future library directors with the skills and knowledge they will need? *Journal of Education for Library and Information Science* **50**(3), 129–142.

McDonough, B. (ed.) (2007). *American library directory*. 60th ed., Information Today, Medford, NJ.

Montgomery, J. G., and Cook, E. I. (2005). *Conflict Management for Libraries*. ALA, Chicago, IL.

Morse, J. M., and Richards, L. (2002). *Read Me First for a User's Guide to Qualitative Methods*. Sage, Thousand Oaks, CA.

Nesoff, I. (2007). The importance of revitalizing management education for social workers. *Social Work* **52**(3), 283–285. Retrieved from http://www.proquest.com

Nichols, J., and Koenig, M. E. D. (2005). Developments in post-masters education for public library administration in North America: With particular reference to the Public Library Administrator's Certificate Program at The Palmer School of Library and Information Science [Abstract]. (P. Genoni and G. Walton eds.). *Continuing Professional Development – Preparing for New Roles in Libraries: A Voyage of Discovery* (16). Munich: Saur. IFLA Publication 116. Retrieved from http://www.ifla.org/IV/ifla71/programme2005-cpdwl-e.pdf

Rhine, A. S. (2007). The MFA in theater management and the MBA: An examination of perspectives of decision makers at theaters in the United States. *Journal of Arts Management, Law, and Society* **37**(2), 113–126.

Richards, L. (2005). *Handling Qualitative Data: A Practical Guide*. Sage, Thousand Oaks, CA.

Riggs, D. E. (1985). Leadership is imperative. *Technicalities* **5**, 9–10.

Salant, P., and Dillman, D. A. (1994). *How to Conduct Your Own Survey*. Wiley, New York.

Saltz, J. (2007). Has money ruined art? *New York* **36**. Retrieved from http://nymag.com/arts/art/season2007/38981/

Weingand, D. E. (2001). *Administration of the small public library*, 4th ed. American Library Association, Chicago.

Williams, J. F., II (1988). Development of leadership potential. In *Leadership for Research Libraries* (A. Woodsworth and B. Von Wahlde, eds.), pp. 99–125, Scarecrow, Metuchen, NJ.

Woodsworth, A., and von Wahlde, B. (1988). *Leadership for Research Libraries: A Festschrift for Robert M. Hayes*. Scarecrow, Metuchen, NJ.

Trends, Issues, and Lessons Learned

Emerging Trends in Native American Tribal Libraries

Elisabeth Newbold

San Diego County Library, San Diego, CA, USA

Abstract

San Diego County (California, USA) contains 18 Indian reservations—more than any other county in the United States. Citizens of these reservations, each recognized as a sovereign nation, have information needs that are highly sophisticated. Coming from a civilization that preserved history through oral tradition, they have only recently made the transition to writing things down and collecting books into buildings. In spite of many tragic events that drastically reduced their population, San Diego County's Indians have retained much of their heritage through efforts of tribal elders and non-Indian historians. With federal and local assistance, tribal libraries were constructed on about half of San Diego County's reservations during the 1980s. Over the next few years, reduction of grant funds adversely affected them, resulting in some closures. Thanks to creative efforts made by many individuals at a local university, the state library, professional associations, and most of all by the Indians themselves, a number of San Diego County's tribal libraries are growing and taking on new shapes. Five local tribal librarians were surveyed twice over a 12-month period regarding their respective libraries. Analysis yielded four key factors for success: (1) the presence of a designated librarian; (2) support from the tribal government; (3) plans and a vision for the future; and (4) partnerships and connections with other entities. The research suggests that these factors are applicable toward ensuring success for small, geographically and culturally isolated libraries in any context.

I. Introduction

San Diego County in California, in the United States, is geographically and culturally diverse by any standard. With a population of three million, it attracts nearly 30 million tourists each year to its beaches and mountains (San Diego County Visitor Industry Summary, 2010). Most residents and visitors are oblivious to the fact that San Diego County is home to 18 Indian reservations—more than any other county in the United States.

The term "Indian reservation" refers to an area of land with boundaries set according to "treaty, statute, and/or executive or court order" (U.S.

ADVANCES IN LIBRARIANSHIP, VOL. 33

© 2011 by Emerald Group Publishing Limited

ISSN: 0065-2830

DOI: 10.1108/S0065-2830(2011)0000033007

Census Bureau, 2000a, b, p. 5-1). Each reservation is governed by a Native American tribal council, not the local or federal government, and is recognized as a sovereign nation. There are approximately 275 Indian land areas in the United States administered as Indian Reservations, covering a total of 56.2 million acres—about 2.3% of the total area of the country (U.S. Department of Energy, 2009). The majority of them are located in the Western United States per map of U.S. tribes at the web site http://www.nps.gov/history/nagpra/DOCUMENTS/RESERV.PDF.

An Indian Tribe is "a body of people bound together by blood ties who are socially, politically, and religiously organized, and who speak a common language or dialect" (U.S. Department of Energy, 2009). According to the Federal Register (2010), there are 564 federally recognized tribes in the United States.[1] Many tribes do not have a reservation, and a few reservations do not have any tribal members. Many Native Americans do not reside on tribal lands for economic or social reasons such as jobs, education, and family.

California boasts the largest number of Indian reservations—99—and the highest American Indian and Alaska Native population in the United States (U.S. Census Bureau, 2000b). San Diego County's Native American population is 25,324, but only 6285 of them reside on the local reservations. Many Native Americans currently living in San Diego County claim heritage from, and identify with, tribes in other areas.

Four tribal groups make up the indigenous population of San Diego County. The largest is commonly known as the Kumeyaay, a name used interchangeably with Diegueño, Kamia, Kumiai, or Ipai-Tipai. Thirteen reservations in the County are home to bands of Kumeyaay Indians. The Luiseño group has three reservations, all in the Northern area of the County. The other two groups, located in Eastern desert areas, are the Cupeño and Cahuilla, which inhabit one reservation each.

II. Purpose and Methodology

The purpose of this chapter is to provide an overview of the history and status of tribal libraries in San Diego County. The methodology used was twofold. Initially, a search was made to locate information on the subject in the current body of professional literature. The only articles written specifically about San Diego County tribal libraries were all written or

[1]As of June 14, 2010, the Shinnecock Indian Nation in New York received final recognition of their official status, making the number of tribes 565.

co-authored by Bonnie Biggs at California State University at San Marcos (CSUSM). They centered on her continuing efforts to strengthen local tribal collections and promote training, networking, and technological advances for their staff. Prof. Biggs, now retired, graciously consented to a telephone interview as part of the author's research. Literature about tribal libraries in general was also reviewed.

The second phase involved selecting and contacting five tribal libraries within the County and interviewing the people who are responsible for their collections. The libraries were selected at random, based on the availability of a contact person for interviews. The five libraries chosen were vastly different from one another, providing a rich sampling of current tribal library status and trends. Each interview was conducted using a structured questionnaire (see appendix) to gather consistent information. The initial interviews took place in 2009.

Two libraries on the Barona reservation were visited in person by the author. Contacts at these two libraries, along with those at Pauma and Santa Ysabel, all completed and returned the questionnaires electronically. The author conducted a telephone interview with the archivist at the Kumeyaay Community College's (KCC) Archives Library, using the questionnaire as a prompt. One year later, in spring of 2010, the sites were contacted and follow-up interviews were conducted with each. The findings from these interviews and questionnaires are summarized below and presented in alphabetical order.

Within the context of this chapter, a tribal library is defined as a collection of materials, including books, manuscripts, photographs, articles, sound recordings, and video recordings, which is maintained by an Indian tribe—a recognized sovereign nation registered with the U.S. (Campo Kumeyaay Nation, 2009) Federal Government. Although tribal libraries contain valuable historic and cultural materials, they also include mainstream current literature that is relevant and useful to their patrons such as information regarding legal matters, health issues, personal development, education, and entertainment.

III. An Historical Look at Native Americans

Through uncounted centuries, the Indians of San Diego County and surrounding areas lived off the land, raised their families, and passed on. Knowledge was not written down but was contained in their many oral traditions, songs, dances, and handcrafts. Their lives were changed forever with the coming of the first "white men," who used many of them as slaves (Campo Kumeyaay Nation, 2009) to build missions and who worked hard to "civilize" the native population with new languages, clothing, religion, and customs. When Spanish immigrants settled in the San Diego area in 1769, the native population at that time was estimated at 12,000. By 1895, the number had fallen to less than 2000 (Four Directions Institute, 2007) due to disease, squalor, and abuse (Dutschke, 1988). Large areas in the Eastern area of the County had been set aside for the Indians, but much of this was claimed by other settlers in defiance of the natives' rights (Carrico, 2008). Indians were constantly on the move, looking for food, and being driven out by land-hungry immigrants. They gradually became aware that they were not welcome in their own lands and were relegated to a meager subsistence on small reservations.

Some members of the local tribes endured the abuse and eked out a living on their undesirable reservation acreage. Others fled farther east to the mountains and deserts, trying to hide from the onslaught of new immigrants. For the next two centuries, tribal elders of various family groups and bands continued the tradition of passing on oral histories and, despite the intrusion of modernization, preserved much knowledge concerning their culture, such as medicinal uses of local plants, arts, legends, tribal government, and native languages.

Although tribal elders still live on most reservations and possess precious knowledge, family structures are becoming fragmented, disrupting the time-honored oral generational transfer of information. This is due to the following several contributing factors:

- the breakdown of traditional family values in the larger society;
- the movement of tribal members into urban areas in search of work, education, and entertainment;
- the flood of money into some tribes from gaming revenues causing a loss of work ethic and self-discipline; and
- easy access to drugs and alcohol.

A. Preserving Tribal Heritage

For centuries, Native American tribes preserved their history and heritage by conveying information orally from one generation to the next. During the past few centuries, western civilization introduced the concept of written language to Native Americans. In a culture where stories and traditions were never transmitted into writing, a library is a relatively new idea (Burke, 2007). The practice of establishing tribal libraries as we know them today has only existed for about 40 years. As oral histories faded into the past, tribal libraries became valued repositories of unique languages, cultures, and knowledge. In the last few decades, tribal libraries have been established in various forms and are now "the logical place for the acquisition and preservation of this information. They have become the place (replacing the 'person') where a tribe's cultural heritage is collected, studied, preserved, and disseminated" (Biggs, 2000b, p. 22).

From the 1700s into the 1900s when tribal populations and reservations were decimated and relocated, much of their heritage was lost through oppression, displacement, and forced assimilation. Families were separated, and Indians were forced to live far from familiar settings. In 1908, one report [regarding the education of Indians] stated,

> the class rooms held three or four students each and it was arranged that no two tribes were placed in the same room. This not only helped in the acquirement of English, but broke up tribal and race clannishness, a most important victory in getting Indians toward real citizens. (Spicer, 1969, p. 235)

Between the 1940s and the 1970s, the U.S. Congress attempted to end the government's relationship with Indian tribes through the dissolution of reservations, with the goal of reducing natives' dependency on the bloated bureaucracy of the Bureau of Indian Affairs. This legislation was known as the "Termination Act." The Native American population was not prepared or willing to be offloaded into the mainstream population, and the effort was eventually abandoned. As Heizer (1978) stated,

> California Indian tribes were to be among the first targets for termination. The commissioner of Indian affairs who inaugurated this policy, Dillon Meyer, was principally known as the man responsible for administering Japanese-American concentration camps during World War II. In 1952, the Bureau of Indian Affairs began to energetically push termination: the Indian Service introduced to Congress several termination bills specifically for California, and in anticipation of that policy, the government ended all Indian Service welfare payments to pauper Indians in the state. (p. 122)

The civil rights movement of the 1960s and the 1970s raised awareness of all minorities, including Native Americans. At the same time, large numbers of Indians relocated to metropolitan areas in search of employment. They became more aware of the "outside world" and the importance of preserving their heritage for their urbanized descendants. The American Indian Historical Society was formed in 1964 by Rupert Costo, a member of the Cahuilla tribe (Metoyer-Duran, 2002). In 1967, the California Indian Education Association (California Indian Education Association, 2009) was founded, closely followed by the National Indian Education Association in 1970 (National Indian Education Association, 2009). In 1971, the American

Library Association served as a catalyst for the formation of a Task Force on American Indians within the Social Responsibilities Round Table. From 1973 to 1984, Native American advocates Charles Townley at the University of California Santa Barbara and Lotsee Patterson from the University of Oklahoma (both members of the Task Force) lobbied, gained support, and obtained a number of small federal grants for training library aides in Indian schools and setting up community libraries on tribal lands in New Mexico (Biggs, 2000a).

As information needs of Native Americans became more complex, tribal libraries began to be recognized as one of the best ways to fulfill those needs. In 1978, Jack Forbes from the University of California Davis outlined and defended information needs of Native Americans at a White House Pre-Conference, concluding his remarks with the following definitive statement:

> The information-knowledge needs of Indian people are very great. Probably no group of people have been and are being called upon to make as complex decisions about claims-cases, land, natural resources, et cetera with almost no information available. This problem, a major source of Indian impoverishment, must be corrected.

> Similarly very few ethnic groups have ever been the target of such intensive cultural genocide policies as have Native Americans. This also creates great information needs relating to cultural-historical subjects.

> Information-knowledge dissemination must, therefore, be a high priority of every tribe which wants to remain in existence as a people and which desires to have a democratic form of government. (Forbes, 1978)

One result of the Pre-Conference was the formation of the American Indian Library Association (AILA) in 1979, which first met as a separate entity in 1980. This organization continues to serve as a vital link among tribal libraries, which are often isolated geographically and organizationally.

With growing awareness, legislation was passed in 1984 amending the Library Services and Construction Act (LSCA) with the addition of Title IV: Library Services for Indian Tribes and Hawaiian Natives Program. This program is now administered by the Institute of Museum and Library Services (IMLS), which annually offers two classes of grants to tribal libraries, a "basic" grant and an "enhancement" grant. Although these funds are not sufficient to run a library, they serve as supplemental income toward necessities such as information technology services and supplies.

The groundswell of attention and support during the 1980s provided an opportunity whereby Dr. Patterson was selected to administer the LSCA Title IV grant nationwide. She applied her experience, knowledge, energy, and passion toward training tribal library staff to make them self-sufficient, and continuing to advocate for tribal libraries at the national level (United States, 1991). One of her most successful programs, funded through the U.S.

Department of Education's Office of Educational Research and Improvement, is still in use today. The Training and Assistance for Indian Library Services (TRAILS) project provided essential training and professional support to the many libraries that came into being during this fertile period.

Seasons of the earth bring cycles of life. So it is with tribal libraries. After an unfruitful period, new growth is appearing. One promising new context that has cropped up recently is the establishment of tribal colleges— including their own libraries—complete with accreditation for high school and college courses (Patterson, 2000). Also, a Laura Bush Librarians for the 21st-Century Grant provided funds for 3 years of historic national gatherings of tribal librarians and archivists (Streams of language, memory, and lifeways, 2009). The first was held in Oklahoma in 2007 with 560 registrants attending, coming from 46 states and 3 Canadian provinces. Immersion Institutes, a series of 3-day workshops, were conducted throughout 2008 on relevant topics such as Digitization and Collection Management and served as a bridge between the 2007 and 2009 conferences. The second national conference was held in Oregon in October of 2009. Despite the economic downturn, 505 people attended from 35 states and 4 countries. The objective of these conferences was to foster networking and collaboration among tribal cultural institutions and programs, specifically tribal libraries, archives, and museums. This goal was not only met but was exceeded. A report was published in 2009 based on participant surveys. Many positive comments are included, such as, "[The conference] offered great networking and what we can do in the future to mentor others. [I] will be able to follow up and make connections locally. Made direct connections to new colleagues," "I learned how partnershipping can work in our library." The document summarizes three positive results perceived by those in attendance:

1. useful information,
2. help in identifying contacts [networking], and
3. important and timely session topics (Cartright and Starr, 2009).

The Librarians for the 21st-Century Program has awarded an additional grant extending these meetings for another 3 years. Six events are planned from June 2010 through June 2012. The project also includes future needs assessment and plans for "a framework to sustain programs for tribal archives, libraries, and museums beyond 2012" (ATALM, 2010).

B. History of San Diego County Tribal Libraries

Tribal libraries in San Diego County can be found in a mixture of settings and serving various segments of the population. Several began as personal

Fig. 1 San Diego County has 18 Indian Reservations—more than any other county in the United States. *Source:* California Department of Transportation. Native American Trust Lands, Division of Transportation Planning, 2009.

collections, whereas some were established through government grants. Most are heavily supported through proceeds from gaming income,[2] and a number are connected with tribal schools. All of them have struggled to overcome various challenges. Each is unique in their history, collection, and plans for the future (Fig. 1).

The first tribal libraries in San Diego County were in people's homes and tribal halls. When federal recognition and sponsorship became available during the 1970s and 1980s, three small library structures were constructed in San Diego County on local reservations—Campo, Pauma, and Viejas—and began to serve their residents. Even though they lived only a few miles from a sophisticated urban center and its burgeoning suburbs, most of the Indian population subsisted at poverty level and were isolated in rural areas.

In addition to federal funds, San Diego County reservations received local support through the San Diego County Library's (SDCL) Outreach

---

[2]A U.S. Supreme Court decision in 1987 reinforced tribal sovereignty and paved the way for reservations to operate gaming halls. In 1988, the U.S. Congress passed the Indian Gaming Regulatory Act that in effect authorized casino gambling on Indian reservations and provided a regulatory framework and oversight body for the industry (Native American gaming enterprises, 2008). Currently, Indian Reservation casinos bring in more money than Las Vegas and Atlantic City combined (777.com, n.d.).

Division that administered the Indian Library Services Project (ILSP) from 1987 to 1989. This effort began as a simple workshop on one reservation but evolved into much more. SDCL assisted a number of reservations with donations of furniture, purchases of library materials, and help with sorting and processing books. SDCL eventually received an LSCA grant that facilitated the growth of the three small existing libraries and the opening of several more over 2 years. Although this "renaissance period" in San Diego County tribal library history was short-lived, significant milestones were reached. Grand openings were held at three libraries; over 100 reservation children participated in a summer reading program for the first time; hundreds of books and media items were added to the library collections; furniture and display cases were built; and four local American Indians were hired and trained to work as library managers. Regarding the core collections that were presented to 10 reservation libraries, Biggs and Whitehorse (1995) wrote,

> These collections became the source of considerable pride for tribal members as they now not only had the opportunity to read about other Indians, but also had access to information about their own people which heretofore had been limited to oral narratives or held in distant and generally inaccessible public, school, or university libraries. (p. 284)

In addition to giving assistance with library collections, furniture, and programs, the ILSP's mission included placement and training of tribal members as library managers. Detailed instruction was provided, along with follow-up visits, and even research tours to local museums. As a result of the tours, tribal library staff came to realize the value and importance of archival records, including photographs of their ancestors and homelands, as part of their library collections.

With economic downsizing looming, ILSP attempted to put permanent functions in place that would ensure a continuing relationship between the tribal libraries and SDCL and immunize them against grant dependency. Unfortunately, "the last served became the first severed" (Biggs and Whitehorse, 1995, p. 287). SDCL was forced to lay off 50 employees, and history repeated a pattern as tribes felt the familiar sting of betrayal. Within their own tribal governments, they also had to make difficult decisions about budget limitations, which dealt heavy blows to the fledgling tribal libraries. During this period,

> Tribal governments did not foresee that the libraries would become as important in the fabric of tribal life as they did for some reservations ... access to information is a tribal imperative which both builds from and feeds sovereignty. (Biggs and Whitehorse, 1995, p. 288)

As the ILSP program closed, other windows were opening. The tribes with successful gaming industries were beginning to generate sufficient recognition and income to sustain their libraries. In the meantime, the California State University system opened a new campus in San Marcos (CSUSM) in 1989. One of the faculty members, Dr. David Whitehorse, professor of American Indian Studies, had been involved in the early development of the Pauma reservation library. He was painfully aware of the plight of the endangered libraries on local reservations and appealed to a university librarian, Bonnie Biggs, for help. They began building relationships of trust by holding cultural events on behalf of the Native American community. As a result of this, Biggs developed the Tribal Libraries Project, which placed interns from the library school at San Jose State University (SJSU) into short-term positions in libraries on nearby reservations. This arrangement required considerable oversight and diplomacy at first. Success was seen in the accomplishments the interns achieved in helping libraries with data entry and collection maintenance (Biggs, 1998). During the next decade, 1995–2005, over 30 students from SJSU's MLIS program participated. Some of these interns have since continued in their career with tribal libraries, and one has served as President of AILA, as well as a professor of Library Science at SJSU.

The multicultural mission of CSUSM includes building bridges with the sovereign nations of Indian tribes. The young university continued to support Native American research and outreach. Bonnie Biggs, who helped initiate the Tribal Libraries Project, was elected President of AILA in 1998. This helped expand her views beyond California as she observed how other states functioned (or did not) in relationships with their tribal libraries. She noted New Mexico's dramatic success through a partnership with their state library and focused her attention on the California State Library (CSL) (Biggs, 2002). One outcome was a grant in 2000–2001, for which she was given 10 months of released time from her faculty position to conduct a Tribal Library Census and Needs Assessment of five counties in Southern California (Biggs, 2001), including San Diego County. Biggs (2004, p. 43) summarized her observations with this comment: "While visiting 34 reservations and their libraries, I discovered that tribal librarians felt isolated and disconnected from libraries in general and other tribal libraries in particular."

Once again, relationships of trust and mutual respect were strengthened as CSUSM hosted and sponsored a series of conferences for tribal librarians who had been inventoried by the Tierra Del Sol Census and Needs Assessment (Biggs, 2003). Eager to communicate with each other, they organized a formal group that became the Native Libraries Round Table of the California Library Association (CLA) in 2003. At last, they enjoyed a permanent network, complete with a listserv (sponsored by CSUSM), that was affiliated with a long-standing state organization. Besides having a voice within CLA, the charter was signed by the CSL, which was showing renewed interest and support on behalf of tribal libraries.

In 2002, the CSL established a full-time position for Library Development Services, with specific duties regarding tribal libraries. Laboring under threats of budget cuts and even a layoff, Susan Hanks, the CSL librarian in this position, has travelled the state, doing needs assessment, offering support, and continuing to build trust with tribal libraries. She developed many resources in print and online (Hanks, 2007). She also provided bibliographies to mainstream libraries to help them maintain appropriate items in their collections that are authentic and not stereotypical or offensive to Native Americans. She advocates with tribal elders, government agencies, and other entities in the cause of California's tribal libraries.

In 2005, a CSL newsletter described some of their challenges:

> Tribal librarians do not have the established networks most California librarians take for granted. Most of the state's libraries are part of bigger networks: public library systems; library consortiums; professional organizations including the California Library Association, the American Library Association, and Special Libraries Association; library cooperatives; and universities. Further, many of these partnerships are regional, which is not the case with tribal libraries. Tribal library networking in California has just recently gone statewide. (California State Library, 2005)

One very successful program sponsored by the CSL was a "Tribal Library Boot Camp" held in 2005 at the Pala reservation in San Diego County. One purpose of the gathering was to provide training in library skills such as cataloging, book repair, Internet resources, and programming. Other purposes were to facilitate the sharing of common concerns and educate tribal librarians about resources at the local, state, and federal level. One of the presenters at this meeting was Jacqueline Ayala, a librarian from SDCL, bringing the story full circle.

SDCL recruited a new director, Jose Aponte, in 2005, who immediately expressed a desire to revitalize the partnership with local tribes that had existed in the 1980s. He teamed up with a colleague—Bonnie Biggs, who was serving as CSUSM's Tribal Liaison—to visit the elders of one reservation (Biggs, April 8, 2009, telephone interview with the author). He assigned Ms. Ayala with oversight of tribal interchange, that is, communication with tribes. She made a presentation at CLA in 2007 illustrating SDCL's efforts (Ayala, 2007). These included a coordinated celebration of Native American Heritage Month, with cultural programs, author talks, web site publicity (including links to local tribal museums and a map of local reservations), and constant monitoring of collections for inclusiveness and appropriateness. Various staff members of SDCL have initiated outreach on a branch level, particularly one location that serves a rural area bordered by five reservations (Puccio, May 7, 2009, personal communication with the author). A SDCL bookmobile makes regular visits to one of the reservations, which does not have a functioning tribal library.

It is a fact that tribal libraries in general have more access to funds, training, and technical assistance from various sources than they did 20 years ago. Whereas some of San Diego County's tribal libraries are under-staffed and under-maintained, a number of them exhibit various stages of development and success, with many encouraging signs for the future. Curtailed by continuing budget woes of State and County governments, the current level of SDCL's involvement holds little resemblance to the 1980s heyday of the ILSP. However, its intent is to continue to respectfully meet with tribes, building a two-way channel of information exchange. A new Native American Services' initiative was launched by SDCL in June of 2009, including a list of action items such as developing a contact list, inviting tribal librarians to meetings, and establishing deposit collections at local reservations. (Executive Team Meeting Minutes, 2009) Due to continuing budget constraints, this initiative has not moved forward as planned.

Tribal libraries are key sources of cultural competency and can fulfill vital information needs of the general San Diego County population. At the same time, SDCL departments and branches can provide forums, programming, grant-writing assistance, and other support to reservations on a case-by-case basis. It is SDCL's sincere hope that communication and networking will continue to become more viable, despite the challenges ahead, and that tribal libraries will become even stronger and more self-sufficient (Ayala, April 27, 2009, telephone interview with the author).

C. Exploring Selected San Diego County Tribal Libraries

Five tribal libraries on four reservations in San Diego County were selected as samples for this study, based on availability of a contact person. These libraries are Barona Cultural Center and Museum (BCCM) Research Library; Barona Tribal Library; KCC Archives Library; Pauma Tribal Library; and Santa Ysabel Tribal Library. In an initial effort to contact tribal libraries for this chapter, several directories were consulted. Each listed a different number of tribal libraries in San Diego County ranging from 6 to 15. This is a textbook example of Patterson's recent statement:

> The most often asked question on the topic of American Indian libraries is, 'How many are there?' My response when asked this question is usually, 'What do you call a library?' Even if I received a definitive answer, I still couldn't respond to the question because the truth is, no one knows. (Patterson, 2008, p. 7)

The most current directories found were an online listing published by the IMLS and hosted by the University of Arizona (2005) and a directory in book form (Peterson, 2007). The most detailed directory available is the inventory conducted by Biggs in 2001, currently accessible on the Tierra Del Sol web site hosted by CSUSM. Although somewhat outdated, it contains useful historical information for each reservation, which remains relevant for anyone doing research on San Diego County Indians.

1. Barona

The Barona reservation belongs to the Kumeyaay/Digueño group and has a resident population of 536. The number of Indians officially registered with the Barona band is much greater, however, because many of them live elsewhere. The tribal organization generates consistent income from its award-winning Barona Resort and Casino. Their leaders recognize the importance of preserving their heritage and providing an education for their children. This has resulted in a reliable budget for the two libraries on the reservation—the BCCM Research Library and the Barona Tribal Library on the Campus of the Barona Indian Tribal School, both in Lakeside, CA, USA.

At the BCCM in 2009, there was one part-time staff member who maintained the Research Library, housed in a lovely new Cultural Center and Museum. She had taken classes at Palomar Community College and had hopes of continuing her education. She started the BCCM library from scratch in 2004. She was hired as Collections Manager for the Museum and "morphed into the library position due to my experience with local Native populations, love of research and books." (Tells His Name, April 23, 2009, personal communication with the author) At that time, there were approximately 1700 books and magazines in the collection, all in good condition, plus four file drawers full of materials. The Library of Congress cataloging system was used due to the research nature of the library. None of the items circulated because many were rare and hard to find. There was no inter-library loan program. There was one computer available for public access and one for library staff use only. There were no existing partnerships with other libraries or organizations.

Funding came entirely from tribal monies, including the budget for computers and technical support. The annual dollar amount had increased over the previous 5 years. The library was open to the public from Tuesdays to Fridays from 12 pm to 5 pm and Saturdays from 10 am to 4 pm. Seventy percent of patrons were adults, 10% children, 10% teens, and 10% seniors. Programs included various story times, cultural demonstrations, and genealogy research. The BCCM published a newsletter online at http://www.baronamuseum.org, which included a column about the library. People also learned about the library through word of mouth. The librarian belonged to a library association. When asked, "Who inspires you?", she answered, "The People of the community inspire me, making me want to provide accurate and current information about them to the public and to change the way people 'think and see' the local Native population."

The greatest challenge in 2009 was finding room for all the materials, and the librarian was hoping to expand the size of the library. Networking with other organizations was something she would have liked to see more of. Her vision for the future of the library was "To be the most sought after and effective research library in Southern California, with references for research including Kumeyaay, Luiseno and others in the area" (Tells His Name, April 23, 2009, personal communication with the author).

When Ms. Tells His Name retired in 2009, the position was reclassified as full-time and filled by the current Librarian/Archivist, Rosa Longacre, who holds an MLIS from SJSU. Ms. Longacre had 5 years of prior experience working in libraries and archives elsewhere when she was hired. Since the 2009 survey, a new Research Center had been added (open from Tuesdays to Fridays from 9 am to 5 pm), and there had been 300–400 archival accessions. A second computer was being used for cataloging the archives. Computers were maintained by the tribal Information Technology department. The library had received some funding through government grants, and their budget continued to increase, despite the general economic downturn. New programs included additional children's crafts and story time and a Heritage Project for middle-school students at the Charter School next door. Ms. Longacre verified that all the other information submitted in 2009 is unchanged and added, "The subject matter . . . inspires me, since some of the information is not always easy to find." (Longacre, April 23, 2010, personal communication with the author).

2. Barona Tribal Library

In 2009, the Barona Tribal Library, housed in a large room on the campus of the Barona Indian Charter School, an accredited school for grades Kindergarten through grade 8, was being run by one full-time employee, Jennifer Ward. As a charter school, they are considered part of the public school system, and therefore, they do not charge tuition, and they receive some of their funding through tax revenues. However, they are not subject to some of the regulations governing mainstream public schools and hence can provide specialized instruction in Native American language and culture.

Students from anywhere in San Diego County may attend, and some are transported long distances to do so.

The library was named after its founder, Joan Phoenix, who started a tutoring center in 1977 and later worked with the SDCL Outreach Division on the ILSP during the 1980s to build the library. Just outside the structure was a large satellite dish, attractively painted with a traditional Kumeyaay basket design, but it was no longer functional. The library manager held an associate's degree and had 9 years of library experience. She attended the 2005 CSL Boot Camp training. The library collection included over 8000 volumes in good condition. It was cataloged using Athena software on the staff computer. Everything circulated except reference materials, with fiction being the most heavily used part of the collection. There was no inter-library loan program in place. Of the three public access computers, two were not working but all were wired for Internet access. The librarian used the staff computer for email, research, ordering materials, and cataloging. The equipment was aging, and the tribal technology department was working on acquiring new computers. A partnership affiliation included the Tribal Library Group (round table). Ms. Ward did not belong to any professional library associations.

Funding for the library was provided largely from the tribe, plus a small amount from grants that covered supplies. The library also received regular book donations from staff and friends. Historically, the budget had increased annually until 2009, when it saw a small decrease. The library was being used primarily by tribal members and students and was open from Mondays to Fridays from 8 am to 2 pm. Although the library was established before the school came into being, the school had grown up around the library so that in 2009, 90% of patrons were children and teens who attended the Barona Indian Charter School. Although they did not have library cards, each student had an ID number that was used to check out items. Programs were limited to story time. The librarian expressed a desire to have summer reading programs, but past efforts had not found much success. One of her biggest challenges was getting the local community involved with the library. People located the library through word of mouth. The school had a website http://www.baronaindianchar-terschool.org where she was listed as the librarian, but the tribal library was not specifically mentioned.

Ms. Ward concluded her thoughts with this comment, "I love books and believe in getting children interested in reading as early as possible. I would like to see our library continue to grow and be a positive experience in reading and research for everybody" (Ward, April 27, 2009; April 19, 2010, personal communication with the author).

A year later, Ms. Ward was still in the same position. The collection had grown to 9000 volumes, with more on the way. The budget for the library had remained level. One computer had been replaced. The remaining information had not changed in the year after initial contact.

3. Kumeyaay Community College Archives Library

This library is located on the Sycuan reservation, which has a tiny resident population of 33. Like the other reservations, many registered members of Sycuan live elsewhere. The reservation owns a large casino that was opened in 1983. KCC, San Diego's first Tribal College, was established in 2003, and its mission is "to promote a quality education for the Kumeyaay/Diegueño Nation, California Native American Indians, and other individuals interested in a unique and supportive educational experience" (Kumeyaay Community College, 2008).

Florence Shipek, an anthropologist, worked with the Kumeyaay for decades. When she passed away in 2003, her research papers were donated to KCC, and this formed the foundation of its library. Her son Carl joined the KCC Archives Library in 2005 and by 2009 served full time as archivist/librarian for the collection, assisted by one part-time employee. Although Mr. Shipek did not hold a Library Science degree, he had many years of professional experience in the field of computer systems. He also had unique personal experience having been involved with his mother's work by accompanying her on trips to Kumeyaay reservations that began when he was a child. In 2009, the collection included over 2000 volumes, 90% of which came from the Shipek collection and 10% from new acquisitions. Some of the older books were very rare and fragile, dating back over 100 years. They were all cataloged and some newer items were available for loan to researchers and KCC students. The KCC collection had no inter-library loan program.

KCC receives accreditation through Cuyamaca Community College, the closest local state-funded community college. Students are able to earn transferable credits toward foreign language and history requirements by taking Kumeyaay language and history classes. Not-for-credit classes were also offered on topics such as pottery, food preparation, and basketry. The library did not have any other formal partnerships but maintained open communication with the CSL and other academic and tribal entities.

The library is entirely funded by the Sycuan Council. The KCC website has a detailed page about the Archives at www.kumeyaaycommunitycollege.com/archives.htm.

It lists the Mission Statement, Policies on Governance and Ownership, and Procedures concerning use and copying of the materials. The library was open at varying hours during the week and also by appointment. Patrons were mainly students and staff of KCC, but researchers from other colleges and universities could access the archives. The Kumeyaay people also used the collection to research their history.

In 2009, Mr. Shipek stated that he enjoyed visiting the Sycuan Learning Center weekly to give programs on "Cultural Fridays" for the Sycuan children. As part of the Sycuan Education Department's public outreach, he also shared, at no cost, his suggested bibliography for general collections in San Diego libraries and provided docent training in support of local historic sites and parks. Mr. Shipek stated that his biggest challenge had been learning how to organize and catalog research notes properly and also to digitize selected items. It was seen as a detailed task, given that his mother's materials included some 4000 file folders and 300 binders of field notes. Although she had labeled them carefully, there was much work to do to index the files and make them accessible through electronic searching. Another item that Mr. Shipek had on his wish list was seeing better coordination among the bands of the Kumeyaay Nation, to avoid duplication of effort. He found great inspiration in his Mother's legacy and his wife's support (Shipek, C., May 5, 2009, telephone interview with the author).

Due to budget cutbacks for 2010, Mr. Shipek was no longer full-time. The KCC Archives Library was secured. To obtain access to library materials, users had to contact the Office Manager of the Education Department (Ring, L., April 24, 2010, telephone interview with the author). With an appointment, Mr. Shipek was available as a volunteer to help patrons with their research (Shipek, C., December 16, 2010, telephone interview with the author).

Meanwhile, the administration was seeking approval to move the library to a new location to make it more accessible. Once this occurs, it was anticipated that Mr. Shipek would be invited back to resume his duties in the maintenance and improvement of the collection.

4. Pauma Tribal Library

Members of the Pauma reservation belong to the Luiseño group. The resident population is 186. The AA'Alvikat (Luiseño for "storyteller") Library was originally set up under SDCL's Outreach Division efforts in the early 1980s. Neighboring Palomar Community College provided vital support to the Pauma library for many years. They formed a satellite campus on the reservation and shared expenses for library staffing. Palomar librarians worked closely with the Pauma library to provide professional expertise. A casino opened on the reservation in 2001, and in 2004, a larger library was opened through an IMLS grant (Aguirre, 2004) written largely by Palomar

College partners. By the end of 2004, Pauma had a fully staffed tribal library that was a mature and healthy facility with dependable funding, a strong support system, and adequate resources. There was one full-time librarian, Jeremy Zagarella, who held an MLIS from UCLA and had 6 years of professional library experience. The library also employed two part-time staff members, both of whom had completed some community college course-work and had 5 years of library experience each. There was also a contract employee who held a B.A. and Teaching Credential. The collection included 5000 volumes in good condition, which was cataloged using the Library of Congress system. Approximately 80% of the materials circulated. The collection was cross-cataloged and regularly shared with the Palomar Community College library. Conversely, Palomar library's collection was available to tribal members, thus greatly enriching Pauma's collection. No other inter-library loan program was available (Zagarella, April 29, 2009, telephone interview with the author).

Mr. Zagarella, a member of CLA, made a presentation on Internet searching at the Library Boot Camp in 2005. He said it was well attended, but there had been little contact among participants since that time. This library boasted 15 public Internet accessible computers and 3 staff computers. The librarian maintained the computer equipment, which was only 2 years old. Partnerships included loose relationships with the Valley Center Branch of SDCL, CSUSM, and Palomar College, which operated a satellite program on the reservation focusing on American Indian Studies. All library funding was provided by tribal monies, except a small grant from IMLS. The budget had increased over the past 5 years and included a line item for computer software and hardware.

The library was open to the public, with 37 operating hours Mondays through Fridays. They issued library cards to all patrons, which consisted of 60% children and teens, 35% adults, and 5% seniors. The programs and classes offered included topics such as tutoring, gardening, GED (a standardized test that may be taken by adults to earn a High School Equivalency Certificate), basic computing, and financial stewardship. Users found out about the library through word of mouth or fliers for events plus the Palomar College web site, catalog, and staff. The biggest challenge at this library, like so many others on and off reservations, was apathy and lack of involvement by the community. In the short term, the librarian hoped to add more classes, including multimedia and movie-making. His long-term vision was to expand the facility and eventually turn the librarian position over to a qualified tribal member.

One year later, Mr. Zagarella continued to manage this thriving library. The staff had been augmented by one full-time member who held a 2-year associate's degree and by an additional contract employee. As of the spring of 2010, plans were to add two new public access computers within the next 6 months, bringing the total to 17—all with Internet access. More programs had been added, including an after-school gardening project where children tend plants, photograph them, and learn about cultivation. Mr. Zagarella was partnering with a librarian at the Valley Center Branch of SDCL, Sandy Puccio, to exchange resources during the 2010 Summer Reading Program. Recent economic pressure had necessitated a budget freeze, but no reductions were anticipated (Zagarella, April 20, 2010, telephone interview with the author).

The Pauma library has a lovely page on the tribal web site, found at http://www.paumatribe.com/pauma-education/pauma-library.html. The information published there includes a tribute to all those who helped it become what it is today:

> The library is indebted to Tribal and General Council members who have supported it throughout its history, and without the vital participation of Palomar Community College; California State University, San Marcos; San Diego County Libraries; and surrounding tribal communities, none of the growth present could have taken place (Education: Pauma AA'Alvikat Library, 2008).

5. Santa Ysabel Tribal Library

The resident population of the Santa Ysabel reservation is listed as 250, with another 450 registered members living elsewhere. This band of Kumeyaay Natives opened a relatively small mountain-lodge style casino in 2007 in hopes that it would "help the band's 700 members climb out of poverty" (Sifuentes, 2007). Unfortunately, the then-booming economy of California and beyond took a nosedive in the ensuing years, and the casino had not, as of 2009, generated the hoped-for profits.

The Santa Ysabel tribal library is in a very unique situation. The tribal librarian, Karen Vignault, is a Native Kumeyaay registered with the Santa Ysabel reservation who holds an MLIS from Drexel University and has 9 years of professional library experience. She is a member of AILA. The library that had existed on the reservation in the 1980s had been closed down by the tribal administration. However, as of 2009, Ms. Vignault stated that there was a collection of 2000 uncataloged books housed in a tribal building that "is not a library" (Vigneault, April 27, 2009, personal communication with the author). Plans were to use the Library of Congress cataloging system whenever she is able to work with the materials. At that time, the tribal government was experiencing problems, with one of the effects being indefinite closure and no access to the collection due to zero funding.

Although the librarian works full time at an academic library in San Diego, she devotes her personal time to maintaining a virtual tribal library online at http://www.santaysabeltriballibrary.blogspot.com, which she launched in 2008. It showcases beautiful archival photographs of the tribe. There are links to scholarship grant applications, an "Ipai[3] word for the day" section, links to Native American web sites, lists of Kumeyaay books, and a link to Native Youth Magazine for young adults. She updates the blog regularly with articles and photographs covering current events of interest. Obviously, her biggest challenge is sustaining the library without a building or a budget. Her perseverance and dedication to her people are evident in the creative way she has adapted to this significant drawback, exhibiting great faith in the future. Ms. Vignault was contacted in 2010 and stated that nothing had changed regarding the status of the Santa Ysabel tribal library and that she was continuing to maintain the blog on her own personal time. She had attended the tribal library conference in Oregon in October 2009 and was serving as co-chair of CLA's Native Libraries Roundtable.

IV. Success Factors in San Diego Tribal Libraries

Several factors are evident that contribute to the survival and success of the five tribal libraries described herein. They are as follows:

1. the presence of a designated librarian;
2. support from the tribal government;
3. plans and a vision for the future; and
4. partnerships and connections with other entities.

In each of the five libraries, the author was able to locate and interview a specific staff member whose responsibility (either through employment or as a volunteer) was to maintain their respective library. Three of these contacts hold an MLIS, a fourth has a 2-year associate's degree and the fifth has completed approximately 3 years of college. The presence of a designated Librarian (regardless of whether they hold an MLIS) offers a consistent point of contact for patrons seeking information. It also ensures consistency in how items are organized and cataloged (whether they are virtual or physical

---

[3]"Ipai" means "people" in the Kumeyaay dialect used in the northern part of San Diego County.

materials). Without someone to take responsibility and ownership of a tribal library and its collection, materials can easily become disorganized and lost over time. Thus, there is less awareness of their existence, they are less accessible, and there is little specific knowledge of their contents. Having a well-educated advocate with a vested interest in the tribal library's success is an essential factor in its survival and growth.

Four of the five libraries in the study were receiving strong support from their three respective tribal governments. This is in large part due to the financial well-being of the Barona, Sycuan, and Pauma gaming enterprises that provide for adequate budgets and infrastructure. These prosperous bands are committed to investing their profits in the future of their members, which includes education and preservation of their cultural heritage. Support of their tribal libraries is a natural outcome. Unfortunately, the fifth library did not receive any support from its tribal government. This was probably due to the reservation's overall lack of sufficient funds. Although there was a new casino in operation, it had not been operating long enough to generate significant revenues. The Santa Ysabel tribal administration has had various problems; however, the author recently learned that a change in leadership is expected to bring much-needed interest and support for the library (Vigneault, December 16, 2010, personal communication with the author).

Plans and goals for the future give impetus to the organization and successful operation of a tribal library. Three of the libraries described are strongly focused on growth, development, service enhancements, and expansion of their influence. Although this factor would appear to be a natural outgrowth of tribal support, the reservation with no tribal support did express a goal of moving the library forward at the first opportunity. On the contrary, in spite of consistent tribal support, there is a temporary lack of momentum due to the current absence of a librarian at one of the sites. Another one of the libraries that receives tribal support is working to maintain their existing level of services, with hopes for future growth and increased community involvement.

Due to the isolated nature of tribal libraries, partnerships and collaborations that could enrich library access have been slow in materializing. Involvement in professional associations such as AILA and CLA offers wonderful opportunities for leveraging technology, sharing knowledge, and combining resources. The three librarians who hold MLIS degrees appear to understand this and apply it in their respective positions. An example of a successful partnership is the cross-cataloging of one of the five libraries with a neighboring community college. This greatly expands information access for members of the reservation and offers unique resources to the non-tribal partner.

A. Levels of Success in San Diego Tribal Libraries

Two of the libraries, the BCCM Research Library and the Pauma Tribal Library, had all four factors present and were running on a solid foundation with a bright future.

The Barona Tribal Library had a designated librarian and support from the tribal government but did not indicate any specific goals for the future, or outside partnerships, other than collaboration with the Barona Charter Indian School and the BCCM Research Library, which are both nearby. It did indicate, however, that its level of services had been steadily maintained. The KCC Archives Library floundered without the presence of a full-time designated librarian because of budget reductions. Due to the ongoing support of the tribal government, it appeared this setback would be remedied and that the library would get back on track with specific goals and increased community involvement.

The Santa Ysabel Library continued to survive despite lack of tribal support. This was because all three of the other factors were present. The virtual library is maintained by a self-designated librarian who willingly volunteers her services. She, along with other tribal members, had goals and a vision for the library's future. She was closely connected with other organizations in the library community and in the tribal community.

B. San Diego Tribal Libraries Summary

The history and ongoing saga of tribal libraries in San Diego County offers a complex and remarkable story of survival. Against all odds, Native Americans and their associates in that area of the country have protected and nurtured a large body of their unique heritage of knowledge. Driven by the realization that languages, skills, and archives are fragile, they have rescued much from the past and are now working toward establishing better, more secure ways of passing it on to future generations. Thanks to the progress of technology, resource sharing across boundaries is easier, organization and retrieval of holdings are becoming more efficient, and methods of preservation are more reliable. In addition to archival holdings, some local tribal libraries are fulfilling their mission to provide current and accurate information on a wide variety of subjects, such as legal matters, health care, educational opportunities, current events, technical skills, and pleasure reading.

Unfortunately, a few of San Diego County's tribal libraries may never rise from the ashes of the late 1980s. For some, hopes lie hidden in boxes of books and small collections of papers in tribal halls. For the tribal libraries that are functioning today, signs indicate trends toward less dependence on—and increasing communication with—outside entities. San Diego County's tribal libraries exist in a culture where independence and sovereignty are highly valued. This is one reason they still survive. Along with their sister libraries throughout the United States, local tribal libraries have growing networks in which they can engage. As they connect with each other, and with similar libraries statewide and beyond, they will face the future with increased knowledge and power. Whether contained in a blog, a bookshelf, or a building, San Diego County's Indians are making valiant efforts to preserve, protect, and offer their heritage to those who will follow in their footsteps.

C. Future Research Opportunities

San Diego County tribal libraries offer fertile ground for further research. The last needs assessment performed was through the Tierra Del Sol project in 2001 and almost 10 years have passed, with many changes since then. The author suggests that a complete needs assessment of all San Diego tribal libraries be conducted on a regular basis. Not only would this add to the body of literature on the topic, but it would provide a catalyst for the various tribal governments and their libraries to connect with each other and to seek better ways to support tribal culture and history. It might also improve tribal leaders' knowledge and awareness of the need to sustain their libraries and culture.

The success of the Tribal Library Boot Camp training in 2005 indicates that this should be a regular event as well. Bringing tribal librarians together promotes networking, knowledge sharing, and open communication among the reservations. Along this line, another potential area for research is a study including other libraries in San Diego County and how to create and strengthen connections between them and the tribal libraries. There are a number of public libraries, university libraries, museum libraries, law libraries, and special libraries in San Diego with collections that could be made more readily available to tribal libraries and their patrons through inter-library loan.

V. Conclusion and Implications for Other Libraries

Beyond the scope of San Diego County tribal libraries, there are lessons to be learned and applied to other libraries in similar circumstances. It is vital to the survival of a small library to have a person who is designated, either by the governing entity or through volunteering, as the responsible librarian. Although an MLIS is preferable, completion of lower division college courses and good technical skills are essential. Support from administrative entities is a key factor, as are shared plans and goals for the future. Partnerships with real and virtual communities are also important to success. The technology is now available for libraries all over the world to connect, communicate, and collaborate with each other. No matter how small, isolated, or impoverished a library may be, a cable or DSL connection can open a floodgate of opportunities. If librarians, or whoever is responsible for a library, are aware of these resources and know how to use them, much can be accomplished on behalf of the communities they serve. Some examples are using a no-cost program such as LibraryThing to create an online catalog, participating in webinars for professional growth, or setting up a library blog, a Facebook page, or other social networking sites to connect with potential patrons and partners.

For small libraries that are ethnically and culturally outside the mainstream environment, their prospects for success and growth may well be determined by the existence of at least three of the four factors aforementioned, with number one being essential: (1) the presence of a designated librarian; (2) support from the governing body; (3) plans and a vision for the future; and (4) partnerships and connections with other entities. Most or all of these factors would seem to apply in any environment or country in which there are geographically or culturally isolated populations struggling to maintain access to information in any form or to preserve their language and culture.

Acknowledgments

The author wishes to thank the staff members of the five tribal libraries surveyed for their thoughtful and sincere responses to her inquiries. She expresses heartfelt gratitude for the enthusiastic support and ongoing contributions of Prof. Bonnie Biggs to this project. Without her willingness to share her time, memories, and insights, it would not have been completed. Prof. Biggs has advocated on behalf of San Diego County's tribal libraries for many years and is extremely knowledgeable on the subject.

Appendix

Tribal Library Questionnaire—May 2009

Staff/Training/Education:

1. Did anyone from your library attend California State Library (CSL) Boot Camp in June 2005 at Pala? Round Table on Nov 15, 2003?
2. How many employees/volunteers work at your library?
3. What is their level of education?
4. What is their level of experience?
5. Do they have goals to obtain more education?

Collection:

1. What is the number of volumes/materials in your library?
2. What is the general condition of your materials?
3. Are your materials cataloged properly?
4. Do all materials circulate? If so, how much? If not, do some of them?
5. Do you allow materials to be loaned to other library systems via ILL (inter-library loan)? Are you set up to obtain ILL items for your patrons?

Computers:

1. How many computers are available for public access?
2. Do they all have Internet?
3. How many computers are used for library staff only?
4. How do you use computers in managing your library? (online catalog, email, etc.)
5. If you have an online catalog, what software are you using?
6. Who maintains the equipment; how old is it?

Partnerships:

1. Do you have existing partnerships with San Diego County Library (SDCL)? California State Library (CSL)? Other tribal libraries? Local universities, or any other organizations?
2. If so, please explain the benefits and functions of these partnerships.
3. Did your library initiate any of these partnerships, or were you approached by others?
4. Do you have any connection with a Friends of the Library organization?

Funding:

1. Where does your funding come from: tribal monies, government grants, private donations, other (please estimate percentage of each)?
2. How is the money divided: salaries, materials, supplies, services (percentage)?
3. Over the past five years, has your budget increased, decreased, or stayed the same?
4. Is there a budget for computers and tech support?

Patrons/Customers:

1. Is your library used only by tribal members, or is it open to the public?
2. What days/hours are you open?
3. What is the breakdown of users in age groups: children/teens/adults/seniors?
4. Do you issue library cards? If not, do you use some other form of ID to check out items?

Programs:

1. Please list any regular programs/events you hold, such as storytimes, cultural programs, computer training, job search assistance, genealogy research, etc.
2. What are some other ideas you would like to implement for programming?

Communication/Networking:

1. How do people find out about your library? Do you publish information in any local newsletters? Do you have a website?
2. Do you or anyone on your staff belong to any library organizations, such as ALA, AILA, CLA, etc.
3. Who inspires you? What motivated you to get a job at your tribal library? What is your vision for the future of your library?

Challenges:

1. What is your biggest challenge?
2. What could other organizations do to help your library succeed?

References

Aguirre, A. A. (2004, March 2). Tribal library opens in Pauma. *North County Times*. Retrieved from http://www.nctimes.com/news/local/article_d2ba5b1d-0ac4-564c-89bd-dfc240c1a24f.html

ATALM (2010). *Association of Tribal Archives, Libraries, & Museums (ATALM) Website*. Retrieved from http://www.atalm.org/

Ayala, J. (2007). *Weaving Partnerships with the Native Americans in Your Community*. Presentation given at California Library Association Conference, Long Beach, CA.

Biggs, B. (1998). The tribal library project: Interns, American Indians, and library services: A look at the challenges. *College and Research Libraries News* 59(4), 259–262.

Biggs, B. (2000a). Bright child of Oklahoma: Lotsee Patterson and the development of America's tribal libraries. *American Indian Culture and Research Journal* 24(4), 55–67.

Biggs, B. (2000b). Tribal libraries: And still they rise. *MultiCultural Review* 9(1), 20–23, 55–56.

Biggs, B. (2001). *Tribal Library Census & Needs Assessment 2001*. Retrieved from http://public.csusm.edu/loc/index.html

Biggs, B. (2002). California's tribal libraries: Equal access? *California Libraries* 12(2), 1–14.

Biggs, B. (2003). California tribal librarians unite. *News from Native California* 16(3), 8–9.

Biggs, B. (2004). Strength in numbers! *American Libraries* 35(3), 41–43.

Biggs, B., and Whitehorse, D. (1995). Sovereignty, collaboration and continuing challenge: a history of tribal libraries in San Diego County. *Special Libraries* 86(Fall), 279–291.

Burke, S. (2007). The use of public libraries by Native Americans. *Library Quarterly* 77(4), 429–446.

California Department of Transportation (2009, July). *Native American Trust Lands, Division of Transportation Planning*. Map generated from Data Source: Bureau of Indian Affairs, January, 2009. Retrieved from http://www.dot.ca.gov/hq/tpp/offices/orip/na/index_files/Native_American_Trust_Lands_Map.pdf

California Indian Education Association (2009). *History*. Retrieved from http://www.ourciea.org/?page_id=14.

California State Library (2005). California State Library team members reach out to Native American tribal libraries and California's Native American population. *Connection*. Retrieved from http://www.library.ca.gov/newsletter/2005/2005fall/tribal2.html

Campo Kumeyaay Nation (2009). *A Look into the Past – History of Campo*. Retrieved from http://goldenacorncasino.com/history

Carrico, R. (2008). *Strangers in a Stolen Land: Indians of San Diego County from Prehistory to the New Deal*. Sunbelt Publications, San Diego, CA.

Cartright, P., and Starr, K. (2009). *An evaluation of the 2009 National Conference of Tribal Archives, Libraries, and Museums: Streams of Language, Memory, and Lifeways*. Retrieved from http://www.tribalconference.org/2009_conf_evaluation.pdf

Dutschke, D. (1988). American Indians in California. In *Five views: An Ethnic Historic Site Survey for California*, Office of Historic Preservation, California Department of Parks and Recreation, Sacramento, CA. Retrieved from http://www.nps.gov/history/history/online_books/5views/5views1.htm

Education: Pauma AA'Alvikat Library (2008). *Pauma Tribe Website*. Retrieved from http://www.paumatribe.com/pauma-education/pauma-library.html

Executive team meeting minutes (2009). Discussion of Native American Services' initiative. *San Diego County Library*, June 16.

Federal Register (2010). Indian entities recognized and eligible to receive services from the United States Bureau of Indian Affairs. Retrieved from http://www.federalregister.gov/articles/2010/10/01/2010-24640/indian-entities-recognized-and-eligible-to-receive-services-from-the-united-states-bureau-of-indian

Forbes, J. (1978). *The Potential Role of Libraries and Information Services in Supporting Native American Cultures and the Quality of Life of Native People*. Paper presented to the White House Pre-Conference on Indian Library and Information Services On or Near Reservations, Denver, CO, October 19–22. Retrieved from http://nas.ucdavis.edu/Forbes/lib.html

Four Directions Institute. (2007). California Indians. Retrieved from http://www.fourdir.com/california_indians_index.htm

Hanks, S. (2007). Tribal libraries. ALASC Luminary Lecture, Colloquia podcast, San José State University Webcast. Retrieved from http://slisweb.sjsu.edu/slis/colloquia/2007/colloquia07fa.htm

Heizer, R. F. (Ed.). (1978). *California. Handbook of North Americans, 8*. Quoted in Dutschke, D. (1988). American Indians in California. In *Five views: An ethnic historic site survey for California*. Office of Historic Preservation, California Department of Parks and Recreation. Retrieved from http://www.nps.gov/history/history/online_books/5views/5views1.htm

Kumeyaay Community College (2008). *Mission Statement. Kumeyaay Community College Website*. Retrieved from www.kumeyaaycommunitycollege.com/mission.htm

Metoyer-Duran, C. A. (2002). The Rupert Costo Archive of the American Indian. Filmed from the holdings of the Rupert Costo Library of the American Indian, University of California at Riverside, CA. Retrieved from http://microformguides.gale.com/Data/Download/9022000C.pdf

National Indian Education Association (2009). *NIEA Profile*. Retrieved from http://www.niea.org/profile/

Native American gaming enterprises (2008). *History of Native American gaming*. Retrieved from http://en.wikipedia.org/wiki/Native_American_gambling_enterprises

Patterson, L. (2000). History and status of Native Americans in librarianship. *Library Trends* 49(1), 182–193.

Patterson, L. (2008). Exploring the world of American Indian libraries. *Rural Libraries* 18(1), 7–12.

Petersen, E. (2007). *Tribal libraries in the United States: A directory of American Indian and Alaska Native facilities*. McFarland & Co, Jefferson, NC.

Peterson, E. (2004). Collection development in California Indian tribal libraries. *Collection Building* 23(3), 129–132.

San Diego County Visitor Industry Summary. (2010). *Calendar Year 2009*. Retrieved from http://www.sandiego.org/downloads/1292987020.72504600_ebe0e3b3e0/December_VISCY09.pdf

Sifuentes, E. (2007, April 12). Santa Ysabel casino opens. North County Times. Retrieved from http://www.nctimes.com/news/local/article_6541a25e-6fc8-59df-bbc2-6cdaba7bd2e3.html

Spicer, E. H. (1969). A short history of the Indians of the United States. New York, Van Nostrand Reinhold Co. Quoted in D. Dutschke (1988). American Indians in California. In *Five Views: An Ethnic Historic Site Survey for California*. Office of Historic Preservation, California Department of Parks and Recreation. Retrieved from http://www.nps.gov/history/history/online_books/5views/5views1.htm

Streams of language, memory, and lifeways (2009). *Tribal Archives, Libraries, and Museums Conference*. Retrieved from http://www.tribalconference.org/history.html

University of Arizona (2005). *Tribal Archive, Library, and Museum Directory*. Retrieved from http://www.statemuseum.arizona.edu/aip/leadershipgrant/directory/directory.shtml.

U.S. Census Bureau (2000a). Geographic Areas Reference Manual (GARM). Chapter 5: American Indian and Alaska Native Areas.

U.S. Census Bureau (2000b). States ranked by American Indian and Alaska Native population, July 1, 1999. (ST-99-46). Population Estimates Program, Population Division.

United States. Congress. Senate. Select Committee on Indian Affairs. (1991). Native American libraries, archives, and information services: Hearing before the Select Committee on Indian Affairs, United States Senate, One Hundred Second Congress, first session, oversight hearing to gain a better understanding of the condition of Native American libraries, archives, and information services, May 23, 1991, Washington, DC. Washington, DC: U.S. G.P.O.

U.S. Department of Energy (2009). *Tribal nations FAQs. Tribal Programs and Native American Agreements.* Retrieved from http://www.em.doe.gov/tribalpages/faqs.aspx

777.com. (n.d.). *Indian Reservations and the American Casino Culture: A Brief History.* Retrieved from http://www.777.com/articles/indian-reservations-and-the-american-casino-culture

Defining Difference: The "Noble and Less Noble" Traditions of Education and Training in Australia

Mary Carroll

Faculty of Workforce Development, Victoria University, Melbourne, Australia

Abstract

The background and context of Australian Library and Information Services (LIS) education and the role LIS education plays in constructing the Australian workplace are explored in this chapter. It provides an analysis of the broader historical, social and educational imperatives which have shaped Australian LIS education. It also examines the pedagogical, structural and epistemological construct surrounding the development of education for LIS in that country. Specific questions are raised about divisions in LIS education and training which lay the framework for further research and discussion. The historical context for LIS education is covered and insights into the nature and background of the broader educational frameworks which have influenced it are provided.

> For clear thinking on the subject of training for library services it is necessary to understand the different kinds of work which must go on in a library. In this report we recognize two distinct types which, for want of better terms we call "professional" and "clerical". Each of these types or phases of library work demands general and vocational education of a particular character. The distinction between the two is only vaguely understood and seldom applied in library organization and practice. (Williamson, 1971, p. 9).

I. Introduction

Over the past three decades the nature of work in the library and information science (LIS) industry worldwide has undergone many changes along with a fundamental shift in the nature of the skills—particularly technological skills—needed by the contemporary workplace. Internationally these changing needs have created pressure to reassess the validity of traditional employment and educational structures. As the skill bases have shifted and

ADVANCES IN LIBRARIANSHIP, VOL. 33
© 2011 by Emerald Group Publishing Limited
ISSN: 0065-2830
DOI: 10.1108/S0065-2830(2011)0000033008

mutated it has become less clear what core skills and attributes are central and unique to the various staff categories within the workplace. This is particularly true of industries, such as LIS, which are at the forefront of technological advancements. These changes have also had implications for education and training. In countries such as Australia there is a nexus between the educational structures and the workplace. The type of education or training an LIS worker undertakes defines the workers place in the employment hierarchy, their tasks and which tasks are deemed inappropriate for their positions. This workplace stratification is based on significant systemic and conceptual distinctions in the delivery of education and training which are central to the development of the Australian LIS industrial model.

In recent years the Australian LIS industry has conducted a number of research projects aimed at determining the impact of changes on the workplace, the future of LIS education and training and the outlook for the workforce. Such investigations have included the Australian Library and Information Association's (ALIA) *Nexus: An Investigation into the Library and Information Services Workforce Final Report* (Hallam, 2008) and *Library Technician Education in Australia: State of the Nation Report* (ALIA, 2010). In 2009, a research project funded by the Australian Learning and Teaching Council (ALTC) titled *Re-conceptualising and re-positioning Australian library and information science education for the twenty-first century,* was begun. This report will be completed early 2011. This project aims to develop a comprehensive picture of education for the Australian LIS profession and identify how its future education and training needs can be developed and sustained.

Historically lines have been drawn in Australian education between what has been called "education for the head" and "for the hand" (Australia, 2003, p. 161). This divided educational model has been subscribed to almost from the establishment of formal LIS programmes in tertiary institutions. Consequently the LIS industry continues to attempt to corral certain aspects of education within the boundaries associated with degrees of "practical" and "theoretical." By using this practical/theoretical divide the workplace has been defined by unacknowledged and often dated constructs, aligned to beliefs about the nature and limits of intelligence, labour divisions, professional territorialism/protectionism and gender equity. Changes in workplace practice have raised questions about these educational divisions and require further examination. This chapter explores the development of education and training for the Australian LIS workforce by first placing it in its broader educational and historical context.

A. Background

Australian library education has existed in two educational sectors for over 40 years. These sectors are university or higher education (HE) sector and vocational education (VE or VET) sector. HE is conducted within universities closely associated historically with similar institutions in the United Kingdom (UK). VE is delivered in Technical and Further Education Colleges (TAFE) and recently, in Registered Training Organisations (RTOs). The sector in which education or training occurs defines what is taught; how it is taught; and by whom it is taught. Over the past 40 years these divisions have aligned with workforce structures defining the roles and responsibilities associated with each classification of worker. These divisions are based on key factors reflective of historical decisions associated with Australian education generally, of professional debates both nationally and internationally, and with concepts associated with labour and industry. A great deal of effort has been expended on institutionalising and conceptualising a rationale for two different sectors of education. Much of this rationale rests on determining divisions in the workplace and drawing of professional boundaries. Differences between the two have been created by systemic and theoretical constraints and are based on broader conceptions which emerged in the late nineteenth and early twentieth century.

These constraints have been based on a pedagogical climate which considered that "high intellectual endeavor can be sorted out into categories, some suitable for study and transmission at special elite institutions called universities and some in less favoured institutions called technical college" (Murray-Smith, 1987, p. 12).

To this end post-secondary education developed a dual sectoral approach to education and training based on a paradigm that articulated knowledge as being of two types, *vocational/technical* and *general*, or *liberal* and assigned responsibility for a particular knowledge type to one of the two educational sectors. Education commentator Guy Neave (1980) ironically simplified this calling this the "noble and less noble" traditions in education. Today they are distinguished each by parameters being drawn around the content and delivery methods of education. The LIS sector has been reflective of the broader context in Australian education. In addition education and training has also been aligned to professional associations such as the Australian Library and Information Association (ALIA) and the Australian School Library Association (ASLA). This has been the case since tertiary education commenced. Today there is both baccalaureate (three year bachelor's degree) and post-baccalaureate (one or two year graduate diploma or masters) entry to the profession. Most HE programmes are generalist though a limited number have specialist focus in areas such as teacher-librarianship. These are delivered in the federally funded HE sector. Paraprofessional or technical (library technician) work supported by a two year vocational diploma delivered by the state funded TAFE colleges or private RTOs.

II. Emergence of Australian Educational Structures

> It is a matter of no little urgency that professional library work be disentangled forthwith from the skilful use of hands in the mechanical operations that play so large a role in every active and useful library. Until this is done, library work will not make a strong appeal to the better type of college man and women (Williamson, 1971, p. 107)

Australian education often developed a hybrid response to its economic and social context. In the nineteenth and early twentieth century European Australia had a desire to model its educational institutions on British and European ones. The first tertiary educational institutions to emerge in the mid-nineteenth century were modelled on "traditional" British/European universities with the so-called "learned professions" such as law and medicine and being underpinned loosely by a "liberal" education. University education was seen as occupying the highest point of the educational structure. It was, and continues to be, perceived as being central to change and innovation, being at the forefront, if not the instigator of developments in thought, process, concept and technology. The HE sector was perceived to be independent of industry. It took a conceptual approach which called for knowledge and broad understanding to create the contexts, climate and possibilities for the application of technical skills.

The economic and industrial climate when the first universities were established in the nineteenth century required a more practical and utilitarian application of education. This meant that what was taught first universities was a compromise between the utilitarian and the learned (Barcan, 1980, p. 119) and included practical disciplines such as law, medicine and engineering to meet the industrial needs. Despite their attachment to the Old World curricula at these universities were often more akin to their New World counterparts. Increasingly access to the professions became dependent on credentials and qualification as was being done in the United States (US). Additionally Australian education in the mid-nineteenth century was developed at a time of increasing industrialisations and the emergence in Europe, particularly in Germany, of so-called "scientific" modes of instruction. Later in the nineteenth century technical training colleges such as the Royal Melbourne Institute of Technology (RMIT) were established to cater to apprenticeship training and emerging adult education needs and to address needs of increasingly industrialised society. The original impetus for technical education came out of changing manpower needs in the second half of the nineteenth century and out of the competitive forces which drove production. The need for such education came about, because

> Trades could formerly be learned by the apprentice system, but that system is now become obsolete. The one influence felt by educators who are not wedded to medieval forms or classical models is the demand of the great masses of the people to be taught the scientific and technical features of their calling. (Stetson, in White, 1976, p. 7)

Exposed as it was to new educational ideas and attached to it British colonial origins Australia developed a dualism in its educational outlook which was to permeate its development into the twenty-first century.

A. The Industrial Imperative

"Technical" or "scientific" training institutions such as RMIT were a product of new industrial models which emerged during the first half of the twentieth century. Such models were "made up of heads of factories at the top, a thin layer of supervisors and foremen standing next to them, and finally, a thicker layer of factory 'hands' at the bottom" (White, 1976, p. 13). This model reflected new pressures for mass production resulting in breakdown of skills into finite, measurable tasks along the Taylorist mode, so that workers "usually wound up working with only one process" (White, 1976, p. 12). There is a clear distinction to be drawn here between the long-established trades steeped in history, tradition and formal organisation established by the ancient medieval craft guilds and their master journeyman apprentice system, and the new occupations that were emerging to meet changing industry patterns: "The old stratification made up of master craftsman, journeymen, and apprentices thus gave way to a different type of stratification" (White, 1976, p. 13). The new structure was reflected in distinctions between education, and vocational training that Moodie viewed as an Aristotelian model, that is "training for work directed by others, education for self-directed work" (2001, p. 6). Moodie and others such as Rushbrook (1997) and Wheelahan (2001) believe this layering of skills reinforced the boundaries between professionals and non-professionals. This industrial model was seen by some to "create labour market advantage by restricting and channeling of access to education pathways" (Rushbrook, 1997, p. 3) through the "sedimentation" of the workforce and the skills needed in the workplace. Later in the twentieth century many of the original technical colleges took on the character of the traditional university. At the same time a new stratum of non-degree conferring colleges were established catering to apprentice training, post-compulsory technical training and further education (TAFE). These TAFE colleges continue to serve this function and remain aligned and responsive to industry.

B. Blurring Boundaries

In 1974, the mission of Australia's technical sector was re-defined as a result of the seminal Kangan Report, *TAFE in Australia: Report on needs in technical and further education* (Australian Committee on Technical and Further Education, 1974). It was seen to have a role in providing "vocational starting points for individuals who frequently did not have a trade background" in "areas which tended to fall outside the province or sphere of the tradesman or professional" (Barker and Holbrook, 1996, p. 219). This report fundamentally changed the face of training for industry, replacing the previous educational paradigm with a new one. This was to re-vitalise training programmes and to change vocational and technical education in Australia. What emerged post-Kangan was the concept that training should be about more than vocational outcomes, that it should also be about preparing people for active citizenship. Specifically, according to Young who developed the first technical or vocational programme in LIS in Australia, it was

> an educational philosophy which recognizes that the ultimate economic stability of the nation will not be realized from a narrow attachment to training for a trade whose usefulness has a limited term but is more likely to derive from young people educated to possess moral, social and aesthetic values, historical perspectives and the capacity to relate effectively to others. (1979, p. 445)

The framework for this new educational model was

- A belief in educating the individual not just for manpower needs of industry
- TAFE education would be available for all
- Emphasis on life-long learning
- Flexibility

This shift began to blur the boundaries between universities and technical education and between their utilitarian and liberal function. In short, the purpose of each educational institution became less distinct. It was in this climate in 1970 that education for Australian library technicians was established in one of the TAFE colleges and the first undergraduate programme for librarians was established in a nineteenth century technical college, the Royal Melbourne Institute of Technology (RMIT).

1. Systemic Distinctions

Institutional or systemic characteristics have been pinpointed by Raffe (2002) as being key elements in sustaining divisions between the sectors in Australia. Qualifications and delivery of instructions are complex. Although there are some variations from state to state, there are systemic differences such as approaches to course mapping, focus on differing client groups, attitudes to credit and admission requirements. Although the TAFE colleges are similar to US community colleges and UK polytechnics, their programmes are considered discrete from those in universities. They have traditionally been considered "terminal" and not intended to lead to further degree programmes. In recent years there has been discussion about VE programmes being pre-professional but this remains a contentious issue. VE training programmes, including those in LIS have been based on Training Packages since the late 1990s. Training packages are a set of standards, qualifications and guidelines that are used to recognise and assess the skills and knowledge that workers need to perform effectively. A training package is not a curriculum but rather a framework of "outcomes" or competencies which have been developed in consultation with industry. They award a series of qualifications from Certificate I to Advanced Diploma, which are national in scope and recognition. The structural distinctions as they currently exist between these two sectors are summarised in Table 1.

2. Conceptual Distinctions

The two sectors operate today in an environment which valorises the notion of "equal but different" and "parity of esteem" concepts which will be discussed further. Some credit into HE can be gained for VE training but the concept of any equivalency between HE and VE is the cause of fierce debate. Difference in have been outlined by the Australian government as HE delivering "education for the head" and VE delivering training "for the hand" (Australia. Parliament, Senate, Employment Workplace Relations and Education Reference Committee, 2003, p. 161). The conceptual distinctions drawn are both epistemological and pedagogical. Epistemological distinctions are based on the presumption that there is difference in the actual content or knowledge base of those being educated at professional level versus those being trained at the vocational level. Pedagogical distinctions are based on a perceived difference in the intellectual depth and complexity of what is required in each sector. It is assumed that what occurs in HE will be more theoretical, abstract and complex than VE. Teaching approaches to subject matter within the two types also differ with VE delivering

Table 1
Australain Educational Sector Characteristics

	Vocational Education and Training	Higher Education
Qualifications awarded	Advanced diploma Diploma Certificates I-IV	Doctorate Masters Graduate diplomas Graduate certificates Bachelors
Length of programmes	1–2 years	3–6 years
Student admission	Open entry	Selective university entry requirements
Usual mode of study	Largely part-time	Largely full time
Funding and policy bodies	State government Federal government	Federal government
Curriculum	Nationally agreed and recognised training packages Consultation with industry to create desired outcomes Competency-based training	Institutional developed programmes Degree conferred by a college or university

Table 2
Conceptual Distinctions between VE and Higher Education

Vocational Education and Training	Higher Education
Knowledge applied to practical outcomes	"Pure" or theoretical knowledge
Closely aligned to industry	Self-directed and independent
"Hands-on" or applied learning	Theoretical or conceptual learning
Associated with the rise of industrial society	Based on classical traditions
Academically simple	Academically sophisticated

programmes in a practical, experiential and context reliant way while HE approaches subjects in a theoretical, generic and abstract way. The conceptual distinctions between sectors have been outlined and simplified and are shown in Table 2.

3. Epistemological Distinctions

> A professional man or woman should display not merely expertise but wisdom; it is a function of education to develop wisdom and a profession should, therefore require a high standard of education in those seeking admission to its membership. (Hagger, 1969, p. 413)

Argument for epistemological differences in education and training reflects a reliance on the concept of there being two "equal but different" occupations within an industry. A philosophy involving "parity of esteem" and is reliant on the concept of two groups of workers fulfilling essentially different roles, of equal value but with a differing sets of core knowledge and skill. It was assumed that each knowledge base is unique and different with each having discrete and identifiable areas of expertise. Thus they practice in complimentary roles within the one discipline.

4. Intellectual Distinctions

Another key element in the arguments for differences is that there is a fundamental difference in the students themselves and in their inherent academic ability. There is a presumption of a "higher" rather than a different knowledge set being required for professional levels. However, very little empirical research has been conducted into academic potential and actual performance. Most assumptions about intellectual ability appear to be based on results in the final year of schooling and on university entrance scores. The correlation between students' intelligence and their results is one that educators treat with caution because it ignores issues of socioeconomic status, family environment, educational opportunity, cultural attitudes and gender. Research on secondary school success pinpoints all of these factors as crucial in educational attainment. When speaking of the disparity of success Teese (in Rood 2006) claimed that "it is doubtful if individuals have a fair chance ... Students from different geographic areas had the same scholarly ability ... but cultural and economic differences meant that the western suburbs concentrated disadvantage while the east concentrated advantage" (Teese, in Rood, 2006, p. 6).

Another factor is the hierarchy of professional prestige. Successful students gravitate towards professions ranked high in the hierarchy whether or not they are truly interested in it. Universities that fulfil these professional aspirations become more successful, leaving other institutions to educate for professions lower in the hierarchy. As a result the latter attract students who have performed less well, with one exception, Monash University. LIS university education falls outside the elite group of universities.

Institutions delivering LIS programmes fall within what Teese (2000) describes as "next on the hierarchical scale after TAFE colleges" and are "former teacher's colleges and technical institutes drawing from the lower half of the achievement distribution" (p. 237). Because of VE's policy of open access, those with poor university entrance results can also be accepted into VE programmes.

5. Pedagogical Distinctions

> The case that technical education should have been making all along is that there is no hierarchy of esteem, not nowise, not no how. There may be educational institutions working in different places, working for different clients, even working at different standards, but that all knowledge is applied, all knowledge is useful, all knowledge is reciprocal. (Murray-Smith and Dare, 1987, p. 16).

The pedagogical argument for difference is based on the concept of "sub-professional" and is related to an incremental rather than discrete knowledge base relying on differences in ability, achievement and quality. To define more clearly the pedagogical factors associated with distinguishing each sector, Gabb and Glaisher (2006) use Biggs' concepts of knowledge to describe pedagogical differences between education and training. These definitions are essentially focussed on the conceptional nature of vocational knowledge itself, rather than emphasising the need for liberal versus vocational education. University education is described as emphasising declarative knowledge, that is, knowing about things, or "content knowledge". VET education, in contrast, emphasises procedural knowledge, that is, knowing what to do, or "know how". Biggs, according to Gabb and Glaisher, believes that, while universities valorise declarative knowledge, both sectors should be aiming to develop functioning knowledge, the knowledge required for practice, needing "both declarative knowledge and procedural knowledge, linked through conditional knowledge so that one knows when, why and under what conditions this knowledge should be used" (Gabb and Glaisher, 2006, p. 10).

These views of education echo those of an early commentator involved in LIS education, who stated

> It is impossible to separate in universities in any acceptable way, education and training ... Parts of any course are concerned with the development of techniques, of routine applications, or manipulative skills, and the repetition of routine applications, or manipulative skill. (Radford, 1968, p. 165)

Gabb and Glaisher believe that both sectors claim to develop functioning knowledge, but that each sector has a particular pedagogical bias. Although the two seek to reach the same end—the attainment of functioning knowledge for professional practice—they use different pedagogical routes and emphasise different knowledge forms, including practical/theoretical distinctions in the way knowledge is attained. This is the root of the concept of "equal but different" in discussions about the nature of knowledge. Simply put, it pits merit-based selection in the university sector against open access mission of VE.

C. The LIS Industry

> No amount of study in a library school can fit for successful library service the individual who lacks the fundamental educational equipment. On the other hand, any persons having the necessary education and native fitness and capacity have taken it up with complete success in spite of a lack of technical training. It is far easier for an intelligent, educated person interested in books and people to make a success of library work than it is for one having all the technique the library school can give him but lacking in general intellectual and cultural background. (Williamson, 1971, p. 14)

Australian LIS has subscribed to the concept of an epistemological difference in those being educated with many attempts being made to distinguish between the knowledge base of the two main groups—librarians and library technicians. Attempts to define difference have included the Library Courses Vocational Standing Committee's *Guidelines for the Education* (1976) and have continued with more recent statements on work level guidelines associated with both function and salary. Defining professional and paraprofessional work by the nature of education has only been partially successful, with many areas of content overlapping between the two. To some extent this has been a result of the complex LIS educational environment in which undergraduate baccalaureate programmes are seen as terminal and as career entry points, and as transfer qualification into higher degrees. In LIS, professional entry can occur through three year undergraduate, one year postgraduate, and one and a half or two year master's level programmes. At the same time library technicians are being trained in two to two and half year Diploma and Advanced Diploma programmes. Programme limitations have led to emphasis on vocational and practical knowledge with distinctions made by different assessment structures.

D. Historical Complexities

Undergraduate education for librarianship and training for library technicians were both established in 1970, under the same state government department, that of technical education. This meant that definitions, curricula and professional identity have always had to take into account the relationship between these two groups. This perhaps has led both groups to define their knowledge base by what it does not contain relative to the other sector. This raises the question of whether education leads the industry in defining difference by equipping the two groups with different core knowledge bases—defined as equal but different. As Wheelahan (2003, p. 34) contends, the VE sector, which includes LIS programmes, generally define themselves not by a set of skills and knowledge different from the HE sector, but residually. That is, they create curricula from what the university sector deems inappropriate for professional programmes. Professional programmes in attempts to equip the "new" professional, have adopted new skill sets, such as those associated with the electronic environment, and have had to shed many aspects of training previously considered to be in the professional domain. In areas such as cataloguing and reference work for example industry is asking VE programmes to equip technician with skills once considered the key professional defining points. This makes for a fluid skill set rather than two unique knowledge bases.

Library education historian Gerald Bramley (1975) believed there were two conflicting possibilities for emerging LIS education system. "The most contentious factor is whether or not there exists a body of theoretical knowledge upon which the practice of librarianship is based" (p. 9). The question of appropriate preparation for the LIS industry continues today. Should it be vocational or practical and best delivered as an apprenticeship, as was originally favoured by Melvil Dewey (White, 1976, pp. 47–48), or should be based on theoretical knowledge that can be carried from one context to another? Should it be a "systematic apprenticeship program on the trades model" (Wilson & Hermanson, 1998, p. 2) or a "purely technical course, coming after general education has been completed" (Wilson & Hermanson, 1998, p. 5)? Did it have enough intellectual depth to provide "conceptual lenses" to "look at a completely new set of problems and suggest ways to deal with them" (Ostler & Dahlin, 1995)? Internationally the educational responses to this have varied. These fundamental debates about professional/vocational continue in Australia where a divide has been a cornerstone of the country's LIS educational structure.

1. A Divided History

The history of education for the LIS reflects the flow of education and the development of other professional groups such as teacher and journalist per Abbott's semi-professions (1998, p. 430). The impetus to create boundaries associated with intellect, pedagogy and gender have been prominent in the development of LIS education. After World War I a large expansion of Australia's public library system occurred along with a decline in apprentice type education. Routine and standardised work practices such as cataloguing and classification emerged. Development of professional associations and an increase in the number of women joining the workforce threatened those with higher professional aspirations. Professional group discussions were dominated by how to raise the status of the profession in the eyes of the public and the academic community. This stratification seemed necessary to stratify the workforce to support librarians" aspirations for professional status. Some of the first efforts were along gender lines, freeing male professional librarians from clerical and mundane housekeeping tasks. This is evidenced in a number of reports that influenced Australia in the first half of the 1900s (Williamson, 1971; McColvin, 1939). Williamson stated

> Two main types of training for library work are required. The first is the broad, general education represented as minimum by a full college course which has included certain important subjects, plus at least one year's graduate study in a library school. ... The second type calls for a general education represented approximately by a four year high school course, followed by a course of instruction designed to give a good understanding of the mechanics and routine operations of a library ... which we may call "sub-professional" or "clerical" (p. 4)

While McColvin stated

> We fear we may be criticized as anti-feminist, but it does seem that, while leaving room for the capable professional woman, it would be a good thing if librarianship were to become predominately a profession for men and an occupation for women ... Let us, therefore, as a general practice recruit women for non-professional work and men for professional work. (p. 114)

These attempts to create gender based groups in LIS failed in the post-World War II period and other means were sought to enhance the professional status of librarians. As Ramsey (1963) stated efforts sought to "free our professionals of a lot of unnecessary responsibility and inappropriate work" (p. 19). The Library Association of Australia (LAA) undertook a quest to establish university education for librarians and to end the apprenticeship and examination system that was in place in the three decades following World War II. The introduction of university programmes resulted in elimination of many trainees or apprentices who performed routine or non-professional tasks. This left a gap for a group of "sub-professionals" who could function between clerks and professionals. It was also felt that librarians' quest for professional status would be enhanced if there were a group that could perform routine library tasks leaving librarians with purely professional duties. Ramsey, a prominent contemporary LIS educator, said the introduction of such training would "free our professionals of a lot of unnecessary responsibility and inappropriate work if we paid attention to the development of a strong body of non-professionals who could carry responsible jobs under professional supervisions" (Ramsey, 1963, p. 19).

Brown, President of the LAA in 1970 said the establishment of the first course at Box Hill Girls Technical College in 1970 was "a major step forward in the field of library education in Australia and one which is hoped will improve division of labour and thus levels of service in all types of libraries" (1970, p. 109). Flowers (1963) noted that

> The workforce will, to some extent, consist of very able women who, having the good sense to realize that their working life is likely to be limited, wish to start working life after matriculation, not after spending four years in higher education. This I would argue is for the common good. Their profitable working life is extended for 4 years. (p. 5)

It was envisaged that this new class of worker would consist of women either before marriage and family or after their family was grown. As professional library education moved into the tertiary sector during the 1960s and 1970s training for this "sub" or paraprofessional group emerged. It was claimed by Brown that "most of the students for the Technicians Course would be of a practical rather than academic turn of mind and would have no interest in further study" (1970, p. 112). The *Eastern Suburbs Mirror* advertising the first course for Box Hill program stated (1970, February 18) "The latter course [library clerk] is one which should have special appeal to the intelligent married woman looking for an interest, with some prospect of employment at the end of the course" (p. 5).

E. Library Technicians

> The library technician assistant is not a watered down librarian, but a skilled person in their own right in particular functions. (Asheim, in Pivec 1975, p. 44)

The first course for library technicians in Australia resulted from an approach made by the Victorian branch of the LAA to the Department of Technical Education in June, 1969. It was approved in October and by December Wesley Young, its first teacher and co-ordinator, had prepared syllabi for a two level course for library clerks and library technicians based on models of similar courses in the United States and Canada. They were sent out for comment on the 23 December 1969 (Naylor, 1991, p. 2). According to Young "the response from women who were thirsting for such an opportunity was overwhelming" resulting in hundreds of applications (personal communication, 23 July 2001). A pilot course with twenty full-time, and 37 part-time students, enrolled including two men was up and running by early 1970 (Pivec, 1975, p. 48). A condition placed by the Department of Technical Education was that the second level be sufficiently advanced to allow good students to articulate into the newly established librarianship undergraduate degree at RMIT.

This was a time of rapid change in the educational environment with a number of key reports that would change the face of LIS education in Australia for the next 20 years. Gates of post-secondary education were opened to a growing number of men and women aspiring to further education but who were not privileged enough to attend university in Australia. All of these changes were to vitally affect the library industry and its workplaces.

1. The Language of Industry

The terminology associated with library technicians is important as it gives a clearer picture of what the LAA had in mind when it began to advocate a training course. Before the course's establishment, Ramsey spent some time pondering the name of such a group, putting forward suggestions such as "chartered librarian", "student librarian", "library aide" and "library clerk" (1963, p. 20). A cursory investigation suggests that it was in the mid to late 1960s that the term "technician" began to be applied in other fields such as engineering. The prominent and influential US educator Lester Asheim spoke at LAA's fifteenth biennial conference in Adelaide in 1969 and used the term "library technician" or "library technical assistant." This appears to have been a defining moment in the naming of this group as well as in the development of key concepts about education. Young (personal communication) was greatly influenced by Asheim's visit and drew many of his ideas from the conference.

The 1970s also saw a new language emerge in the educational lexicon which was to shape the future of education and to profoundly influence LIS education. It was the language from the Kangan Report. What began to appear in the contemporary LIS literature was a shift away from the use of terms such as sub-professional towards the use of the term paraprofessional. The use of the term paraprofessional is an important conceptual shift, connoting a collaborative in which "parity of esteem" and "equal but different" would be possible. The term paraprofessional applied to middle level workers in libraries. The term emerged in the 1960s and seems to have become attached to the LIS field in the early to mid-1970s when Emma R. Christine from the Department of Librarianship at the Queensland Institute of Technology wrote an article for the *Australian and Academic Research Libraries* (AARL) journal entitled "Paraprofessionals: Plague or promise?" (1974, pp. 201–205). This change in language was important since it changed in the way in which work and education were perceived and promoted. What emerges from the late 1970s and into the 1980s is an increasing adherence to the concept of the technician as a discrete professional group with a set of its own skills and specialisations. As Noel Watkins of the Education Department of Victoria's Technical Division wrote

> I believe the middle level paraprofessional courses prepare students for vocations which have an integrity in their own right. I believe that they are not mere extensions of the technical psychomotor skills of the tradesman or tradeswomen. Neither are they watered down, diluted aspects of the full vocational preparations one expects of a professionally educated person. (1976, p. 5)

These views were to dominate educational rhetoric for the next 25 years and were to guide much of the employment structures and educational curricula during that time. Courses for library technicians were described (perhaps a little unfortunately) as terminal rather than pre-professional (Smeaton, 1983, p. 34) a viewpoint stressed strongly by both LIS educators and industry.

Although rhetoric espoused this view, reality was somewhat different. Within this paradigm is a belief that the skill sets and thus the education of the paraprofessional and professional were unique and the people inhabiting each group had different abilities and were somehow "different". This view was not unique to the LIS sector but underpinned most of the educational structures at this time. With the establishment of the first Library Technicians course in 1970 Williamson' 1929 vision for a divided profession, though perhaps not quite as he had envisaged it, had largely been fulfilled.

III. The Current Context: Re-assessing the Concept of Difference

> There is a very real danger that the objectives of library technician' courses, vis-à-vis the objectives of the professional courses, are going to be confused and intermingled. (Watkins 1976, p. 5)

In 2010, the divisions associated with education and training continues both in execution and outcomes. Curtis views the current perception of difference between the two sectors as being associated with funding sources, accreditations arrangements and qualification arrangements (2009, p. 2). The Australian educational landscape continues to be complex with the federal government funding HE and each state and territory being responsible for funding VE at TAFE colleges. Issues surrounding sectoral boundaries, the nature of vocationalism and the validity of sectoral distinction have emerged in recent years as a major global concern. Traditional constructs are believed by some to be based on an obsolete, irrelevant or dated paradigm with more of a social or political dimension than an educational one. Wheelahan (2001) believed "the difference was not whether one system was general and the other vocational, but rather the differences arise from difference in status and wealth" (p. 4).

In 2002 the Australian government paper, *Striving for Quality*, asked,

> If the vocational education and training sector provides "education and training for work", how different is a higher education course for a professionally oriented degree? Is there a point at which higher education, by emphasising the development of professional expertise, loses its distinctiveness and perhaps its significance? Is there something that distinguishes a higher education from vocational education and training, beyond the preparation for work? (DEST, 2002, p. 2)

Recent major reports into Australian tertiary education, including the *Review of Australian Higher Educations* commonly called the Bradley Review (DEEWR, 2008) and *Transforming Australian Education* (DEEWR, 2009a, b) addressed many of the systemic issues associated with transfer and equivalency between HE and VE. They recommended "infrastructure synergies", "structural adjustments" and an "interconnected training and education system" (DEEWR, 2009b, p. 1). Although attempting to abolish many of the systemic differences between the sectors, these reports retain the epistemological and pedagogical delineations which have historically kept the two sectors discrete. These reports also suggested the need to recognise "the distinctly different roles that each sector plays" (DEEWR, 2009b, p. 1). The Bradley review restates many of the existing epistemological and pedagogical distinctions. Outlining what is believed to be the key characteristics of the two sectors the review states:

> The principal characteristics of a fully effective tertiary system would be:
>
> - the equal value given to both VET and higher education, reflecting the importance of their different roles in the development of skills and knowledge and their contributions to our economy and society;
> - the recognition that institutions may have a primary mission in one sector, but should still be able to offer qualifications in the other sector as undercurrent arrangements;
> - a shared and coordinated information base and approach to anticipating future labour market needs, industry needs and demographic trends;
> - a capacity for the whole system to provide integrated responses to work force needs for industries and enterprises, including those in specific localities and communities like outer metropolitan and regional areas where there is significant population growth, low levels of educational attainment and participation and uneven provision;
> - an efficient regulatory and accountability framework and
> - clearer and stronger pathways between the sectors in both direction (DEEWR, 2008, p. 179).

The final report re-stated the traditional characterisation of the role of VE and HE. VE is to continue to respond to the needs of industry as

> The vocational education sector is a vital contributor to the development of a skilled workforce. It has the capacity to respond quickly to employers' labour and skill needs, provide access and opportunity to the tertiary sector for millions of Australians, and contribute—through skills training and partnerships with business—to the nation's productivity and, ultimately, prosperity.

Although HE was to continue "graduating citizens capable of leading the world in their areas of expertise" (DEWWR, 2009a, p. 43).

These concerns have been part of a long-term international movement focussed on the unification of education and training systems. Patterns of systemic unification are occurring in countries such as Norway, Sweden, Australia, New Zealand and Scotland. They are however are finding different solutions (Raffe, 2002, p. 10) to create parity of esteem (Raffe, 2002, p. 2) between university programmes and vocational education and training (VET). Pressure for educational unification is the result of a number of factors, including changing aspirations of students, global changes in the labour market, increased emphasis on generic skills and focus on the concept of lifelong learning. These global changes bring focus on the reasons for having two education sectors in Australia and raise questions about the validity of this division.

A. Australian Qualifications

Since 1995 Australian qualifications have been awarded under the auspices of the *Australian Qualifications Framework* (AQF) a nationally accredited system of qualifications intended to make them all transportable nationally. Before this, VET programmes and qualifications in particular were state based and not recognised nationally. According to the Australian Government's Department of Education, Science and Training (DEST) the AQF is a

> single, coherent framework for qualifications from Senior Secondary Certificates through to Doctoral Degrees.
>
> The framework links together all these qualifications and is a quality-assured national system of educational recognition that promotes lifelong learning and a seamless and diverse education and training system.
>
> It covers qualifications issued by secondary schools, vocational education and training (VET) providers and higher education institutions. All qualifications are nationally recognised. (DEST, n.d., para 3)

Table 3
Australian Qualification Framework by Sector

Schools Sector	Vet Sector	Higher Education Sector
Senior secondary	Bachelor degree (Victoria only)	Doctoral degree
Certificate of education	Advanced diploma	Masters degree
	Associate Degree	Graduate diploma
	Diploma	Graduate certificate
	Certificate IV	Bachelor degree
	Certificate III	Advanced diploma
	Certificate II	Associate degree
	Certificate I	Diploma

Qualifications are prescribed as appropriate for, and the responsibility of, different educational sectors with some degree of overlap. They span all post-primary education sectors. The concept of "qualification" and "level of competency" (or skill level) are seen as distinct and independent of each other and are not equivalent. Each educational sector was deemed to have primary responsibility for particular types of qualification although, in recent years, there has been greater fluidity in the delivery of qualifications between sectors. Secondary schools and TAFEs now deliver qualifications outside their original mandates. Key qualifications and sectoral responsibility are outlined in Table 3.

Key objectives of the AQF were to:

- provide nationally consistent recognition of outcomes achieved in post-compulsory education
- help with developing flexible pathways which assist people to move more easily between education and training sectors and between those sectors and the labour market by providing the basis for Recognition of Prior Learning (RPL) including credit transfer and work and life experience
- encourage individuals to progress through the levels of education and training by improving access to qualifications, clearly defining avenues for achievement, and generally contributing to lifelong learning; Sectoral arrangements for the delivery of qualifications are outlined below. As shown in this table there is considerable overlap in the qualifications which can be delivered within the sectors (Australian Qualifications Framework Advisory Board, 2002).

Associated with the AQF were the Australian Standards Framework (ASF) levels, a set of eight competency levels established by the National Training Board in the mid-1990s to serve as reference points for the development and recognition of competency standards.

- Level 1, generally regarded as entry level-the skills needed to function in the workplace
- Level 2, generally regarded as operator level-basic production skills
- Level 3, generally regarded as basic trade level or equivalent 1
- Level 4, generally regarded as advanced trade level
- Level 5, generally regarded as post-trade, technician or supervisor level
- Levels 6–8, covers the management levels of work

These levels were associated with employment outcomes, skills levels and knowledge forms. They became an area of contention in the early twenty-first century were finally discontinued in 2002. However while the designation of *level* was discontinued, performance outcomes or descriptors associated with qualifications, largely reflect these original performance levels.

The aim was to make qualifications national, make the outcome transparent in order to enable increased articulation across sectors. It was imposed without any major shift or alteration in the existing systemic differences. The opposition by universities to levels hinged to a large extent on uneasiness about the relationship between these levels and qualification, particularly areas of overlap and the contentious issue of equivalency. In addition, the advent of Training Packages and Competency Based Training (CBT) into VET training imposed further systemic and pedagogical differences upon the sectors. This seems to have made the aim to have transparent pathways more, not less, difficult. There are also inherent differences in assessment in the VET and university sectors which make it difficult to determine the ability of students and their success, for articulation purposes.

B. The Construction of LIS Education

LIS industry continues to attempt to corral certain aspects of education within the boundaries of practical and theoretical. According to the Australian Bureau of Statistics' (ABS) 2006 Australian census (ABS, 2007) there were approximately 10,000 librarians, 6500 library technicians and 8000 library assistants employed in the country. The distinction between these groups defined by the Australian Library and information Association (ALIA) in its salary scales and work-level guidelines (ALIA, 2009). Changes occurring in workplaces challenge these divisions in education and raise questions about the nature of professionalism itself, how we measure aptitude for entry to higher education, and what constitutes education as opposed to training.

LIS as it exists today still presumes that one education sector meets the requirement of one level of job description, such as "library assistant" (Certificate III) "library technician" (Diploma or Advanced Diploma), and that the other sector meets needs of professional librarian (undergraduate,

graduate diploma or masters). The reality, as Radford commented is that the library workplace is so varied and fluid that workers of any designation may be called on to perform any task within a skill range, whether they be classed as professional or non-professional (Radford, 1977). Radford, on this issue stated:

> Many who write about the preparation of people for work in libraries choose to distinguish between the words education and training, using the first to signify the theoretically based preparation of professionals and the second to signify the practical preparation of non-professionals. Others speak of the education of the librarians when referring to his study and knowledge of subjects other than librarianship, and the training of the librarian when referring to his studies in librarianship. In this chapter the words will be used interchangeably, in the belief that neither of the customary distinctions is worth making. Indeed, they are neither of them valid. (1977, p. 491)

Such early comments highlight some of the issues continuing today. LIS education is involved in ever-shifting, mutating curricula which blur the boundaries between professional and vocational work. As a consequence there is need to address the function and validity of distinctions between those who train as professional information workers such as librarians and those who are library technicians.

IV. Contemporary LIS Education

In 2009, as previously outlined, the Australian Federal Government began to promote an increasing integration of education and training as part of an educational reform agenda. These reforms were to emphasis the removal of many of the structural divisions remaining between education and training while retaining the conceptual divisions. The government in *Transforming Australia's Higher Education System report* stated

> Tertiary education in Australia should be a continuum of delivery, with better connections between sectors in both directions while avoiding one sector subsuming the other ... To achieve these goals what is required is an education system that is less fragmented and easier for students to navigate. It should be straight forward for students to enter post-school education and move between vocational and higher education as appropriate to enhance their skills and qualifications. (2009, p. 43)

Such a statement highlights increased credentialism, greater mobility nationally and internationally and transparent pathways (or articulation) between VET and HE. Such realignments in the national education system, as well as increasingly globalised educational practices, impose increasing pressure on all industries to examine traditional employment and education structures.

Given the current context for education in Australia and the dynamic nature of skills needed in the field, LIS education needs to address a number questions including

- To what extent does LIS university education teach a core of immutable principles that remain central and unique to identification of the profession?
- How relevant, valid and necessary are the distinctions and barriers which exist between LIS education sectors?
- Does education for the industry stand up to scrutiny when seeking to define difference, or is education a tool used to impose, define and reinforce workplace differences?
- To what extent have educational structures led to continued debate about the requirements for entry to the profession, task confusion and role blurring?
- What place does liberal education or education in a field outside LIS have in the creation of the professional?
- Do professional associations have a vested interest in maintaining educational distinctions?
- What is the extent to which the shape and form of LIS education reflects competing interests, expediency, professional gate-keeping and outside agendas?
- How can LIS education achieve the continuum of delivery set out in 2009 in *Transforming Australia's Higher Education System*? In short, how can LIS education become less fragmented?
- What authority/authorities should have the power to grant or deny entry into LIS professional practice?

V. Conclusion

Like elsewhere, Australian LIS is confronting an increasingly complex and challenging environment. Changes in the workplace, alongside a changing educational landscape, has had an impact on both content and structure for education in the library and allied industries' sector in Australia. At present, both content and structure have been in place for over 40 years and led to long standing patterns in both how students are educated (pedagogy) and what they are taught (epistemology). Today's changing landscape has brought into question many of the distinctions which have existed to date between education for professionals and training for paraprofessionals.

As the country moves its educational reform agenda along, LIS will need to answer a number of elementary questions. Education must continue to address its role in the preparation of those who will work in the industry and it must do so with vigour. The need to clearly define and articulate both the skills set and the role of those within the industry is becoming ever more urgent. Increasingly there will be pressure to align LIS education with broader educational policies. This will involve greater articulation between previously divided sectors and increasingly open access to all sectors of education. This in many ways reflects the changing nature of the current policy landscape and changes in the workplace. How LIS education will accommodate these new climates and how it will move forward, needs to be carefully considered. Today, as in the past, the answer to many essential questions about the nature of the profession and its education it remain unanswered. Understanding how and why Australian LIS education has developed as it has can help to answer tough questions in the future. This chapter has brought a perspective from the past to the discussion table. Thus it helps to set a framework for future discussions and decisions. Given this background, answers key questions about the nature of the discipline and its workforce may be easier to find, particularly as they serve to clarify and define the direction that education must take to survive and thrive in the future.

References

Abbott, A. (1998). Professionalism and the future of librarianship. *Library Trends* 46(3), 430–442. Retrieved from Academic Search Premier.

ALIA. (2009). *Salaries for Australian librarians and library technicians 2009–2010.* Retrieved from http://alia.org.au/employment/worklevel.guidelines/

ALIA (2010). *Library Technician Education in Australia: State of the Nation Report.* ALIA, Deakin, Australia Capital Territory.

Australian Bureau of Statistics. *Work in selected culture and leisure activities, Australia, April 2007,* (Catalogue. number 6281.0). Canberra, Australia: ABS. Retrieved from http://www.abs.gov.au/AUSSTATS/abs@.nsf/0/D32427E1211847C7CA257 6550013EFCD?opendocument

Australian Committee on Technical and Further Education (1974). *TAFE in Australia: Report on needs in mechanical and further education.* Australian Government Publishing Service, Canberra, Australia.

Australia. Parliament, Senate, Employment Workplace Relations and Education Reference Committee. (2003). *Bridging the Skills Divide.* Canberra, Australia.

Australian Qualifications Framework Advisory Board. (n.d.) *About the Australian qualifications framework.* Retrieved from http://www.aqf.edu.au/aboutaqf.htm# cross

Australian Qualifications Framework Advisory Board (2002). *Australian Qualifications Framework Implementation Handbook.* AQFAB, Carlton, Australia.

Barcan, A. (1980). *A History of Australian Education.* Oxford University Press, Melbourne, Australia.

Barker, R., and Holbrook, A. (1996). Meeting the demand for vocational courses. *Vocational Aspects of Education* 48(3), 214–219.

Bramley, G. (1975). *World Trends in Library Education.* Clive Bingley, London, England.

Brown, W. L. (1970). Training for sub-professional library staff in Victoria. *Australian Library Journal* 19(3), 109–112.

Christine, E. R. (1974). Paraprofessionals: Plague or promise. *Australian Academic and Research Libraries* 5(December), 201–205.

Curtis, D. (2009). *Student Transfer at a Glance.* National Centre for Vocational Education Research, Adelaide, Australia.

Department of Education, Science and Training. (2002). *Striving for quality: Learning teaching and scholarship.* Retrieved from http://www.backingaustraliasfuture. gov.au/publications/striving_for_quality/default.htm

Department of Education, Employment and Workplace Relations (DEEWR). (2008). *Review of Higher Education.* Retrieved from http://www.deewr.gov.au/Higher Education/Review/Documents/PDF/Higher%20Education%20Review_one%20 document_02.pdf

Department of Education, Employment and Workplace Relations (DEEWR). (2009a). *Transforming Australia's higher education system.* Retrieved from http:// www.deewr.gov.au/HigherEducation/Documents/PDF/Additional%20Report% 20-%20Transforming%20Aus%20Higher%20ED_webaw.pdf

Department of Education, Employment and Workplace Relations (DEEWR). (2009b). *Transforming Australia's higher education system: Fact sheet 12.* p.1. Retrieved from http://www.deewr.gov.au/HigherEducation/Documents/PDF/Pages%20from% 20A09-303%20Budget%20Fact%20Sheets-12_webaw.pdf

Flowers, E. (1963). Objectives of training for library service. *Australian Library Journal* 12(1), 3–10.

Gabb, R., and Glaisher, S. (2006). *Models of Cross-sectoral Curricula TAFE and HE.* Victoria University, Footscray, Australia.

Hagger, J. (1969). Principles into practice: Anew course of librarianship at RMIT. *Australian Library Journal* 18(11), 413–416.

Hallam, G. (2008). *Nexus: An investigation into the library and information services workforce final report.* Queensland University of Technology. Brisbane, Australia.

Library Courses Vocational Standing Committee. (1976). Guidelines for the education of library technicians: Report of the national workshop, Melbourne 24–27 May.

McColvin, L. R. (1939). *Library Staffs.* George Allen and Unwin, London, England.

Moodie, G. (2001). Identifying vocational education and training. *AVETRA Conference*, Griffith University. Retrieved from www98.griffith.edu.au/dspace/ bitstream/10072/6624/1/identifying1.pdf

Murray-Smith, S. (1988). *Behind the Mask: Technical Education Yesterday and Today.* Beanland Lecture. FIT 1987. Victoria, Australia.

Murray-Smith, S., and Dare, A. (1987). *The Tech: A Centenary History of the RMIT.* Hyland House, South Yarra, Australia.

Naylor, P. (1991). Who created us? *Library and Information Studies Newsletter* 4(5), 1–2.

Neave, G. (1980). Accountability and control. *European Journal of Education* 15(1), 49–60.

Ostler, L., and Dahlin, T. C. (1995). Library education: Setting or rising sun. *Library Journal* 26(7), 683–685.

Pivec, C. S. (1975). Middle level library education in Victoria. *Australian Library Journal* 24(2), 48–53.

Radford, W. (1977). Educating and training staff. In *Design for Diversity* (H. Bryan and G. Greenwood, eds.), pp. 491–536, University of Queensland Press, St Lucia, Australia.

Radford, W. C. (1968). Education and training in Australia. In: *Anatomy of Australia.* pp. 152–173. Sun Books, Melbourne, Australia.

Raffe, D. (2002, April). Bringing academic education and vocational training closer together future of education. *Work Education and Occupation Conference,* Zurich, Switzerland.

Ramsey, Margery (1963). Solutions in search of a problem. Department of Education, Employment and Workplace Relations (DEEWR), *Australian Library Journal* 12(1), 15–20.

Rood, D. (2006). East beats west: But some make it against the odds. *The Age,* p. 6, November 5.

Rushbrook, P. (1997). Tradition pathways and the renegotiation of TAFE identity in Victoria. *Discourse* 18(1), 1–12.

Smeaton, H. (1983). Library technicians in Australia: past present and future. *Australasian College Libraries* 1(1), 34–37.

Teese, R. (2000). *Academic Success and Social Power.* Melbourne University Press, Carlton, Australia.

Watkins, N. (1976). Middle level education and its implications for library technician courses. *Report of the National Workshop Melbourne Library Courses (Vocational), Standing Committee* (pp. 4–10).

Wheelahan, L. (2001). Are TAFE and higher education different? *Keynote presentation to the Tertiary Teaching and Learning: Dealing with Diversity Conference.* Darwin, Australia: National Teacher Union

Wheelahan, L. (2003). Global trends and local bends: Australian VET developments. *Journal of Adult and Continuing Education* 9(1), 32–50.

White, C. M. (1976). *A Historical Introduction to Library Education: Problems and Progress to 1951.* Scarecrow Press, Metuchen, NJ.

Wilson, A. M., and Hermanson, R. (1998). Educating and training library practitioners: a comparative history with trends and recommendations. *Library Trends* 46(3), 467–504. viewed 03/03/2003, retrieved from Academic Search Premier.

Williamson, C. C. (1971). *The Williamson Reports of 1921 and 1923.* Scarecrow Press, Metuchen, NJ.

Young, W. (1979). The future for the library technician: Education and continuing education. *Alternative Futures,* pp. 444–447, Library Association of Australia, Canberra, Australia.

E-Texts in Research Projects in the Humanities

Suzana Sukovic

School of Philosophical and Historical Inquiry, Faculty of Arts, University of Sydney, Australia

Abstract

This research paper explores the roles of electronic texts in research projects in the humanities and seeks to deepen the understanding of the nature of scholars' engagement with e-texts. The study used qualitative methodology to explore engagement of scholars in literary and historical studies with primary materials in electronic form (i.e., e-texts). The study revealed a range of scholars' interactions with e-texts during the whole research process. It uncovered a particular pattern of information-seeking practices in electronic environments called *netchaining* and the main types of uses and contributions of e-texts to research projects. It was found that e-texts play *support* and *substantive* roles in the research process. A number of influences from electronic environment are identified as challenges and aids in working with e-texts. The study does not have statistical significance. It indicates a need for further research into scholarly practices, training requirements, and new forms of service provision. Study results are relevant for the development of digital collections, information services, educational programs, and other forms of support for the use of technology in research. The results can be also used to inform approaches to text encoding and development of electronic information systems and have implications for organizational and industry policies. The study found a range of scholars' interactions and forms of intellectual engagement with e-texts that were not documented and analyzed by earlier studies. It provides insights into disciplinary variations in the humanities and contributes to the understanding of scholarly change catalyzed by information technology.

I. Introduction

A great emphasis on knowledge and learning in contemporary industrialized societies is associated with a dramatic impact of information and communication technology (ICT) on knowledge acquisition, production, and sharing. Text and ICT, as key entities in information and knowledge cycles, have been brought together in the composition of electronic text.

ADVANCES IN LIBRARIANSHIP, VOL. 33
© 2011 by Emerald Group Publishing Limited
ISSN: 0065-2830
DOI: 10.1108/S0065-2830(2011)0000033009

131

Changes in technologies for presenting and transmitting text are associated with significant cultural transformations. The print revolution is often mentioned in relation to far-reaching changes brought about by computer technologies. This common comparison signifies that the shift in production and transmission of text is a central part of the perceived revolution. Libraries as traditional book repositories are at the center of this transformation. Considering that a library is often described as "humanists laboratory," changes in the way these academics work have important implications for research libraries.

Text is fundamental for scholarship in the humanities, which is based on studying recorded texts and reflecting on their nature. McGann (1998, p. 609), a humanist scholar, wrote, "Textual studies is ground zero of everything we do. We read, we write, we think in a textual condition. Because that is true, the new information and media technologies go to the core of our work." One of the central questions related to effects of ICTs on scholarship in the humanities concerns the effect of electronic text on the way in which scholars think about and work with text. The potential importance of investigating interactions of humanists with e-texts has been recognized by a number of authors. Brockman *et al.* (2001) noted that

> [e]lectronic texts are potentially the most radical element in the construction of the evolving technology environment in the humanities. The explosion of electronic texts promises to alter the way in which scholars conceive of the activity of research in a way paralleled only by similarly major developments in the history of printing. (p. 30)

Although text has a central position in our culture in general and scholarship in the humanities in particular, very few studies to date have focused on the use of e-texts. Those that did usually investigated the use of a particular database or an archive.

In an attempt to uncover a part of the change that involves people, text, and technology, this study into the roles of e-texts focused on academic researchers in literary and historical studies, because they are known for their intense use of textual sources. These scholars have a long tradition of engagement with text in various forms from all periods, and therefore, they are in a position to reflect on recent changes. In modern academia, literary studies include traditional historical, critical, and theoretical research as well as creative writing, all of which provide possible access to changes in creative and analytical approaches to e-text.

This chapter has the following parts:

- *ICT in the humanities*: Background of ICT adoption, and adoption and applications of e-texts in the humanities.
- *Methodology*: The study's design and research methods.

- *Interactions with e-texts*: A range of issues and activities related to working with e-texts, namely:
  - ○ *Defining electronic text* provides a background for defining electronic texts and considers how study participants perceived e-texts.
  - ○ *Interactions with selected e-texts* considers issues of reading and how scholars in the study worked with oral texts, personal digital collections and databases.
  - ○ *Information seeking in electronic environment* looks into seeking behaviors and focuses on netchaining as a particular pattern of information practices which emerged from the study.
  - ○ *Investigation of the research topic* considers how scholars used e-texts to aid their intellectual engagement with their research. Core aspects of e-text functionality are also considered in this section.
  - ○ *E-texts and writing* are about influences of work in electronic environments and interactions with e-texts on writing techniques, styles, and genres.
  - ○ *Experience of working with e-texts* considers participants' thoughts and feelings associated with interactions with e-texts.
- *E-text in the research process*: Interactions with e-texts in research stages, the main types of uses of e-texts, and their contributions to research projects and the two main roles that e-texts play in the research process.
- *Challenges and aids in the electronic environment*: Factors that aid interactions with e-texts or act as obstacles.
- *Implications for academic libraries*: Implications of humanists' engagement with e-texts for services and academic libraries.

II. Information and Communication Technology in the Humanities

Scholars in the humanities have appeared to be on the margins of technological changes for a long time, but a short historical overview in this section outlines significant transformations in scholars' practices in the past three decades.

A. Adoption of ICT

Humanists were initially slow and reluctant adopters of new technologies, and even when they used computers, it was mainly for word processing. Stieg (1981) noted that most historians ignored computers, whereas Stone (1982) observed that "the impression is given at times of humanists as rather inadequate individuals unable to face up to technological change" (p. 300). Humanists' needs for a wide range of materials and finding aids, as well flexible searching across full-text documents, made the first databases of bibliographic records of limited use.

As digitization projects provided a constantly growing number of documents and finding aids online, electronic collections became increasingly useful. Dalton and Charnigo (2004) followed up Stieg's study and found an increased use of electronic catalogs and indexes to identify sources of information. Electronic bibliographic tools and reference works became a preferred format (Palmer and Cragin, 2008; Summerfield et al., 2000). A study of Jewish studies scholars found that while they had positive attitudes adopting technology, they had reservations when a technology or source could not support their needs (Baruchson-Arbib and Bronstein, 2007). Despite limited availability of materials and lack of technologies responsive to humanists' needs, these scholars have made extensive use of electronic sources (Brockman et al., 2001; The British Academy, 2005), usually for "tried, tested, and somewhat traditional research functions" (Greenstein in Brockman, et al., 2001, p. vi).

Technological advancements over the past three decades have made ICT more suitable and acceptable for humanists. Although hard copy books and primary materials remain important, some digital tools and sources have replaced their analog counterparts. At the same time, problems related to access, availability of sources, technical limitations, and scholars' knowledge remain an impediment to the adoption of digital technologies.

B. Applications and Adoption of E-Texts

The provision of text in adequate electronic form is crucial for the qualitatively new employment of technologies in the humanities. The first attempts to apply computer technology to the humanities in the middle of the 20th century, and consequent advancements in digital humanities research, were based on work with text. The appearance of personal computers in the 1980s and widespread use of the Internet in the 1990s were significant developments that brought computers to humanities scholars. Major developments of scholarly text in electronic form was enabled by the development of the World Wide Web, SGML (Standard Generalized Markup Language)—a metalanguage for defining methods of representing texts in electronic form, and TEI (Text Encoding Initiative)—a system for encoding text (Hockey, 2004; Ide and Veronis, 1995). Advancements in digital imaging in the 1990s have also contributed to provision of pictorial resources in conjunction with electronic texts.

Word and concept retrieval across full texts, multiple uses of a text, integration of resources, and flexible and remote access are some of the developments associated with electronic texts, which directly address a variety of researchers information needs.

1. E-Text Applications in Digital Scholarship

Different ways of using ICT in research affect scholarship, but digital scholarship relates to uses that directly influence knowledge production. Digital scholarship in the humanities has become more elaborate in recent years and now refers to several related forms:

a. building a digital collection of information for further study and analysis;
b. creating appropriate tools for collection-building;
c. creating appropriate tools for the analysis and study of collections;
d. using digital collections and analytical tools to generate new knowledge, interpretation, understanding; and
e. creating authoring tools for presenting these new ideas, either in traditional forms or in digital form (American Council of Learned Societies, 2006, p. 10).

This report identified (d) "as the core meaning and ultimate objective of digital scholarship" (p. 10). The main uses of e-texts in the humanities are based on the text retrieval and analysis. The prominent areas of e-text applications are as follows:

1. concordances and text retrieval programs for text-analysis;
2. dictionaries and lexical databases;
3. literary and linguistic analysis;
4. stylometry and attribution studies;
5. electronic editions and archives (points 1–5 based on Hockey, 2000); and
6. digitally born literature and media art.

The last point was added by the author in response to a growing interest and advances in electronic literature and art. The value of electronic editions for textual criticism and a wide multipurpose use has been discussed more often than any other application of electronic texts. Electronic editions and archives can provide large amounts of dispersed materials, different versions of the text, images of originals, and scholarly annotations as well as links to context-building information. The presentation of e-texts includes specialized services such as presentation of text in different languages, an option to reconfigure the same materials for different purposes, and online help and contact details for enquiries. Many advantages of working with e-texts arise from the speed of processing. Hockey (2000) pointed out that work that had taken years and decades in traditional ways could be performed more accurately in a matter of minutes or even seconds.

Although e-texts may have a great potential for scholarship, it appears that they have not been widely accepted. Palmer (2005) said that the effects of interrogation of the full-text corpora were appreciated in literary, linguistic, and cultural fields where these interrogations guided formulation of research questions, interpretation, and textual analysis, but these methods were not widespread. Hockey (2000) suggested that the reluctance of scholars to adopt these methods had been based on a perception that they are alien to the nature of the humanities research.

2. Adoption of E-Text

In the first decades of humanities computing, advancements in e-text development were not readily accepted outside of a rather small group of scholars who worked in this field. Olsen (1993, p. 309) wrote that "the role of electronic text in literary research remains surprisingly limited" and presented an overview of relevant literature as evidence.

A number of editing and digitization projects since the 1990s provided a base of e-texts that made their way into mainstream research. Studies indicated a growing, but uneven adoption in use. In a study by Wiberley and Jones (2000), only two of thirteen participants used primary materials in e-form. Summerfield *et al.* (2000) found that monographs and texts for the humanities were not heavily used, but usage had been growing. Users usually browsed books online, printed them for reading, and searched them to find a quotation or a citation. Scholars in Massey-Burzio's (1999) study did not respond enthusiastically to technological advancements, but their view of full-text databases was very positive.

Searching provides a critically important functionality. Few participants in the study conducted by Brockman *et al.* (2001) used full-text databases but those who did were very satisfied with them, particularly with the products that provided access to primary materials: "The thoroughness with which searching is possible across any of the corpora covered by these databases means that once they have been recognized by a group of researchers in a particular field, their use is obligatory" (p. 16). Davies (1997, p. 387) found that the way "computers can 'crunch' through texts, comparing usage of given words or idioms, has completely altered the questions which humanists can ask." Similarly, scholars in American literature valued searchable texts because they allowed them to make "intellectual connections that were previously impractical, if not impossible" (Brogan and Rentfrow, 2005, p. 21).

The ease of searching allows students to ask questions by interacting with e-texts that were once answered only by reading and experience (Ruhleder, 1995, p. 49). Cherry and Duff (2002) studied the use of *Early Canadiana* in research and teaching and found that the main advantages of it were access to remote and dispersed materials, the convenience of working from one's own office and searchability.

The main obstacles to engagement with e-texts were lack of trust in the scholarly standards of electronic collections, the availability of materials with contextual details, and the lack of direct access to sources. Researchers in the humanities did not think that a critical mass of relevant materials was available (RULOIS, 2002). This study found that scholars were very interested in e-texts of manuscripts and primary documents, but the tradition of physical contact with objects and manuscripts was found to be important. Andersen (1996) noted that historians needed to check original primary sources, even when they were found in a print version.

A study of e-book use (Levine-Clark, 2007) showed that the acceptance of e-books varied among humanistic disciplines. Historians consistently preferred print, while almost a third of participants in languages and literatures had a preference for electronic form.

Many questions and assumptions about nonuse, disciplinary differences, and the way in which e-texts are used have not been clarified. The majority of studies aforementioned asked questions about e-text use as part of a broader investigation of other issues A small number of studies surveyed users of a particular collection of primary materials (Cherry and Duff, 2002; Duff and Cherry, 2000; Flanders, 1998; Noguchi, 2001). Although they provided valuable pointers, the objectives of these studies did not allow deeper investigation into users interactions with e-texts. Interviews conducted by Ruhleder (1995) with users, tool developers, and editors of *Thesaurus Linguae Graecae* elicited interesting results about various aspects of the use of sources, but this study, which was focused on one of the first large electronic projects, is now dated.

III. Methodology

This study of scholars' engagement with e-texts aimed at a broad investigation of participants' interactions with e-texts and their experiences of working with these sources. It focused on scholars in literary and historical studies because they are known for their intense and sophisticated work with textual materials. Projects aiming to develop computer applications in the humanities were excluded from the scope of this study. Primary materials are the main source of information for many scholars in literary and historical studies and for that reason this investigation focused on interactions with primary sources.

The term "electronic text" in this chapter means any textual material in electronic form, used as a primary source such as literary works and historical documents. Digitized archival copies of magazines and newspapers or web sites could be electronic texts when they are used as primary sources.

Electronic texts could be written or spoken (e.g., oral histories), digitized or created electronically, stand-alone documents, or part of electronic databases and editions.

The roles of electronic text in research enquiry in literary and historical studies were explored to deepen understanding of the nature of scholars' engagement with e-texts. Qualitative methodology was used to answer the following research questions:

- How do academic researchers interact with e-texts?
- What do e-texts contribute to their research projects?
- What are some of the challenges and aids influencing the interactions with e-texts?

A. Study Participants

Sixteen historians and literary scholars from two major Australian cities and one participant from the United States, all active academic researchers, took part in the study. The group was not representative in any way but was composed of people with different characteristics. Historians and literary scholars were approximately equally represented as were people of both genders (Table 1).

Participants provided data about 30 projects covering a wide range of time periods, approaches, and disciplinary orientations. Projects in literary studies ranged from Old Icelandic to contemporary Australian literature and from creative writing to theoretical considerations of literature in English. Historians discussed projects in Australian, English, American, and Asian history and included studies of religion, political, and cultural history.

Details about participants and their projects were carefully disguised to protect participants' privacy and ownership of their ideas. Numerical codes were used to label data from the participants. The role of study participants is a topic of numerous discussions in the literature about qualitative methodology, including those specific to the field of library and information studies such as McKechnie *et al.* (2006). Numerical labeling was chosen as an

Table 1
Study Participants

Total number	Gender	Field	Career stage
16	9 female 7 male	9 historical studies 7 literary studies	2 early career 5 mid-career 9 senior

effective and neutral way of labeling data. The numerical labels used are in the form 1/1, 2/1 or 1/2, 2/2, and so forth, meaning "Participant's number/ Data gathering stage." For example, 1/2 means participant 1 in stage 2.

B. Data Gathering

The study had two stages. The first stage included in-depth semi-structured interviews and other forms of data gathering, such as examination of participants published works and e-texts discussed in interviews. Participants were asked to discuss two projects: a finished and a current project in which they had used e-texts at least once. Focus on a particular project enabled better understanding of e-text in the research process and provided a distinct framework for discussions. Protocol for semi-structured interviews in this stage was tested in a pilot study, which consisted of three interviews. Data from the pilot interviews were not used for analysis.

The second stage involved a smaller group drawn from participants in the first stage. They recorded detailed information about one of their current projects by using data-gathering forms and audiotapes on which to record comments. Finally, they discussed details of the research project and their view of electronic texts in the research process in the second interview. A two-stage research design enabled prolonged engagement with the field providing opportunities for insights into the development of research projects.

Table 2
Data-Gathering Summary

Stage of the study	Method	Number of participants
Pilot study	Interview	3
First stage	Interview	16
	Examination of participants' works	15
	Examination of e-texts	If possible
Second stage	Interview	4
	Audio tape with comments	2
	Form	2
	Examination of participants' works	3
	Examination of e-texts	If possible

Overall, the main form of data gathering was 20 interviews with 16 participants who discussed 30 research projects. Table 2 summarizes the data-gathering methods, which were used in the study. Additional details about data-gathering methods can be found in Sukovic (2008).

C. Data Analysis

Data were analyzed throughout the process of data gathering. Audio tapes were fully transcribed, and all data were analyzed by using grounded theory techniques described by Strauss (1987), Strauss and Corbin (1998a, b), and Glaser (1998). The software *Nvivo* was used after an initial coding scheme was developed.

IV. Interactions with E-Texts

Engagement with electronic texts includes a wide range of interactions, from working with written and oral texts, reading, and developing electronic collections to a variety of searching practices and uses during the research enquiry. Understanding the complex nature of electronic text underpins discussion about interactions; therefore, it is necessary to start by defining what is meant by e-text.

A. What is E-text?

Modern meanings of "text" include traditional understanding of text as a linguistic phenomenon as well as a very broad postmodern understanding, which encompasses linguistic and nonlinguistic forms of expression. An understanding of text in this work starts from traditional definitions of text as an essentially linguistic phenomenon. Text is defined as an autonomous linguistic chain, oral or written, that constitutes an empirical unit, fixed by writing or recording (Rastier, 1997; Ricoeur, 1991). Textuality is the "totality of the properties giving cohesion and coherence and that render a text irreducible to just a succession of utterances" (Rastier, 1997, p. 265). This definition, grounded in the experience of working with previous textual technologies is useful, not only because it says what text is but also because it provides a reference point with which to contemplate new meanings associated with electronic texts.

Although e-text can be a plain string of text in a digital form, it is usually presented as hypertext linking different textual objects, media, and formats. Multimedia is an essential part of electronic textuality. Connections between diverse types of information enable combinations of the linguistic, visual, or musical expressions of an idea. Smith (2004) wrote that a "more radical approach to the co-presence of words, sounds and image is ... that of 'semiotic exchange': the negotiation of different media so that each takes on the others characteristics and cultural connotations" ("From analogue to digital: The technowriter"). According to Smith, semiotic exchange is not about just bringing different formats together, but also about the way they are shaped by each other so that text, image, and sound adopt each other's properties. The presence of other media with and around text changes its meaning. Multiplicity becomes part of its semiotic field.

Multimedia and associated transformations of textual meanings provide the basis for changes in values. Kress and Van Leeuwen (2001) noted a distinct preference for mono-modality in Western culture in the past, so that dense text, for example, was used for the most highly valued genres such as literary novels, academic works, and official publications. The prominence of visual qualities of electronic text and new possibilities for the inclusion of other media have shaken the singular authority of text and promoted multimodality.

1. E-Texts as Fluid Objects

Discussions with researchers who participated in the study revealed that multiplicity and semiotic exchange were very much part of their perceptions of e-texts. Blurry boundaries between media and formats are not the reflection of any temporary lack of clarity, but rather of the consistent and prominent characteristic of e-texts.

Images, bibliographic records, and full text are very difficult to distinguish in the fast move from one object to another, "all of which is somehow electronic text" for a researcher (participant 6/2). Different types of materials are meshed in results "thrown up" by search engines. A possible reason for this perception was described by participant 6/2: "I treat the Google search engine as ... perhaps not a database but an entry point into many, many possible databases or many, many configurations of text." Some participants referred to both visual and textual sources when they talked about e-texts used in a project.

Fluidity is an essential characteristic of electronic texts (described in some detail in Sukovic, 2008). When trying to distinguish electronic text from other media and formats, participant 10/1 said that "it becomes like the air you breathe. It's very difficult to talk about because it's everywhere." Ocean metaphors were a prominent part of discussions about e-texts referring to their fluidity and unpredictability of online searches. It is a "vast ocean of information out there and I can draw on that when I feel like it" (participant 9/1), or exploration of a textual database is like "going in fishing, pot luck to see what turns up" (participant 6/1). A researcher would go to the Internet "just to see what it threw out" (participant 1/1).

B. Interactions with Selected E-Texts

Interactions with e-texts are often integrated in the research process in a way that makes it difficult to distinguish clearly between activities such as using and reading e-text. Using e-text involves active searching, interaction, watching, different ways of reading textual and visual signs, downloading and manipulating text, and only occasionally sequential reading as one would read a book.

Scholars are less likely to read books online for a long period of time but use them for browsing and searching (Hillesund, 2010; Liu, 2005; Summerfield et al., 2000). Brown (2001) found that sequential reading, cover to cover, had been used less often than segmental reading: "Readers of digital text search, scan, select, cut, paste and create a 'personal library' of related files that hold their citations and texts" (p. 395).

Researchers in this study reported that they usually bookmarked selected sources and would then read them on screen or print or work with the text in audio form. Interactions with selected e-texts included downloading and organizing copies on researchers' own computers.

1. Reading and Printing

Different types of reading are an essential interaction with e-texts that enables either assessment of the retrieved text for further use or intellectual engagement. Most researchers who read e-texts on a screen did so to "scan read." They mentioned speed-reading a whole book from less than an hour to maximum two hours (e.g., participant 4/1 read a novel in this way). A few participants practiced reading from the screen even when they read in a more focused way and for extended periods of time. Participant 6/1, for example, usually read from the screen while taking notes. He found reading from computer screens quite comfortable compared to reading from microforms.

The majority of participants tended to make printouts for in-depth reading or for speed-reading of longer texts, because they found it tiring to read on the screen. This finding is consistent with the dominant view in the literature. Some researchers preferred to take printouts to read in an armchair instead of at their desks and talked about a different physical settings required for focused reading.

Another reason for printing was that participants found it difficult to assimilate intellectually material in electronic form. This finding supports results of Hillesund's (2010) study. Participant 2/1, for example, felt that she had not read the text properly if she read it on screen. Participant 13/1 needed to make printouts at some point for synthesis because it was easy to keep adding files without any intellectual grasp of the material. It was easy to be "lost in that tunnel that the computer is," scrolling up and down, this researcher said. The printed text was usually marked and annotated.

It was useful to print e-texts while working in physical collections. Participant 7/1 described how she worked in overseas archives. She would conduct a catalog search and save it and then start ordering materials in hard copy. While waiting for hard copies to arrive, she explored their electronic representations or used e-texts to make printouts. Participant 6/1 said that he would save time in archives by finding an electronic copy of a page to print rather than making a trip to another archive or waiting for a librarian to give permission to copy it.

2. Working with Oral E-Texts

Interaction with e-texts in oral form depended on what was permitted by the electronic system. If texts were presented as simple audio files for listening, the researcher would transcribe whole documents or summarize and transcribe sections of it. Participant 10/1 tended to read documents into a tape recorder when he could not make photocopies. He would transcribe the tapes and use electronic copies of the transcriptions as e-texts.

Participant 2/2 used audio files in archives. One particular archive had a database, which provided text transcriptions as well as sound waves for some recordings. There were also keywords marking sections of the audio file, which aided retrieval. Access to sound waves was useful because it enabled more options in interaction with texts and provided for more efficient marking of relevant sections. The interaction was compared with editing of audio recordings.

3. Making and Organizing Electronic Copies

The majority of participants (13 participants) reported downloading or copying the whole or part of e-texts to their personal computers. When they discovered materials in archives, they sent electronic copies to their e-mail address, or archivists made electronic copies for them. These files were stored and named in a way that made sense to the researcher, often in predetermined ways that organized the whole lot of data for a project. The downloaded e-texts were used in conjunction with all other materials in the personal library. Some participants mentioned using written notes or cards to organize access to these files. For participant 13/1, cards were the first step in synthesizing downloaded texts.

The extent and frequency of adding e-texts to a personal digital library varied. Participant 2/1 maintained a very large and elaborate digital library, accessed through the bibliographic software *EndNote*. This researcher downloaded e-texts and other files in various formats. She would normally copy and paste all details into *EndNote*, index the file by keywords devised for personal use, and then type either her own notes or copy excerpts from the text into the record. *EndNote* records had links to file locations on the computer. This participant usually had her laptop computer when working in physical collections, and therefore, she added records and annotations as she worked with materials. The researcher developed a very extensive library that required a great deal of effort to back it up—culling the hard drive and maintaining links from *EndNote* records to file locations. She found that the benefits of easily accessible and well-organized materials were worth the effort.

4. Developing Collections of Own E-Texts

E-texts written or prepared by the researcher provided important materials in some projects. Participants mentioned producing and using e-texts in two ways, which were relevant for this study:

- they produced textual databases or collections for their own use for purposes of a particular project, or
- they published e-texts in one project and then used them as primary materials in another project, which aimed to produce traditional output.

Four participants (6/1, 8/1, 10/1, and 12/1) prepared their own databases to be used as tools in a project. In another four instances (participants 12/1, 13/1, 15/1, and 16/1), they used their own e-texts produced in previous projects. The interactions with e-texts produced by the participants in a previous project did not differ from working with any other e-text.

More interesting from the perspective of interactions with e-text was the first group of projects, in which textual databases or collections were prepared to provide a tool for information retrieval and analysis in the particular projects. These databases and collections were not publicly available. The content and the use of the database varied, depending on a particular topic and the researcher's sense of how she/he wanted to conduct the research. The following two examples outline different projects in which participants developed textual databases for their own use. Unlike e-texts retrieved online, these collections were not normally used for reading and printing but for searching.

EXAMPLE 1: WORKING WITH A COLLECTION OF DIGITIZED DOCUMENTS

Participant 10/1 wrote a biography of a contemporary writer and developed an extensive collection of documents and interviews. The researcher found that the only way to work with the collection was to enter it into the electronic form. The production of a searchable collection was a major digitization project in which the researcher transcribed all interviews and numerous other documents. None of the library holdings that the researcher used were digitized.

The researcher handled all of the primary materials in electronic form by using a word-processing program. He had electronic folders according to the material type (e.g., interviews and letters), and inside each folder, there were files alphabetically arranged under various names. These e-texts were used in conjunction with photocopies of documents arranged by date and then by name.

EXAMPLE 2: WORKING WITH A DATABASE OF LITERARY MOTIFS

A relational database of literary motifs was developed to support research into a national folk literature. Participant 12/1 explained that the purpose was to compile a database of motifs and to compare them with existing analyses or other relevant compilations of folk motifs.

This participant did not normally use keyword searches in electronic editions of works she regularly consulted or in the database of motifs, because she thought that keyword searching of primary materials was "a rather low grade." The researcher felt that she needed to know texts very well and to understand how motifs fit in the whole narrative, so that there was no substitute for reading. The relational database allowed the researcher to explore connections between texts and motifs.

Researchers who developed their own digital collections and databases of primary materials invested significant time and effort in tasks such as digitization, indexing, and database development, with or without assistance. Approaches to these processes depended on requirements of a given project and personal work habits. In most cases, scholars produced highly valuable resources, which remained unknown outside a researcher's circle of colleagues.

C. Information Seeking in Electronic Environments

Information seeking and gathering have always been key parts of the research process. Unsworth (2000) used the term "scholarly primitives" to "refer to some basic functions common to scholarly activity across disciplines, over time, and independent of theoretical orientation" (para 1). Discovering was identified as one of the primitives. With online sources available where scholars work, information seeking becomes an integral part of the investigation and thinking about the research topic.

Users in general, and humanists and social scientists in particular, conduct evolving searches. They start with a query and then move to a variety of sources, constantly adjusting the query by selecting bits of information. Bates (1989) discussed this way of working and called it a berry-picking model, which described online and other information retrieval. The question is which strategies scholars use to pick their "berries" in constantly evolving electronic environments.

Humanists traditionally use a wide variety of materials, and this is unlikely to change. Preference for traditional library catalogs and finding aids also remains, as reported by the Digital Library Federation (2002). At the same time, keyword searching has become a notable online practice (Duff and Cherry, 2000; Wisneski, 2005). A recent study showed that a network was increasingly a research starting point rather than library-specific tools (Schonfeld and Housewright, 2010).

Use of citations in information seeking is a well-documented practice. Ellis called it chaining and defined it as "following chains of citations or other forms of referential connection between material" (1993, p. 483). Palmer and Cragin (2008) identified chaining as one of the best examples of an information work primitive. Tibbo (2003) found that 98 per cent of primary materials were found by following leads in printed sources. Brockman et al. (2001) wrote that chaining helped scholars "maintain a conceptual network of the field into which they envision their own work being placed" (p. 9). Buchanan et al. (2005) thought that the provision for browsing in digital libraries was inadequate, but that chaining was used often and replaced browsing.

Researchers consult colleagues and prefer informal and semiformal channels to finding information (de Tiratel, 2000). Recent studies have indicated that ICT has influenced the strengthening of informal networks and even collaboration. The number of British humanists who rated colleagues, conferences, and research networks as essential information providers was very close to that of scholars in social sciences and sciences (Education for Change, 2002). Scholars in Israel have significantly increased their cooperation with colleagues in other countries because of the Internet (Baruchson-Arbib and Bronstein, 2007).

Study into the roles of e-texts confirmed the importance of established research methods and sources but also uncovered some behaviors emerging from traditional practices. The multiplicity of sources, formats, and textual information that could be quickly brought together form a basis of exploration that allows scholars to see different meanings and aspects of the topic.

1. E-Texts and Searching

Participants described searching for primary sources of information as a constant movement between online and hard-copy sources, indexes, and full-text documents. Searching for information sources included electronic searching, examination of editions that gather materials in different ways, consultations with archivists, searching through card catalogs, and sending advertisements to particular groups to find people who might have relevant information. Reading and travelling to collections and sites of interest was also part of information gathering. An important part in some projects was access to memories or experiences of particular groups of people through interviews, informal conversations, blogs, discussion lists, and bulletin boards.

Searching the Internet was widely used for discovering bodies of material and for finding particular information. Searching by keywords or personal names, a standard practice in historical research, was often used in online searches. Google was often mentioned as a starting point for an Internet search. When the researcher wanted to discover what was available, she/he would type a name or a keyword, aiming for a rather broad but manageable search. Skim reading a large number of recalled items was often the only way to distinguish relevant items from frustratingly long lists of irrelevant ones.

Web surfing starts from a subject gateway or a well-known site on the topic and develops by following links. Researchers in literary studies described a process where they started from a journal of electronic poetry or a writer's web site, then went to other sites where works of interest were published. From there, they followed links to discover new literary works. This includes browsing and searching at different sites.

Database searching is a regular starting point for interactions with e-texts for some researchers. Many researchers had one or two favorite databases, which they used often (e.g., JSTOR, EEBO: English Books Online). Researchers interrogated these databases to discover any relevant e-text, but some researchers usually consulted known works or searched for specific authors and works.

Monitoring can be a part of interactions with a database when it provides information and digitization is in progress (e.g., EEBO). Some researchers found this information useful because they would check periodically to see whether the text had become available. Scholars who studied contemporary literature monitored web sites to find out when new works became available online.

Information embedded in other sources was used to retrieve relevant primary materials. Sometimes researchers discovered primary text in secondary sources either as references or as content embedded in secondary sources such as books or journal articles. Researchers found it most useful when databases provided access to both secondary and primary sources.

A *combination of searching electronic and analog sources* sometimes led to e-texts. Participant 14/1 used e-texts to find leads to analog materials, and therefore, he examined summaries of particular historical documents available from a database as an indication of where he could find required information. Participant 2/2 described the way she worked in an archive of audio recordings kept in analog and digital formats and retrieved them through different systems available in the archive. The researcher would try to think laterally and to understand the reasoning behind the retrieval system, but found it was easier when a professional acted as an intermediary. Some researchers also needed professional help when working on topics with very high recall.

Any system of retrieval and organization adds an intervening layer to the material, and therefore, participants stressed that they needed to know systems of representation, and some participants needed to have direct contact with material as much as possible.

2. Netchaining

The possibility of fast searching across dispersed and diverse sources, the lack of physical boundaries, and technologies for social interactions provide conditions for new information practices. Explorations in this study indicate that some online behaviors and adaptation of old practices for the new

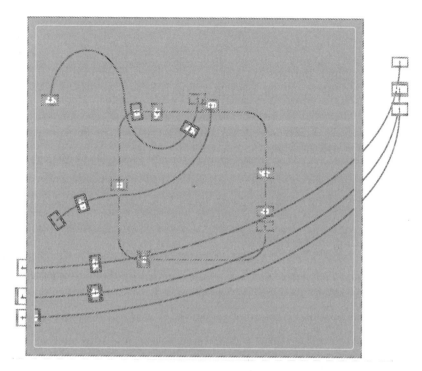

Stefans (2010), http://collection.eliterature.org/1/works/stefans_the__dreamlife_of_
letters/image_19.htm. *Source*: Reproduced with permission, © 2000 by Brian Stefans.

environment are becoming integrated in qualitatively new information-
seeking patterns.

Study participants discussed information-seeking practices, which
combined aspects of networking, searching, chaining, browsing, and web
surfing in a distinct pattern of online information-seeking behavior called
netchaining (Sukovic, 2008). Netchaining is an emerging pattern of
establishing and following information chains, which connect people and a
variety of online sources. For example, the practice of browsing in the
electronic environment may include browsing of distinct digital collections,
as well as web surfing, as a way of looking for relevant information by
searching and following hyperlinks in a range of sources. Chaining is often
combined with searching, browsing, and web surfing. Study participants
described various instances of going to an academic e-text or a site, which
they visited regularly for current awareness. When they found a relevant
source, they would follow the lead to an author's web site of the author or

archive, retrieve another source, and seek further information from an archivist, the author of the work or colleagues on online forums.

Participants explained how an initial search may open paths in different directions in which information seeking, retrieval, and communication play part in the exploration of the topic and, possibly, become part of long-term networking:

> Sometimes … if an article is really fascinating, and there are some writers on [country] who write so well and so interestingly, I would look up their web site, find them, email them, you know, make a note of them for future potential research stream. (participant 1/1)

Participant 16/1 talked about web surfing, searching or browsing journals, and visiting authors' web sites. This researcher would contact authors to make enquiries about technologies, which have been used in the production of a work. When asked whether authors were willing to respond, participant 16/1 answered,

> Yeah, yeah, I think people who make electronic texts are probably more forthcoming about that than, say poets writing on a page.
> *Why?*
> Well, I suppose just because they are, there is the more kind of obvious technology. They know that in the end that you could probably really trace that thing yourself and because I think they're probably more medium interested, they're perhaps more interested in the process, they're interested in the technology and how you do things so that they're perhaps quite interested in passing that on to somebody. (participant 16/1)

Although netchaining does not have to include communication with other people, it is a distinctive characteristic of online interactions. Researchers contacted other people because of one of four main reasons: to find information, to aid with access to a physical collection, to confirm information and for current awareness. These reasons are explained in Sukovic (2008). Table 3 summarizes why participants initiated netchaining activities that involved communication with other people. Reasons and netchaining activities can be combined and so one reason can include several netchaining activities from the same category. In the first category, *To find information*, contacting another person is the first step.

Through netchaining, a researcher identifies immediately relevant information, but also establishes information chains for future use and broadens networks of people. Traditional research environments also enabled the establishment of information chains, but the difference in what was immediately available, as well as communication norms, promoted a different range and type of connection. In online environments, speed, immediacy, coexistence of a wide range of sources, and ease of

Table 3
Reasons for Initiating Netchaining Activities Involving Other People (Sukovic, 2008, p. 277)

Reasons for netchaining	Netchaining activities
To find information	
• If interested in further information about a document	• Contacted a person who may know
• To confirm detail(s) from e-text	• Looked up author's web site
• If information is crucial	• Made a note for future use
• If author's authority could not be discounted	• Contacted the responsible person and asked question(s)
• Interested in technical details of electronic literature	• Connected that person into own network, invited to a conference
• If curious	
To aid access to a physical collection	
• To confirm details about a collection	• Contacted archivist listed on the web site
• To arrange a visit to an archive	
To confirm information	
• When worried about trustworthiness of a document	• Posted a question to a discussion list
	• Contacted the responsible person
For current awareness	
• When coming across new work, wondering what other people do	• Contacted the author
	• Initiated online discussion about the type of work people are doing
	• Contacted people outside the discussion list

Source: Reproduced with permission, © 2008 by The University of Chicago.

communicating with people who share the same interests all contribute to the establishment of connections, which may go in many different directions.

The concept of intertextuality is particularly relevant for considerations of e-texts in general and netchaining in particular. Hypertext, multimedia, and social technologies promote textual connections and polysemy, which are the central ideas of intertextuality. Textual connections appear in what Kristeva (1980) described as three dimensions or coordinates of dialog:

> writing subject, addressee, and exterior texts. The word's status is thus defined *horizontally* (the word in the text belongs to both writing subject and addressee) as well

as *vertically* (the word in the text is oriented toward an anterior or synchronic literary corpus). (p. 66)

In online environments, horizontal connections are promoted by social technologies, which make connections between author and reader explicit and evident in many everyday communication exchanges and acts of collaboration. Vertical connections are emphasized not only by hypertext but also by netchaining practices that promote links formed around a particular information need and task. The range of exterior texts has widened significantly in the process. Easy access to sources is changing the sense of center and periphery and blurring boundaries between authoritative and nonauthoritative knowledge.

As Bolter (2001) pointed out,

> this passing on of the text from writer to reader, who then becomes a writer for other readers, is nothing new; it is the literal meaning of the word 'tradition'. The previous texts were also part of textual connections, but [w]e are now using the computer to simplify the technology of intertextuality so much that we seem to be refashioning the idea of tradition itself. (p. 179)

D. Investigation of the Research Topic

This study found that participants' investigation of their research questions with the aid of e-texts took the following four main forms:

- exploration of patterns and connections by searching and comparing diverse bodies of electronic texts;
- production and interrogation of textual databases to explore research questions;
- exploration as part of academic research to be used in creative writing; and
- investigation of digital literature.

1. Exploration of Patterns and Connections

This is a prominent online practice described by researchers in historical studies. The researchers searched for a variety of materials from different sources to build a profile of the topic. Critically important aspects of the search are search engines, which retrieve information in a systematic way and provide access to a wide variety of genres. Participant 13/1, for example, searched for information about a historical personality known in aboriginal oral history and found that "oral history often gets captured in the blogging culture." He looked at a variety of online sources and found "a whole range of different registers of different genres of text all turning up in the electronic version." I asked the researcher about the place of e-texts among other resources used in the project, and he responded,

> through the project, I became more and more reliant, really, on search engines. Not for the final conclusive material necessarily but to help me see patterns, to search on a particular set of search words or look for a particular piece of evidence or try to trace a character. (participant 13/1)

Simultaneous access to online and personal sources along with inter-actions with computers promote serendipitous discoveries. One of the parti-cipants explained how this process works:

> when you've got your computer going and you've got a couple of different documents open and you're cutting and pasting or you're toggling between two or three documents, ... you're just feeling ideas come out of this idea, idea no. 1 and idea no. 2, when they pop up against each other often completely other idea, idea no. 25 will, sort of, turn up out of that. (participant 6/2)

Some serendipitous discoveries emerge in moving relatively quickly through large amounts of diverse materials when juxtaposition of ideas and information trigger novel combinations.

2. Production and Exploration of Textual Databases

Production and interrogation of textual databases to explore research questions are described by scholars in both literary and historical studies. The aim is a focused in-depth exploration of a limited range of texts. Although it is possible to work in this manner online, all participants who referred to interrogation of textual databases worked offline, either because they worked with a stand-alone database or because it was easier to examine downloaded texts.

The simplest use of textual databases or editions is to check a detail and compare different versions of a text, which was reported by some participants, but this is not seen as a practice that contributes directly to the exploration of research questions. Interaction with a full-text database, however, can change the way exploration unfolds. The previously mentioned database of literary motifs was not used for full-text keyword searching, but the added intellectual value was useful to the researcher because it supported searching, clarifying ideas, and exploration of connections.

In other projects, keyword searching was an essential part of exploring hunches and providing a basis for further analysis. Participant 8/1 developed his own database and found the process of constructing the database an important part of developing research questions. The researcher used this database to explore links between concepts and to prove his hypothesis that a widely held view in his field was not quite correct. It was hardly possible to prove his understanding by using more traditional research methods. The required texts existed only in translation in a print version at the time of his study and word counts would take a long time. The slowness of the process would not allow the exploration of all possibilities; therefore, the researcher decided to develop his own database. When a more extensive readily available database of relevant primary materials appeared later, the scholar started using it to explore initial thoughts about his topics.

Similar to explorations of large amounts of diverse materials, in-depth exploration of a small number of texts allows researchers to investigate connections. Participant 6/2 talked about his interrogation of a particular version of the Bible. He would search for certain phrases, make concordances, and then make comparisons by examining the electronic version of the Book of Common Prayer. Although these texts are available in the library, there is an advantage in exploring electronic versions because they promote understanding of "relationships amongst bodies of knowledge" (participant 6/2).

Use of textual databases depends on their availability and a match between the scholar's needs and what the particular database can provide. Participant 6/1 noted, "It's not straightforward because certain things will not become apparent unless you're asking the right sorts of questions. The program really isn't written with my questions in mind so it will have its limitations" (participant 6/1).

Exploration of research questions aided by interactions with e-texts, whether focused or broad, was valuable because it enabled academics to see connections, deepen their analysis, and test hypotheses. Another significant but less tangible benefit was that e-texts allowed scholars to follow half-formed ideas, to explore them in a fluid movement among search queries, sources, and links. The speed of retrieval enables investigation of hunches: "And you can do that, you can chase that quite quickly whereas I can remember having those kind of hunches 25 years ago ... but to chase those would take literally 36 hours and by that time that hunch is gone, you know, that tip-of-the-tongue feeling is gone" (participant 6/2).

3. Exploration of E-Texts for Creative Writing

Literary scholars talked about two other forms of online exploration: exploration of e-texts to support traditional creative writing and analysis of digital literary works. Exploration of e-texts as support for creative writing for print is led by the scholar's own sense of what can be used creatively. Participant 1/2 talked about her research project at the point when she finished all research in archives and libraries and then searched the Internet to go beyond print and find details that were not available in hard copy. She looked for any source that could shed some light on the experiences of people who lived in the time and space of her writing. The search was broad and open-ended because various pieces of information could be used in novel ways.

Interactions with e-texts contribute to building a background on the topic. In some instances, it may be just to give character a thought rather than to develop a full argument that would be required in academic genres. A variety of historical and personal information on the Internet allows the researcher to develop a sense of what is possible.

4. Investigation of Digital Literature

Investigation of digital literature involves on-going searching to discover new literary works on the Internet. In most instances, works such as electronic poetry cannot be explored offline, especially not outside the electronic environment, and therefore, investigation of digital literary works necessarily happens online. Researchers who studied electronic literature watch the work, inspect the code, and then repeatedly watch the same short section to aid analysis. The main interest in this investigation is in revealing different meanings enabled by the multisensory experience of interaction with electronic literature and understanding the experimental nature of the work.

5. Core Aspects

A number of the described practices can be observed in traditional research environments, but the core aspects that provide the unique functionality of e-texts distinguish interactions with e-texts from working with analog materials. Participants' discussions about the way they had interacted with e-texts uncovered the following three core aspects of e-text functionality:

- electronic searching
- availability of e-texts
- speed

The importance of availability and speed confirms indications from the literature that the content and scope of online materials, convenience, the speed, and savings in scholars' time are critically important for the adoption of ICT.

Electronic Searching. Study participants searched metadata and full-text documents to retrieve specific information or explore a topic. In most cases, they perceived searching by a search engine as more reliable than the same function done by people, because it was more thorough and accurate, although there were situations in which the assistance of a human intermediary such as archivist was desirable or even necessary. Electronic engines provide a unique facility for retrieval of dispersed information. Participants 10/1 and 12/1, for example, emphasized the importance of searching across different types of dictionaries that covered historical language uses, which could not be adequately reproduced in other ways.

The reliability of electronic searching was so important to participant 14/1 that he repeated searching, completed in traditional ways to make sure that he did not miss anything. Although he had big files with photocopied materials that he had explored over the years, he repeated searching when these sources became available in databases of primary materials. Electronic retrieval across bibliographic records and other forms of metadata as well as full-text documents provide results that could be hardly achieved by searching in traditional ways.

Availability. Functionality of electronic searching is based on the availability of e-texts. A wide range of e-texts provides,

- basis for searching, text analysis and manipulation,
- a substitute for materials that are not readily available in hard copy, and
- obscure and unique materials.

Access to electronic copies of materials that are available to a researcher in hard copy is valuable because of electronic searching and the convenience of not being place-bound. Researchers often worked with hard and electronic copies for their unique advantages. In many cases, hard copies were not readily available, and therefore, electronic copies were substituted, which enabled work with the text until a hard copy could be inspected if needed. Researchers were able to identify these materials through bibliographic aids or already knew about their existence.

Obscure and unique sources such as original documents and materials that are not available in print are either difficult to identify or the researcher would not attempt to find them if they were not available online because of difficulties involved in finding and accessing rare materials. E-texts allow the researcher to go "beyond books" (participant 1/1) by providing interaction with obscure digitized documents and materials that have never existed in hard copy. The value of obscure sources was illustrated by participant 11/1, who found an electronic copy of a work that contained more extreme statements than other works by the author under investigation. This title was not included in printed selections of the author's work, but it provided important insights for the participant's study. Study participants also used e-texts to find personal information about people from the past through oral stories contained in blogs and online postings as well as information that could be obtained only in direct communication or online. Unpublished literary works that exist only in electronic form and digital literature are unique sources of information for a literary scholar.

Availability of e-texts influenced the formulation of a research focus and exploration of a topic. The provision of e-texts and gaps in provision form a pattern that can inform exploration. Participant 14/1 found that electronic searching across available materials is valuable because "you can get a few things, and you can trace absences as well as presence, if you like, the presence of a particular research topic."

Access to sources of information is a key aspect in any research enquiry, but the study participants who explored their topics online suggested that availability of e-texts and the way search engines retrieved information might have particular significance in affecting development of the enquiry. Participant 1/2 expressed concerns that Google and the way it retrieved available sources may take the researcher in a certain direction. The same is the case with analog sources, but the impact of the availability of e-texts can be attributed to different ways of interacting with print and electronic texts. Participant 13/1 found that interactions with electronic sources required the researcher to assume a more active role. Rather than relying on the author of the book for guidance, the researcher formed his view through the interaction with available materials:

> The electronic or digital presumes or requires a subjectivity which is more investigative than receptive, if that makes sense, that you're more delving into the thing, *putting together your own thesis in* relation to *the patterned information that's available*, whereas if you're in the presence of a really great book, you tend to allow the author to carry you along. Every now and then you'll pause and try to know your own mind in relation to the way the author is carrying you along. [emphasis added; participant 13/1].

This participant also discussed the usefulness of search engines that retrieve information in a patterned way. The researcher formed a view through a dynamic relation to patterns emerging from electronic searches and in relation to available information, rather than in relation to a path set by the author of a book, who may take the reader in a certain direction. In the electronic environment, the pattern emerging from searches is likely to have a stronger impact.

A variety of materials and representations as well as the breadth of contextual information were aspects that made available e-texts more or less useful. Participant 3/1 thought that the availability of a wide range of e-texts and other materials allowed her to compare different representations and make connections better than ever before, whereas participant 6/1 commented that digitized materials did not provide sufficient contextual information. Participant 14/1 stressed that different interest groups presented e-texts for their own reasons, and therefore, special caution was required in evaluating from which perspective the e-texts were presented. The electronic presentation of materials with contextual details and transparent selection processes makes available materials more acceptable for research purposes.

Speed. Speed of access and retrieval aid quick searching for specific information and the assessment and selection of sources. Fast retrieval of large amounts of information aids pattern recognition. It also aids tasks that would take a long time, such as the production of concordances or comparisons of passages in different translations.

Researchers used e-texts to explore questions that could not be investigated practically in any other way. A quick electronic search across a large amount of materials is enabling new research possibilities: "to be able to search everything that relates to a particular topic over some decades and across a number of newspapers is just fantastic. And it gives a whole added ability to make comparisons and to do better research" (participant 3/1). Exploratory interactions with e-texts—compared with playing jazz, partially because of quick, sudden moves, sometimes in a seemingly random fashion— were dictated by the unfolding of investigation and the researcher's interest. Speed enables following hunches and tip-of-the-tongue feelings that would change or disappear in a longer process.

Hayles (2003, p. 215) wrote about the critical importance of speed for the development of understanding: "When information enters in a short time-frame — a few seconds — it can be stored as a block. When it enters more slowly, much more effort is required to integrate it with existing information." On the other hand, e-text can make intellectual processing more difficult. Study participants printed e-texts when they wanted to gain an intellectual grasp of content. Hard copies are easier to use for careful reading and reflection, which may be partially related to the fast interactive nature of working with e-texts.

E-texts also influence the use of time in other aspects of the research process. More effective organization of the research process, quick retrieval of factual information, and faster construction of a paper were possible because of the possibility of retrieving information, contacting people, and manipulating text quickly and easily. Participants also pointed out that some intellectual aspects of the research process cannot or should not be fast.

E. E-Texts and Writing

Working with digital media and hypertext and writing for academic purposes are two aspects of the research process, which often do not coexist easily. Diverse information paths and multifarious online voices, which are taken into account during the research process, are usually filtered to outline a linear argument with a strong authorial voice. Although digital media provides opportunities for different presentation of research results, it has been rarely used. According to Bolter (2001) writing is a culmination of scholarly research, and the way it is presented is more than a matter of style. "In order to be taken seriously, both scholarly and scientific writing must be nonfiction in a hierarchical-linear form" (p. 105). A promotion of visual elements in e-texts has not been perceived as advantageous in a culture where a serious argument has to be developed in verbal form. Bolter noted that the success of the World Wide Web, based on borrowing from many media, had promoted its wide use, but that it tended "to devalue the Web for many scholars in the humanities, especially those influenced by French theory with its tendency to distrust visual representation . . ." (p. 113). Despite intense debate about the nature of academic work and value of digital outputs in recent times, academic output has essentially remained unchanged.

Study participants discussed their experiences and thoughts about academic writing in relation to the way they conduct research. Some participants said that interactions with e-texts had an impact on their thinking about, and choices of forms and genres, for the presentation of research results. They discussed their need to develop new electronic genres, which was limited by existing academic standards and traditions.

The fact that references to e-texts were largely absent from participants' published work reflects scholars' perception of acceptable academic practice (Sukovic, 2009). E-texts have some influence on scholarly research and writing, but this is often invisible to the reader.

1. Writing Techniques and Styles

E-texts were used by the majority of participants to copy and paste excerpts into their own writing. Some researchers typed notes and quotations because they felt their computer skills were not good enough to manipulate e-texts. Although there was danger in not inserting quotation marks promptly (participant 2/1), participants who used this method found it quicker, easier, and more accurate than retyping quoted passages.

The ease of manipulating text leads to new ways of using e-texts in writing. "Mix and match," "remix," and "montage" were some of the expressions used to describe ways of manipulating texts into novel combinations. Considering that the experience of working with e-texts was compared with playing music, it is hardly surprising that participant 15/1 described what he called "remixing methodology" in the following way: "It's like a DJ who has a stack of records that they mix in a live performance so I do that with my virtual stack of writing." Another participant talked about digital montage, which becomes part of an exploration of ideas and creation. Participant 6/2 explained the meaning of the practice by comparing it with Jamaican music in the 1960s when people were able to hear music from many countries on the radio and became comfortable with different styles: "Many, many Jamaican musicians talked about how, when they're just trying to get their ideas formed, they'll often just move down the dial quickly and get a little grabs of different stuff and in those conjunctions some sort of new set of ideas turns up."

Traditional genres emphasize the division between creative and academic styles, which have different conventions of what and how should be presented. Participant 1/2 talked about using e-texts differently for different kinds of writing—"emotional resonance" is required for creative writing, whereas rational argument is needed in academic writing:

> You're using it for the kind of emotional resonance of it whereas in academic writing you're brought up ... to kind of get rid of all that stuff. I don't know that's always right to do it but academic writing has to be coldly, thoughtfully presented in ways that scour off all of the emotional stuff. Whereas in fiction you want it, you deliberately use it to create a reaction for your reader. (participant 1/2)

In some instances, researchers did not want to maintain the division between intellectual and emotional or fictional and theoretical. Participant 6/2, for example, wanted to write an "emotionally and intellectually moving" scholarly book. The division between different genres started to disappear for some people interested in experimenting with new forms of textuality.

> I saw myself also writing fiction and the fiction becomes theoretical and I saw myself writing artist theory and the artist theory becomes fictional. So all these different kinds of styles and modes of writing were starting to mix into the merge and I decided that I would explore that. (participant 15/1)

The process of change is not contained in boundary areas. The experience of working with multiplicity and moving between ideas and texts in different directions is brought into traditional forms of academic writing. Participant 6/2 commented on his historical book in which he used literary and academic writing styles. He found that "in an indirect way the existence of electronic texts and certainly the existence of the Internet, and digital forms themselves" encouraged "overlaying and mixing and putting into conjunction with each other, things [that] would have a slightly different tone or a different mood or a different voice or a different set of protocols." This way of working "if well managed, can be quite stimulating" (participant 6/2). The researcher thought that living and working in the climate of digital montage, mixing and overlaying just set conditions for thinking, "Uh, I could write this book this way I don't have to write it in one voice necessarily."

2. Genres and Formats

Bringing qualities of electronic media into writing for print happens on different levels and for different reasons. A number of researchers commented that traditional academic formats did not provide the right fit for the presentation of research based on multimedia sources.

Researchers interested in experimenting with new media and styles stressed that similar experimentation existed before, but computer technology provided new means for exploration. However, academics still need to present research results in standard academic formats. It is similar to writing for print about cinema or music. Participant 2/2 commented that if a researcher was working on television or radio history, it would be appropriate to produce an academic output for the same media rather than write for print. Similarly, participant 16/1 explained limitations of writing about multimedia work for print.

Academic writing for electronic media has not significantly changed, but possibilities and interest exist:

> when I'm writing for the Web it has to some degree changed how I do things. It doesn't necessarily make much difference to my actual argument, my argumentative style but it does mean I link in more to other things on the Web or have visual elements or sound examples. So, yes, it does impact on it quite a bit. It doesn't necessarily make me put the argument together in a totally different way, but it could do ... I can see there are a lot of possibilities which I would be interested in exploring. (participant 16/1)

The same participant showed examples of introducing visual nonlinear elements in her academic book by using the page layout to emphasize different aspects of the subject and to bring different examples without following a strictly linear structure. The researcher attributed the decision to present material in this way to the influence of the visual appearance of text on the computer screen.

Print media and online publications mimicking print provide limited options for the development of new academic styles. It is easier to bring sound and visual aspects into conference and live presentations. Participant 2/2, for example, said that it was easy to include audio files in conference presentations. Manipulation of text from audio files supported her thinking about issues and demonstration of the points for the audience: "I think when I presented papers, people have been really pleased to hear the audio. That just wouldn't be possible without the digital side of things" (participant 2/2).

A number of participants talked about presenting research results in different formats. They started with an aim to write books or journal articles, but realized that they would not be able to present part of their research in that way and thus decided to add a piece in digital format. Participant 7/1 planned to develop a web site to make a series of images and oral texts available. Another reason for thinking of alternatives was to find a better way of analyzing connections and presenting results. Participant 3/1 wanted to link materials in different formats into a multimedia work, which would allow her to explore connections and later present them to the audience. Participant 6/2 talked about the decision to prepare a book and add a multimedia presentation to do justice to different aspects of the research findings. The part of the research that could be presented as a full argument was written as a book because the author was able to acknowledge all different facets and perspectives, but also to develop a conclusive argument. The researcher described the reasons for adding a multimedia work:

> So, there, I look at the material and I say, "Well, this is extremely moving and important material, it's extremely narrative but it's inconclusive, you'll never put a kind of an 'Amen' to all of this, it will always be stimulating possible narratives. Therefore, in order to attend to or bear witness to that quality of the material I need to make something which is organized and authored and persuasive but endless and inconclusive." And explicitly inclusive, so that leads me to think, "Oh, that needs to be a computationally driven and delivered thing of some kind." (participant 6/2)

For other researchers, the decision on how to present their work is driven by the reality of job demands to produce books and journal articles:

> I have to produce written material ... that's refereed journal articles and book, monograph books, that's what will get another job ... Then if I had extra time or extra funding or something, it would be extra to make an audio thing. (participant 2/2)

Although the research output has been changing, it is still dictated by existing publishing conventions. Participant 16/1 commented that she was rather conservative in the way she wrote journal articles because she often did not know in advance whether it was going to be published in an electronic or print journal.

F. Experience of Working with E-Texts

Study participants talked about the nature of their experiences and thoughts and feelings associated with interactions with e-texts. They compared interactions with e-texts and other media and provided accounts of positive and negative thoughts and feelings, which shed some light on what interactions with e-texts meant to them. They often described their interactions with e-texts in relation to other media and art forms.

1. E-Text and the Print

Study participants, whose education and work experiences developed within the print culture, defined e-texts in relation to print and traditional libraries. The meaning of the "word" and "text" was strongly associated with the print in some statements made by the study participants. The "written word" is associated with the traditional library and the book in the comment that "if you've come through that kind of arts, literature study you kind of . . . there is a little tag that still pulls you back to the old library and the book and the written word" (participant 1/1). Participant 4/1 talked about possibilities offered by electronic editions and said that "you can do it in a text as well, to include facsimiles and so on . . . ." In this comment "a text" refers to print editions.

The book is used as a reference point that defines e-texts but does not necessarily indicate a preference for one or another. Saying that "my non-electronic books arrived" (1) participant 7/1 turned the common expression "electronic books" around by calling hard copies "nonelectronic books," and participant 8/1 said that "a database is just essentially a shelf of books on one particular thing" describing e-texts in terms of books.

The nature of working with e-text is explained by comparing interactions with e-texts and books. One of the researchers acknowledged the difference in interactions with the two media without stating a preference: "it's seamless in as much as I move from one to the other without anxiety but I'm also very aware that the conditions of encounter are quite different" (participant 13/1).

While electronic media provide an increasing number of options to incorporate technology in the research process, physical aspects of the interaction with print are an important part of the experience, so some participants thought that print was likely to be used regardless of the e-text development. Although some participants, like participant 5/1, doubted that electronic scholarship will ever completely replace work in physical collections, others appreciated the physical aspects of the book and would not like it to disappear, regardless of its practical use in research. Participant 9/1, for example, said, "I never, ever, ever want to see the book go, I love books, they're beautiful objects" (participant 9/1).

2. Nontextual Experience in Interactions with E-Texts

Understanding of the e-text included a variety of media and formats, and the experience of the exploration with e-texts was sometimes distinctly "nontextual." Engagement with electronic texts connected verbal with intuitive and sensory ways of knowing. Some participants talked about similarities between working with electronic texts and playing music, particularly about the resemblance to jazz improvisation emphasizing exploratory nature of interactions with e-texts and the existence of a range of skills that enable creative investigation. Participant 13/1 talked about quick jazz-like explorations in which the scholar "jumps" to possible relationships elsewhere, then comes back to the main theme and its variations. Participant 15/1 also used a comparison with jazz improvisations to answer a question about the creative process of producing an academic text based on e-mail messages:

> it's like asking a jazz musician, how did you come up with that improvised solo in the middle of that last set ... In this case, the instrument is, the artist is the instrument, which is playing with whatever source material is available at any given time. In this case that would be a cluster of e-mails. (participant 15/1)

Interactions with e-texts promote use of other senses and exploration of ideas that are only partially formulated on a verbal level. Following "tip-of-the-tongue" feelings is an example of how the search may start with a vague verbal definition, which often becomes better defined in interactions with e-texts. In some instances, interactions with e-texts support sensory rather than verbal ways of knowing. The experience of interaction and the process of knowing are perceived as intuitive and multisensory, as described below in relation to the exploration of half-formed ideas:

> And multisensory and also temporarily, like, emerging and losing in time, emerging and disappearing in time. That's the other thing I think, that's what the [database] is trying to explore in a way, this feeling that ... that tip-of-the-tongue sensation in a way that 'Uh! Just for a moment I knew something and then it went away.' (participant 6/2)

The intuitive or nondiscursive type of knowledge has different qualities, it supports "an intense momentary way of knowing" (participant 6/2), but it can be systematically developed, similarly to the knowledge acquired by dancers and musicians.

Another participant was focused on different systems of meaning in different media that come together in electronic textuality. In the following passage, participant 16/1 talked about poetry, but this comment can be applied to other participants' experiences of interacting with e-texts in other genres:

> So it's, to some degree it's bringing together different systems of meaning. It's bringing together music as a system and writing as a system and it's saying that kind of logical sense isn't everything, that there's the sound to the words and to the way we immerse ourselves in text. (participant 16/1)

The task of a literary scholar who analyzes electronic literature moved beyond textual analysis and now includes analysis of aspects of different media and technical aspects of electronic literature such as coding. The way writers work with text for the electronic presentation includes strong visual aspects: "You think of it in a spatial way and you think of writing in a spatial way so to some degree you're almost writing, *you're writing a kind of picture*" [emphasis added; participant 16/1). The participant pointed out that concrete and visual poetry, for example, experimented with visual elements before, but the Internet "brought it to the fore a lot ... And also, of course ... it's kinetic and that you think about what can happen when a word moves from one point of the screen to another point in the screen" (participant 16/1).

3. Researchers' Responses to E-Texts

A range of thoughts and feelings accompanied interactions with e-texts. Some participants found work with e-texts to be predominantly a positive experience, which enabled them to do more than before. Work with e-texts and the participation in electronic networks of people contributed to a sense of identity for participant 15/1. Participant 3/1 felt empowered by new possibilities commenting that "I find it enormously empowering, for both access to secondary analysis and for access to those texts and images which have been digitised. I know there's a lot out there that hasn't been and it won't be and I know there's a lot of political decisions about what does get digitised, but there is with libraries and hard copies as well ... And I have access to far more than I ever did before."

Participant 5/1 relocated from a place where she had regular access to research materials, but e-texts provided a convenient way of working and made her feel more confident about continuing research away from original primary materials. An additional benefit is that "it probably allows me to look at more sources in a shorter amount of time because it's very easy to do that" (participant 5/1). The researcher commented that e-texts made her feel closer to the sources of her research.

Researchers' perception of the adequacy of their skills was an important factor in how they viewed using e-texts. Some expressed confidence in their skills saying "I am an old surfer of the Web" (participant 8/1), and participant 9/1 stated, "I think I'm quite good at that sort of thing," talking about selecting e-texts from a large number of hits. Participant 12/1 had concerns about the quality of e-texts and said, "That's the sort of thing I say to my students. But ... I think I can usually determine for myself whether the source is reliable."

A number of researchers, however, were uncertain about the adequacy of their skills and practices, making them confused and insecure: "I think it is just more the way the process and the protocols ... that are kind of being more confusing to me than anything else" (participant 1/1). Participant 14/1 was not sure how to present web addresses neatly and commented in a light-hearted manner: "But this reflects, of course, my ignorance, no doubt." A number of other participants were not sure what they were supposed to know or do either. One was not sure whether he should have taken more interest in electronic editions, whereas another thought that she probably was not good at doing a particular task. Most participants were not sure what the standards were and what their colleagues were doing. Some opinions were accompanied with statements indicating the lack of certainty about what the acceptable answers may be. Participant 1/1, for example, when asked what she did not like about e-texts, answered, "Portability—and I know it sounds ridiculous ... " meaning that e-texts could not be physically moved around easily.

Interactions with e-texts sometimes caused feelings of being out of control in situations that ranged from the handling of particular tasks to defining the research project. Participant 7/1 had a sense that an overwhelming amount of available materials was a threat because it became difficult to contain the project within certain boundaries:

> Yeah, I guess another sense that, you know when you can search and see that so many things are available that there's a bit of that sense of being overwhelmed ... Once upon a time, you were just allowed to be interested in a modest, small thing ... following the whole passion of academia where you could just be contained. And there's something about the proliferation of electronic texts that makes that impossible.
>
> *How does it affect you?*
>
> I think that ... I just can't ... almost like they're a threat. That somehow or other all that stuff will get you or will slip into your little project or something. (participant 7/1)

The same researcher also feared that "if it's electronic, it can be wiped. Entirely" (participant 7/1). It is indicative that some other participants mentioned fear: participant 14/1 in relation to handling references to e-texts and participant 6/1 in relation to e-texts themselves. Other participants commented on being impatient or frustrated by interactions because something did not happen as expected or as quickly as expected.

Considering the sense of insecurity and the lack of control, it is hardly surprising that some participants felt more comfortable with books. While talking about the usefulness of e-texts, some researchers stressed their love of books. Participant 2/2 talked about a more intimate relationship the researcher establishes with a physical object found in traditional ways:

> You know, you actually have a relationship to it by finding it. And maybe using index or something, but you actually went, made the step to find the object whereas in an electronic version it's all the same. The file, the .mp3 file, has within it the metatext, which tells you where it is, just magically comes up. (participant 2/2)

At times, there was a sense of contradiction between different responses. Participant 7/1 explained how she was immersed in the electronic world while feeling it was threatening her ability to determine the development and boundaries of her own project:

> once I start thinking about it and articulating it, everything I do is an electronic text. Each e-mail I send, each effort to build bridges around my project is done electronically, like 'don't send me that', that's sent by an e-mail. [...] So I'm completely in an electronic world. But, there is ... a sense of, I guess ... I become anxious about not being able to tell the difference any longer between what I want to know and what I should know. Or what they or the force of all that electronic production thinks I should know.

Despite confusion, insecurity, frustration, and the difficulty of pinpointing different aspects of interactions, most participants expressed openness to using e-texts in part due to the attitude of openness to the research enquiry. When asked about a certain use of e-texts, participant 4/1 responded, "Well, it's quite possible I might at some future stage, yes, because with this research you never quite know where it might take you." Another researcher commented, "I think that I am really committed to research, and I am quite happy to research in all sorts of ways." Researchers also demonstrated their openness to e-texts by investing considerable time and effort in preparing their own databases and digital collections to aid their research, by deciding to develop electronic works to be able to present some aspects of their findings. The vibrant tone in participants' descriptions of interactions with e-texts provided vocal evidence of their engagement with e-texts and open-ended research enquiries.

V. E-Texts in the Research Process

Considerations of interactions with e-texts along the continuum of the research process provide a view of the roles that e-texts play from the inception to the close of a project. This approach also provides opportunities to tease out differences between some similar behaviors depending on the goals in a particular research phase. Analysis of types of uses, contributions, and roles that e-texts play in projects provide insights into multifarious ways in which e-texts enhance research processes.

A. Research Process in the Humanities

Academic research is information-intense work in which information-seeking and use are integrated into all research stages. Research processes in different disciplines in the humanities are likely to have the same general patterns considering similarities between process models across time. For example, Uva's model of the research process in history, developed in 1977, was suitable as a basis for some revisions made by Gilmore and Case (1992). Chu (1999) developed a research-phase model in the work of literary critics based on a study of scholars from a wide range of fields. Chu's comparison of this model with Stone's (1982) model in the work of humanists and Uva's (1977) model of research projects in history identified comparable parts of project development. Brown (2002) found significant similarities between Chu's model and research processes of music scholars, attributing differences between the two models to the nature of the work of literary and music scholars.

Byström and Hansen (2005) considered the dynamic nature of the information-seeking process and found that "the ISP model is, in certain work settings, suitable as both a work task model and a model for the information seeking task" (p. 1055). In the case of the academic research process as an information-intensive task with information- seeking, use, and knowledge production as its integral parts, the ISP model is suitable as a work task model and an information-seeking model.

Most models of information-seeking and research processes show development in sequentially ordered phases, but Case (1991) found that stages do not present the reality of historians' research process, nor that various stages "can go on concurrently, both within and across individual projects" (p. 79). Palmer and Neumann (2002) wrote about "long, unpredictable" paths of inquiry in the humanities, which "often overlap from project to project." This practice "creates a relatively unique path of information seeking for each project" (p. 99). Some of the models presented in the literature described or directly included the dynamic nature of processes in the models. Foster (2004) compared information behavioral patterns of interdisciplinary scholars with "an artist's palette, in which activities remain available throughout the course of information-seeking" (p. 228). Brown (2002) also stressed that the process is "iterative, not sequential or linear in nature" (p. 90) and represented the process as a free movement between the stages.

The dynamic nature of the research process in the humanities underpins traditional and electronic research practices, often described as random and serendipitous because of their unpredictable patterns.

B. Research Process in the Study

Development of research projects considered in this study follows Chu's (1999) model of research phases in the work of literary critics, as in the following: Idea Stage; Preparation Stage; Elaboration Stage; Analysis & Writing Stage; Dissemination Stage; and Further Writing & Dissemination Stage.

A comparison between the use of primary sources in Chu's model and the use of e-texts in this study showed that Chu's model was applicable to descriptions of both literary and historical projects carried out by participants. The data strongly supported views from the literature that the research enquiry is a dynamic rather than a sequential process.

Chu's observation that the idea stage can be based on previous research was confirmed in this study. The initial idea can start in unexpected ways in situations outside the context of a specific research project. For example, participant 7/1 saw an intriguing poster during a holiday trip, then kept the poster at home, collected pictures, and read around the topic of the poster for 10 years before she formally started the project when she received a research grant. In short, researchers often did not know where initial ideas would lead while they collected information, but significant ideas were often formed long before formal engagement in a research project. Researchers said that they would follow a lead wherever it took them and that they would do whatever was needed to be done. While observing limitations in time and resources, they generally approached research as an open-ended process.

In the preparation stage, the emphasis is on intensive collecting of material that may have relevance to a topic. Some researchers started to prepare their own textual databases for further interrogation at this stage and used e-texts to familiarize themselves with holdings of physical collections and organize trips to these collections.

The elaboration stage is mostly a mental process, but e-texts were used to aid the formulation of the research focus. Some researchers worked on formulating an approach to interrogation of textual databases while they were making decisions on how to investigate the topic. This involved some experimentation with searching textual databases.

Variety of Investigation becomes important during the analysis and writing stage. Although researchers knew the focus of their projects, they actively looked for a wide range of evidence, including alternative and contradictory sources. During the writing stage, some researchers looked for information that would be incorporated in novel ways and they worked in creative ways with e-texts This was particularly the case in creative writing projects, but the process of assembling a piece of academic writing was often described as exploratory. Some participants decided toward the end of the project that they needed to present their findings in different forms such as electronic outputs as well as traditional academic papers to present different aspects of their work. Conclusions arising from collected information remained unsettled until the last stages of the project.

Some changes were made to the last two stages of Chu's model after analyzing the study data. For the purposes of this study, Chu's stage 4, analysis and writing, was renamed as analysis and presentation of results, because participants discussed presentation of research results in different formats, such as journal articles and books as well multimedia works and exhibitions.

The last two stages of Chu's model, the dissemination stage (5) and further writing and dissemination stage (6), were contracted into one, called *dissemination and further presentation of results*. A large part of the data from this study related to active projects, which had not reached the final stages. Data about finished projects suggested that different phases of dissemination were not significant for purposes of this study. Therefore, the research stages used to present findings in this study are as follows:

1. Idea stage
2. Preparation stage
3. Elaboration stage
4. Analysis and presentation of results stage
5. Dissemination and further presentation of results stage

Projects by the researchers in this study generally went through the outlined stages, but some could have been completed earlier as part of another project. Research phases could not be completely omitted, but they could be repeated at any time and in any order. Tasks undertaken in different projects could be combined to complement each other so that stages from different projects could be connected. Participant 12/1, for example, talked about a project based on years of research in the same subject area. The researcher said that she wanted to write a book in which she could put insights from previous projects into a bigger picture. The work on the book was complemented by another parallel project on a textual database. She explained the connection between the book, her previous projects, and a current complementary project in acknowledgments in her book. Participants 15/1 and 16/1 talked about academic and creative work in different projects that used results of one project to approach them from a different perspective in another project. Strong links between different projects were described by a number of other participants as well. Although linear representation of the research process does not show its dynamic nature, it was used to make the representations of uses and roles of e-texts clearer.

C. E-Texts in Research Stages

Comparison of the use of e-texts with the use of information and primary sources in Chu's model revealed that some aspects of use of e-texts were present, which were not in Chu's study. Table 4 outlines characteristics of stages and the use of primary source in Chu's model and the use of e-texts in research projects in the study.

1. In the idea stage, Chu noted the use of information to define or develop one's ideas, but did not include the use of primary sources (Chu, 1999). Chu found minimal use of information at this stage. Study of e-texts in projects in the humanities indicated that interactions with e-texts, particularly searching, have a role in supporting the development of ideas. Scholars searched e-texts to see what was available, to get trends and explore ideas while thinking about the topic. According to study participants, e-texts used or produced for previous projects also influenced their thinking about a new project.

2. In the preparation stage, some additional aspects of the phase described by Chu were noted in relation to the e-text use:
   - using online collections to plan further research,
   - additional support in working with hard copies and in archives, and
   - preparation of own e-collections.
   Text analysis is used for the initial exploration that would provide a basis for further work.

3. The elaboration stage included considerations of the ways to interrogate textual databases to explore questions.

4. In the analysis and presentation of results stage, Chu found "extensive use of information with slight to moderate amounts of information searching" (p. 261). Analysis in the study showed that
   - more intense use of e-texts, including different types of searching, happened in this and the preparation stage,
   - researchers' analysis was sometimes based on interrogating textual databases,
   - e-texts had a stronger and more direct role in writing than identified in Chu's model, and

Table 4
Chu's Model of Research Phases and E-Texts

Chu's model (Chu, 1999, pp. 259–260)	Use of information	Use of e-texts in this study
1. Characteristics of idea stage Generation of idea Initiation of project Initial formulation of idea Decision on literary texts for study Discussion of idea(s) *Minimal use of information*	**Use of information** Define or develop one's idea(s) Identify which literary text(s) to use	Search e-texts • To support thinking about ideas, 'follow hunches' • To get trends; see what is available • To formulate project Netchaining to gather and clarify information To develop ideas over a long period of time
2. Characteristics of preparation stage Searching for primary and secondary materials or resources Using/reading primary and secondary sources Taking notes from primary and secondary sources Trying out idea(s) Application for funding *The highest use of information*	**Use of primary sources** To relate the materials to other known information To look for support for argument of the study, for example, quotations, answers, images, themes To look for something specific in the text(s) because of the literary critical approach one uses To read from a different perspective in the second reading To familiarize oneself with the text in the first reading To understand the time period when text(s) were published To understand the time period covered by work To learn more about specific literary critical approaches To help in formulating questions	To gather material Text analysis • To locate information and work with hard copies • To explore ideas Explore broadly • To follow hunches, possible relationships, compare contexts • To find clues and pointers • To clarify meanings of unknown words/names/events Work with traditional sources and e-texts • To complement work in archives, supplement what is not available in hard copy • To plan further research • To prepare own digital library or database

3. Characteristics of elaboration stage

Thinking of focus for each section of the work

Mapping/sketching idea(s) for work, creation of an outline

Organization of notes to represent structure of work or create shape of argument

Discussion of idea(s)

Application for funding

Mainly a mental process

Use of information

To determine what will be central and what will be peripheral to the study

To focus more precisely on the exact area of interest

Parallel with the preparation stage or break during the preparation
- To get intellectual grasp

Selection of material to think about support for own argument
- To decide how to explore research questions by text analysis

4. Characteristics of analysis and writing stage (Chu)

Drafting the work

Revision of the work

Obtaining help with work

Searching for more information

Re-reading text(s), notes and other materials

Preliminary exploration of dissemination channels

Extensive use of information with slight to moderate information searching

Use of information

Re-reading text(s), notes and other materials

To verify a citation

To see if there are "connections" which may have been missed

To refamiliarize oneself with the information because time has elapsed between the last reading of materials and start of writing

To obtain more support for argument of work, for example, quotations, answers, images, themes

Searching for more information

To know about something that is still unclear

To obtain more support for argument of work, for example, quotations, answers, images, themes

To see if there are any new developments

Collect additional information, go back to material and notes from previous projects, go back to known e-texts, participate in online discussions about new issues
- To find evidence for argument
- To make connections and explore patterns
- To be used creatively
- To add factual details, additional point of view
- To fill in gaps, write explanatory notes, inform someone working on a section of a project

Work with personal digital library and printouts:
- e-poetry—look over and over again; codes
- occurrences of certain words
- interrogate texts to explore research question
- analyze text from printout

To analyze

To explore patterns

To check different translations (combination of textual database and analog materials)

To aid document and information retrieval

Table 4. (*Continued*)

Chu's model (Chu, 1999, pp. 259–260)		Use of e-texts in this study
		To check details, copy quotes and bibliographic details
		Monitor digitization projects and certain web sites
		Introduce various aspects of e-texts in writing, remix e-texts to combine creative and analytic processes; to enhance understanding
		Order pictures and confirm publication rights; check newspapers and images at book production stage
5. Characteristics of dissemination and rewriting stage (Chu's 5 and 6 combined)	**Use of information**	**Use of e-texts**
Exploration of dissemination channels	To refine the argument of the study	• Pirate online dissemination to provide alternative dissemination
Publication or presentation of work	To improve the content of the study	• To find additional material
Application for funding	Reading and Re-reading text(s), notes and other materials	• To add primary material (testimonials and blogs)
Exploration of dissemination channels	To find more support for argument of work, for example, quotations, answers, images, themes	
Searching for more information	To see if there are "connections" which you may have missed	
Reading and/or re-reading text(s), notes and other materials	To verify a citation	
Re-writing of work	To refamiliarize oneself with the information	
Publication or presentation of reworked document	To help in modifying argument	
	Searching for more information	
	To see if there are any new developments	
	To follow up on leads which have not yet been checked	
	To search for critical work to incorporate	

Source: Information from the source used with permission, © 1999 by Elsevier.

- e-texts aided preparation of manuscripts for publication (e.g., reproduction of images and confirmation of publication rights).
5. During the dissemination and further presentation of results stage, online delivery of published works may provide an alternative dissemination channel.

This study indicated that e-texts aid technical aspects of conducting a research project and have a more direct role in intellectual aspects of the research process, such as formulation of research questions, refining a research approach, analyzing texts, and presenting research results.

D. Uses of E-Texts

The following four types of uses were found in the research projects:

1. *Supplementing* a document, when e-texts were used to supplement or replace primary material in hard copy.
2. *Locating*, when e-texts were used to locate relevant information and documents.
3. *Exploring*, when e-texts were used to investigate ideas and evidence contained in a range of documents. Researchers accessed as many documents as possible and brought these documents together to reveal patterns and common threads.
4. *Analyzing text*, when researchers worked with one single text or a thematic textual database to investigate connections between ideas and linguistic expressions. Analysis may involve stylistic analysis or tackling various linguistic expressions to reveal ideas. Focus is on revealing connections and meanings in the text.

1. Supplementing

E-texts were used to supplement or substitute for hard copies. Researchers who used e-texts as a supplement, said,

> I used electronic texts a reasonable amount, actually, a reasonable amount, to supplement the books that I was using. (participant 6/1, 1)
> it was still a supplement to my own original research in the archives. (participant 5/1, 5)

Participants who used e-texts in this way searched text for a particular passage, browsed the content, read it online, and printed it. E-texts provided content and it was used in a similar way to hard copies. In this use, evaluation of e-texts was often based on the comparison with hard copies. Participant 11/1 described using an electronic copy of a book as a substitute for hard copy, which was not available to the researcher. As the e-text appeared to be a reliable reproduction in a pdf file from a library, trustworthiness was not an issue.

E-texts were used to supplement work in physical collections and archival materials when the researcher was elsewhere. Certain web sites were visited regularly to monitor the appearance of new texts, which would supplement or substitute for hard copies. In 4 of 30 projects, e-texts were used only to supplement hard copies. These were three historical and one literary project described by three participants. Two participants said that they normally used e-texts in this manner.

2. Locating

Use of e-texts by researchers for locating relevant information and documents aided the research process. Participants searched a variety of sources to find relevant documents and information. Locating use involved searching, netchaining in a form of an online version of traditional chaining, evaluation and selection, reading on- and off-screen, downloading of retrieved e-texts or preparation of researchers' own e-texts, investigating the topic to support traditional creative writing, and copying and pasting of text in writing. Researchers also used e-texts to locate factual detail, to compare details of different versions of a text, and to find evidence for their argument.

Locating provided a convenient way of searching for and accessing information. Sometimes e-texts provided texts that were not available from other sources, but the use did not change the intellectual engagement with the topic in comparison with working with hard copies. Participant 10/1 used e-texts extensively to locate particular information and textual passages and described the advantage of this type of use of e-texts: "it is much easier to both store, and search and access materials in electronic form than it was in a handwritten form. But the key techniques are very much the same" (participant 10/1).

The difference between searching in *locating and supplementing* is that for supplementing, researchers went to a specific source, where they expected to find a particular passage or document. Locating involved searching across a variety of sources to find relevant documents and information in them, which might not have been known in advance. In six projects in literary studies, e-texts were used for locating information and documents. Supplementing uses occurred as well.

3. Exploring

E-texts were used by researchers for exploring during investigation of research topics. Exploration of patterns and connections, which was described earlier in relation to the investigation of a topic, is found in this category of projects. A broad range of available sources and search engines enabled different approaches to explore research interests. This type of use can involve all practices described in the section "Interactions with E-texts", including the full range of netchaining activities, not just the electronic form of traditional chaining, which was the case in the locating use. Exploring was used to follow half-formed ideas in interactions with e-text, along with retrieval of large amounts of materials from different sources to investigate connections and patterns of information. This type of use also promoted the introduction of different voices and perspectives.

In supplementing and locating, retrieved documents and information helped the research process and provided needed texts. Participants' descriptions of the process suggested that thinking happened "outside the screen." In exploring, investigation and thinking happen through searching and interaction with e-texts. Researchers who used e-texts for exploring described how they interacted with e-texts:

> So there's a movement backwards and forwards between a whole range of sources, not a substitute (participant 3/1)
> through the project I became more and more reliant, really, on search engines. Not for the final conclusive material necessarily but to help me see patterns. (participant 13/1)

E-texts were used to explore ideas and evidence and to establish patterns and connections in 12 historical projects. Locating is a necessary part of the exploring type of use and supplementing appeared in these projects as well.

4. Analyzing Text

Text analysis is a study of textual material, including e-texts, aided by a digital representation and encoding. Although various tools for text analysis can be used to find words, patterns, generate statistics or create visualization, study participants reported the use of a search engine only.

Investigation of the topic included the production and interrogation of textual databases as well as exploration of electronically born literature. Some participants talked about text analysis as an ongoing activity. For example, the analysis of e-poetry has been a regular activity for a literary critic (e.g., participant 16/1), interrogation of a textual database happened whenever a researcher had a question on mind (e.g., participant 8/1) and a database created for an earlier project was regularly used to support thinking (e.g., participant 13/1). Interrogation of a textual database enabled finding evidence to confirm a hypothesis. An example of working with the database of literary motifs described to illustrate the development of personal databases belongs to this category of use. This type of use also involved text

Locating. Participant 10/1 has had a large collection of primary materials in electronic and analogue forms. He used transcribed interviews and other e-texts to locate information and find pointers to retrieve documents in analogue form (for details about the collection, see *Developing collections of own e-texts*).

Exploring. Participant 3/1 developed a collection of transcribed interviews, downloaded e-texts and other materials. Her main interest is in exploring connections between a wide range of materials. The researcher worked with transcribed interviews to reveal ideas. She also used her digital collection to locate information.

Analysing text. Participant 8/1 used a textual database to aid the exploration of ideas. He looked for linguistic expressions in the texts and analysed their distribution to provide evidence for a hypothesis. He also used the database to aid information retrieval in materials in analogue form.

Figure 1 Different uses of researchers' own digital collections.

manipulation in creating a new work. Analyzing text assists intellectual engagement with a research topic.

E-texts were used for analyzing text in eight projects: three in historical and five in literary studies. Some participants created databases for their own use to support text analysis. All other types of uses were reported by participants who discussed this use.

Textual databases developed by researchers were often used for analyzing text, but these databases could support other uses as well. Figure 1 shows examples of different uses of digital collections and databases developed by researchers. The supplementing use does not appear in the comparison, because researchers who used e-texts only for supplementing did not talk about developing their own digital collections.

5. Complexity of E-Text Uses

Levels of e-text use grow in complexity. Supplementing is the basic use type of use. In a small number of projects, e-texts were used only to supplement hard copies. In some projects in which e-texts were used for locating, supplementing was described as well. In projects that used e-texts for exploring and analyzing text, all four types of uses were reported as well.

Four types of uses make contributions to the projects by assisting in (1) finding particular documents and information (level one: supplementing and locating) and (2) finding patterns and connections (level two: exploring and analyzing text). Finding particular documents and information means that a researcher used e-texts for some input needed for research, but intellectual

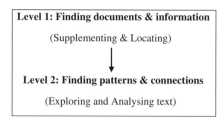

Figure 2 Two levels of e-text's uses.

engagement with the topic is not changed by the unique functionality of e-texts. Finding patterns and connections, on the contrary, relates to uses that directly contribute to the understanding of the topic. The unique characteristics of e-texts enable intellectual engagement with the topic that is not possible or is too difficult to be practical by using hard copies. Level two uses included level one uses as well. Figure 2 represents the growing complexity of e-texts uses, which does not relate in any way to the complexity of projects.

Table 5 summarizes how different aspects of use contribute at different stages of the research process. Research phases used in the table are a modification of Chu's model. The table was developed by overlaying two levels of use with research phases. Uses are divided within the stage to outline the growing complexity of interactions. For example, e-texts may be searched to find relevant material in level one uses. On level two, they can be also searched to find trends and explore ideas. Some contributions appear in level 2 uses only. Ongoing activities are added to research phases because they may inform all projects conducted by a researcher.

6. Disciplinary Differences

The uses of e-texts indicated possible differences between literary and historical studies. Although it is possible that they appeared accidentally, disciplinary differences are likely. The differences could relate to different research approaches and to limitations of existing e-texts and tools for the two different fields. E-texts were used primarily for exploring in historical projects and for locating in literary projects. The study did not explore reasons for the differences, but it is possible that they are based on different ways of working with primary materials in literary and historical studies. Literary scholars usually need to find particular texts and then analyze them in depth. Historians are often interested in everything related to the topic, so they can find, they can find connections, gaps, and disagreements between different sources.

Table 5
Uses of E-Texts in Projects

	Uses of e-texts: Level 1	And	Uses of e-texts: Level 2
1. Idea stage	Search e-texts to see what is available	+	Search to get trends, explore ideas Use of e-texts from previous work
2. Preparation	Search e-texts to gather relevant material	+	Netchaining; selecting e-texts authored by the researcher to gather relevant material
	E-texts used to complement work in archive; prepare and work with own e-collections	+	Use of online collections to prepare visits to physical collections; use pointers in data from textual analysis to work with hard copies Explore research topics
3. Elaboration	Choosing search strategies for more focused search to retrieve documents and information	+	Choosing search strategies for analysis Elaboration while analyzing pilot interviews and searching Locating information that will support own argument
4. Analysis & presentation of results	Checking and clarifying details Monitoring appearance of e-texts Filling in gaps and background		
	Working with own digital collection to retrieve documents & passages	+	Working with own digital collection: all possible searches to support analytical processes
	Analysis: e-texts read, checked to refresh memory	+	Analysis: combination of information gathering, analysis and writing; word occurrences to confirm hypothesis; analyzing patterns in searches; analyzing e-poetry

Table 5. (*Continued*)

	Uses of e-texts: Level 1	And	Uses of e-texts: Level 2
	Writing: copying passages; ordering materials	+	Writing: bringing different voices into writing; elements of electronic textuality in traditional writing; remix methodology
5. Dissemination & further presentation of results			Adding primary data from testimonials and blogs
Ongoing activities	Monitoring for current awareness Checking details	+	Ongoing netchaining

It is possible that a literary historian or a literary scholar working on a theoretical project may want a wider variety of materials in which she/he would follow patterns in a similar way to how historians conduct their research. There are two possible reasons why the literary scholars in the study did not use e-texts for exploring. Firstly, there is a limited range of literary texts available online. Some literary scholars in the study (e.g., participants 1/1 and 11/1), who worked on projects with a significant theoretical component and required a range of texts, stressed that materials which they needed were either not available because there was not a great deal of interest in them or because copyright arrangements made digitization impractical. Secondly, the existing texts have limited value for literary scholars if they cannot be brought together for searching and if special software tools are not available for analysis. Analyzing text requires focused work with texts. It is indicative that the study participants in both disciplines conducted text analysis offline unless they worked with electronic literature.

Keyword searching may have a different value in literary and historical studies. The use exploring involves keyword searching across a wide range of texts, which may be less useful in studying literature than history. For example, participant 1/1 talked about "searching beyond the obvious" and inability to retrieve relevant information hidden in relationships between literary characters and their characteristics. Participant 12/1 developed her own database of literary motifs to support exploration of relationships that could not be revealed by simple keyword searching.

There is a limited provision for textual analysis of large bodies of online materials. Large online databases with special analytical tools such as *Perseus Digital Library* provide valuable resources and tools, but they are available only in a small number of fields. More sophisticated ways of exploring a wide variety of texts would be useful in historical studies, but it seems that historians are currently in a better position to use e-texts for exploration than are scholars in literary studies. The use of specialized textual databases for analyzing text in both disciplines points toward the need for further investigation.

7. Uses and Accompanying Thoughts and Feelings

Uses of e-texts have been considered in relation to comments about a particular use, in the context of a whole research project and in relation to the categories with data about participants' attitudes and affective responses. The analysis showed that participants' comments about some thoughts and feelings featured in relation to different types of uses.

An attitude of openness to different research approaches and positive feelings associated with the use of e-texts were reported in relation to all types of uses. Participants who used e-texts mostly for supplementing and locating perceived traditional research methods and analog materials as the most important in their research. Although many participants mentioned their love of books, some researchers who used e-texts as a supplement to hard copies also said that they were more comfortable with materials in analog form. Some of the participants who used e-texts for locating discussed their belonging to the "old school," which promoted values of the traditional library and book.

Participants who used e-texts for exploring felt overwhelmed with the amount of irrelevant material while appreciating the richness of available e-texts. Feelings about the inadequacy of the researcher's own skills were mentioned by participants in all types of uses except analyzing text. People who used e-texts mainly for analysis were more likely to express impatience and frustration when something did not work as expected in relation to any interaction with e-text.

Table 6 summarizes types of thoughts and feelings that were mentioned in relation to four types of uses.

Study participants who discussed only level 1 uses expressed either their preference for traditional research or talked about the advantages of traditional research, although they found e-texts useful and often enjoyable. The researchers who reported level 2 type of uses talked about the limitations of traditional research, advantages of electronic research, and emergence of new academic styles, genres, and disciplines, although they expressed

Table 6
Uses, Thoughts, and Feelings

	Supplementing	Locating	Exploring	Analyzing text
Traditional research and hard copies preferred	✔	✔		
Comments about limitations of traditional and advantages of electronic research			✔	✔
Comments about participants' relation to the emergence of new disciplines and styles			✔	✔
Open to all sorts of research	✔	✔	✔	✔
Positive feelings related to e-texts	✔	✔	✔	✔
Negative feelings related to dealing with amount of information and feeling out of control			✔	
Inadequacy of one's own knowledge & skills	✔	✔	✔	
Impatience				✔
Expectations and interpretations of availability			✔	

negative thoughts about e-texts and electronic scholarship as well. These differences associated with the two levels of use may indicate that level 2 uses were associated with more prominent electronic forms of research, with a stronger integration of e-texts in different activities, and a greater likelihood of thinking about electronic research as a distinct form of scholarship.

Participants who reported using e-texts for exploring also commented on the availability of e-texts and feelings of being overwhelmed with the amount of information, possibly because of frequent interactions with large bodies of text. Researchers who talked about analyzing text felt impatient at times, but it was the only use that was not associated with feelings of inadequacy. Possible explanations are that only confident researchers undertake this sort of work or that any feeling of inadequacy disappears in this type of interaction. Intense work on a smaller range of text allows researchers to have a sense of control and engagement, which may inspire feelings of confidence.

E. Contributions of E-Texts to the Research Projects

Contributions of e-texts in the projects are realized through scholars' interactions with and uses of texts. Four main contributions of e-texts emerged from the study. First, *Support in finding documents and information.* Computer search capabilities combined with the provision of full-text documents assist information discovery. E-texts provide support in information retrieval and discovery of primary materials. They lead to other sources, help in working with analog sources, supplement hard copies, and contribute to the current awareness. This is the most fundamental contribution. All participants who discussed interactions relating to the following three contributions used e-texts for retrieval of documents and information. Not only do information discovery and retrieval provide a basis for all other contributions, but the nature of scholars' interaction with e-texts during the retrieval underpins other contributions to a large extent (e.g., contribution 3). Second, *Aid in managing the research process.* Access to e-texts allows scholars to plan visits to remote collections; aids the publication process and provides sources for some research activities such as ordering digital images, confirming publication rights, and exchanging files with collaborators and publishers. Third, *Aid in investigation of the topic.* The multiplicity of sources, formats, and textual information that could be quickly brought together is a basis of exploration that allows scholars to see different meanings and aspects of the topic. This helps scholars to identify trends, recognize issues, explore hunches, and work on formulating and confirming hypotheses by text analysis. A range of unique online sometimes provides support for arguments or evidence for a point of view that is difficult, if not impossible, to identify in other ways. Fourth, *Contribution to writing and presenting research results.* E-texts allow copying and pasting of passages, which improves the speed and accuracy in writing. Traditional academic writing was affected by electronic textuality, which influenced a range of changes from subtle alterations in presenting an argument to generating more radical combinations of academic and creative writing styles. These new styles of writing tend to blur traditional distinctions between emotional and rational, and creative and academic styles. Interactions with e-texts also encourage considerations of alternative modes for presenting research findings that do not fit traditional academic genres. Producing e-texts becomes an option for presenting research results that cannot be presented in other ways.

F. Roles of E-Texts in Projects

The four types of contributions of e-texts have two roles in research projects, depending on how they support the development of the project. They are as follows:

- aid in providing basis for research (support roles) or
- aid in exploring the topic and presenting research findings (substantive roles).

1. Support Roles

E-texts provide the basis for research, or play support roles, when they make the research process quicker, easier, and more accurate. The first two contributions, support in finding information and aid in managing research process, have support roles. The fourth, contribution to writing and presenting research results, has a support role when e-texts help in improving speed and accuracy. Table 7 provides some examples of comments about support roles.

Table 7
Comments about Support roles

"To reproduce that [electronic search for information in e-texts] on paper version will take years of searching and you'll still probably miss most so there are certain kinds of searches which you can do electronically and only electronically" (participant 10/1)

"It hasn't influenced my interpretation. It hasn't influenced my methodology or interpretation I think at all. What it has influenced is the level of accuracy" (participant 14/1)

"If I wanted to be absolutely sure when I have the page proofs in front of me, I'll just zap into the Internet and check a date or a spelling or a title or something like that" (participant 1/1)

About an electronic edition used to check the textual details: "I don't think that the fact that the standard edition was available in electronic form made me work in any different way from what I would've done had I used it only in print form because in the form I have it, it's not interactive" (participant 12/1)

Table 8
Comments about Substantive Roles

"Now, we couldn't have even begun to do those searches with the limited amount of
    time and resources, if we were doing them in hard copy. And we wouldn't actually
    have imagined making those sorts of links because it wouldn't be simple to do so
    we wouldn't have even bothered." (participant 3/1)
"One of the things that electronic text does allow is pursuing the sort of question
    that just'd be so uneconomic to ask, going in fishing, pot luck, to see what turns
    up." (participant 6/1)
"But even in those days, it allowed you to ask questions you wouldn't bother asking
    otherwise because it would take too long to find out and you wouldn't know
    whether the answer was significant." (participant 6/1)

---

2. Substantive roles

E-texts aid in exploring the topic and presenting research findings, or play
substantive roles, when they take part in shaping the scholar's thinking
process. The third contribution, aid in investigation of the topic, has a
substantive content-oriented role. In contribution to writing and presenting
research results, e-texts play a substantive role when they influence the
writing style and presentation of research results. Table 8 provides some
participants' comments about substantive roles.

3. Roles in Research Phases

E-texts play a role in each phase of the research process. Three contributions
(support in finding documents and information, aid in managing the research
process, and aid in investigation of the topic) are present in all phases, whereas
the fourth, contribution to writing and presenting research results, is apparent
during the phase "analysis and presentation of research results." In the idea
stage, e-texts in support role aid information retrieval, whereas e-texts in
substantive roles enable identification of trends and following half-formed
ideas and hunches. During preparation, e-texts substitute for unavailable hard
copies, enable information-gathering, and assist in organizing trips when they
play support roles. In substantive roles, they aid exploration of relationships
and support decision-making about research.

    E-texts do not play a support role during elaboration but interactions
with e-texts have a substantive role when they contribute to the formulation
of research focus through preliminary text analysis. The phase of analysis and
presentation of results is supported by interactions with e-texts for
supplementing and information retrieval, for example, when e-texts play

support roles. E-texts in substantive roles aid understanding of the topic and influence writing at this stage. In dissemination and further presentation of results, e-texts play support roles by providing additional information.

Table 9 outlines support and substantive roles in the research process.

None of the study participants, even those who initially thought that their interactions with e-texts were very limited, used e-texts in one way only. An assessment of the roles of e-texts, which does not take into account a variety of these seemingly simple engagements, is likely to miss their cumulative effect.

The unique qualities that e-texts brought to a number of research projects can be illustrated by the participants' use of their own textual databases and collections and by their choices for the presentation of research results. Half of the study participants (eight) developed e-texts, and four of them put a great deal of time and effort to developing textual sources designed to support the investigation of a particular topic. Some of these databases and collections played support, some played substantive roles, but they provided a unique functionality for the researchers when they decided to put the time and effort required into the development of these sources, usually for personal use only. Palmer (2005, p. 1146) saw digital resources created by researchers as "indicators of how scholars wish to engage information technology in their research". As this study indicated, thematic textual collections may provide a significant form of engagement with e-texts.

Production of e-texts and multimedia for the presentation of research results is another area in which researchers showed that e-texts brought some unique qualities to their projects. It seemed that the interactions with e-texts brought a new dimension to research or emphasized the awareness that some aspects of research could be appropriately explored and documented only by electronic media. Although in some cases the awareness of new research possibilities may be attributed to the general discussions in the scholar's field, many of the study participants clearly stated that e-text use was not discussed in their area of research. Scholars' initiatives in using e-texts often related more to their own sense of what was needed in their research rather than to any other influence.

VI. Challenges and Aids in the Electronic Environment

Humanities researchers use a wide range of materials from all periods, and therefore, availability and accessibility of materials are significant issues in the provision of adequate online environments for them. Content and scope of online materials, speed, savings in scholars' time, and convenience are

Table 9
Roles in Research Phases

Stage	Support roles	Substantive roles
Idea stage	(1) IR (broad)	(3) Aids initial exploration to formulate project—identifying trends, following hunches and half-formed ideas; insights for reflection
Preparation	(1) Substitute for unavailable hard copies; supplement archival material	(3) Aids exploration of relationships, presences and absences, issues, comparison
	(1) IR (detailed; collecting scattered texts in own database)	(3) Supports decision-making during preparation of own textual database
	(1) Lead to information and aid work with hard copies (after interrogating database to explore ideas)	(3) Helps in formulating or disregarding hypothesis
	(2) Aid in assessing physical collections and organizing trips	
Elaboration		(3) Aids in formulating focus (selection, preliminary analysis)
Analysis and presentation of results	(1) Supplement/substitute for hard copies (checking details, refreshing memory)	(3) Provides material for thinking about ideas (after locating)
	(1) Provision of current information through monitoring	(3) Supports exploration of ideas and connections during analysis; analysis of e-poetry; confirmation of hypothesis; analysis of patterns in results of searches (text-analysis)
	(1) IR—checking details, finding additional information, alternative point of view; search own database	(3) and (4) Aids the combined process of information gathering, analysis and writing

Table 9. (*Continued*)

Stage	Support roles	Substantive roles
	(2) Support ordering materials, confirming copyright; provision of sources (4) Copying quotes and bibliographic details	(4) Influence on writing—remix methodology; introduction of different voices; nonlinear elements (4) E-text used to present results
Dissemination and further presentation of results	(1) IR—additional information, primary data	
Any stage	(1) IR—current awareness	(3) Provision of insights for reflection
	(1) Provision of primary data (testimonials, online forums)	

LEGEND. Contribution (1): Support in finding documents and information; Contribution (2): Aid in managing the research process; Contribution (3): Aid in investigation of the topic; Contribution (4): Contribution to writing and presenting research results; IR: information retrieval.

critical issues for adoption (Andersen, 1996; Gardiner *et al.*, 2006; Palmer, 2005; Wiberley and Jones, 2000), while limited access and availability of materials are obstacles (The British Academy, 2005). Problems related to equipment or software include poor search engines, slow response time, difficulty in navigation, and frequent format or interface changes (Dalton and Charnigo, 2004). The scholars' own lack of knowledge and training have also been recognized as obstacles (Dalton and Charnigo, 2004; Ellis and Oldman, 2005). Interactions with e-texts are enhanced if there is a range of available materials that are easily accessible and presented in a way that supports researchers' technological skill levels. However, each of these aspects is complex and imposes a number of challenges as well.

A. Search for Information in E-Texts

As knowledge and information are contextual, what constitutes useful information depends on a particular person in a given situation. Considering that researchers in the humanities tend to work with a wide variety of materials to form their own interpretation, it is hardly surprising that the study participants found different aspects of e-texts informative. Information can be contained in anything—from personal experiences to "seemingly banal things, like a box of toffees called Captain Cook Toffees" (participant 7/1). Everything a researcher reads and sees forms the background that becomes a source of information. Participant 1/2 said,

> In the past, if I'm researching a novel at home, I have a filing cabinet full of folders with things I cut out of the newspaper, with photos of people that I think my characters might look like, with addresses and maps and all sorts of things that I used to create a kind of portfolio background material. So I would use the Internet in a very similar way to that.

Researchers' interest in a particular aspect of a topic and their interpretation of a pattern also shape their searches. The search for relevant information may be for particular aspects of texts that cannot be identified easily. Participant 1/1 talked about the difficulties of finding key texts that could not be discovered through bibliographic records or plot summaries. For example, a researcher mentioned discovering a key literary text with a narrative part that enhanced a particular aspect of the research topic. Participant 7/1 searched an online newspaper archive and discovered a picture with accompanying text which became a key source in the project, not because of the meaning in the original context, but because the source provided context for the researcher's interpretation. As participant 1/1 called it,

> if the book was called *Sue Smith's dilemma* and there was nothing in the blurb that suggested her father was, for example, a [war] veteran and this was critical to the text, then it would fall through the web, so what we would need to do once we get this initial bibliography done, really go out and *search beyond the obvious*. [emphasis added; participant 1/1].

Researchers often searched this way. Even a simple search for factual information may quickly move "beyond the obvious" when the researcher becomes interested in interpretation and different contexts in which factual information appears. Flexible searching across full-text documents supports the search for information, but various boundaries of disciplines and ownership impose limitations to searching.

Although the disciplinary lines have been often reinforced, the line between data, information, and creative work may be difficult to establish and maintain. Participant 15/1 talked about poetic metadata and described creative work based on available sources as a way of creating metadata:

> Well ... you have the data and then you remix it and shape it in your own stylised signature effects, which you bring to the Net. And by doing that you're, being self-aware of the way you are doing it, you're creating some kind of metadata experience. (participant 15/1)

When the creative work is based on mixing and reshaping sources, it becomes more evident that the creative use of data says something about data, and therefore, the researcher called the creative interpretation poetic metadata.

B. Availability

In considering aids to the use of e-texts, the central question is what e-texts are available and how they are made available. Participant 12/1 saw the availability of scholarly sources through the university network as the central issue when she discussed barriers to the use of e-texts. Participant 10/1 mentioned web site on which the Biblical text was available in several languages, with commentaries and oral recordings. The researcher pointed out that this single web site replaced a whole theological library. The availability of relevant sources can compensate for limitations encountered during their use. Participant 11/1 spoke about the lack of flexibility in interacting with a particular text he used and the physical discomfort of reading from the screen. However, the fact that the text was available compensated for its limitations.

Participants appreciated the availability of different editions of the same text (participant 12/1) and original documents rather than specific editions (participant 7/1). Researchers preferred to have page images to examine details of originals as well as searchable transcriptions. Participant 3/1, talking about an online newspaper archive, said that its limitation was lack of the whole context of page with the layout, advertisements, and other details, but he still thought searching across the database was valuable. Transcripts and images have their advantages, but for manuscripts, both transcription and high quality images are required.

It was preferable to have more than one way of seeing text (e.g., images and transcripts and different editions), although it was doubtful that e-texts can ever provide the variety that may be needed in research. Participant 6/1 said that at times he needed a particular copy of a book or manuscript because he was interested in the owner or particular annotations. Although the researchers needed a very detailed representation of texts, even abstracts and summaries were helpful in making a decision about ordering material.

Availability of a wide range of texts meant that there were lots of materials that were not perceived as valuable in any way. However, the variety was appreciated because it provided unique material, which was used to access different accounts of a story, view different perspectives, and gather accounts of events or phenomena. Participants also commented on the value of interacting with obscure documents and their surprise that these sources were available.

Although researchers appreciated available materials and, at times, found them overwhelming, they often commented that the sources were related to a rather limited range of interests and national cultures. Participant 1/1 noted that material related to an ethnic community in America was available and was not for the community in Australia. As the study was about Australia, the American material was marginally relevant. Participant 3/1 found that indigenous peoples' history was not well represented because there was not enough funding to digitize relevant sources and participant 2/1 stressed that material she used was not available because it was not of national significance. The participants also discussed the politics of representing knowledge on the Internet. Participant 14/1 commented that the wealth of information on the Internet was restricted to some nations, but there was a "poverty of knowledge about many areas of the globe":

> I think that the use of the Internet is very much conditioned by certain kind of politics which is politics of access to knowledge and the politics of the provision of knowledge. [...] If I want to look up anything about American history, I can find it out very easily on the Net. And I think that encourages more knowledge about America. But ... if I want to go back and I want to find out how the colony of Liberia was established and how Sierra Leone developed and freed slaves, etc., I'm much better off going back to books.

C. Accessibility

Easy access to available materials from any location is another appreciated aspect of interactions with e-texts. As participant 3/1 said, "to have access to those at home, any time of the day or night, is just magic." Participant 9/1 commented,

> What promotes use of electronic texts are convenience and speed. I very rarely go to the library these days, which I think is quite funny because when I was an undergraduate and postgraduate, I almost lived there. But now you can do everything from here (i.e. office).

Online access was particularly valuable in viewing remote collections. Participant 4/1 talked about the importance of online access to Australian materials, which are rarely reprinted because of the small audience. Distance made it difficult for researchers to access these materials within the country, not to mention researchers overseas who work on Australian topics.

Free access to sources was seen as advantage, but was not expected. However, some researchers commented on frustrating and unnecessary limitations to access. Participant 7/1 found it particularly frustrating that, while searching for a full-text copy of a document on a library network, various databases offered the same bibliographic details rather than the full text, without an initial indication of what was not available, and therefore, the searcher felt like going around in circles. Participant 2/1 found that the request for payment in some archives was limiting access unfairly, especially when they with were public documents, funded by "public money."

D. Information Overload

The wealth of information promotes the use of e-texts, but it is also an obstacle to an effective use. The opinion that "one of the problems now with doing research, you know, the idea of being really on top of the field, it's not even in theory possible because there is so much material splurting out from every possible place" (participant 9/1). This view was shared by some researchers. Participant 14/1 noted that an expectation that researchers would know about constantly increasing literature in a field might impede creativity, especially for younger researchers.

One approach to dealing with information overload may be some form of specialized assistance. Participant 7/1 worked on an interdisciplinary project that could be informed by a vast range of materials and the researcher needed help from highly specialized reference librarians who could recommend relevant material. The participant also needed a more efficient way of making selections from retrieved sources: "And it's, again, if there could be an intervening index between these things somehow. So it's an irony, isn't it? On one hand we look to the Net for this incredible extension and, on the other level, all I want is an index" (participant 7/1). Although the researcher had to deal with the 'flood of stuff from everywhere', this academic distrusted the stability of the Internet and feared that currently available materials could easily disappear.

E. Presentation of E-Texts

The way in which e-texts are presented within a collection or a database influences interactions by enabling some and limiting other possibilities of discovery and use. Organization of e-texts is one of the first features researchers note when entering an online collection. They appreciated a collection where relevant texts can be found easily, without "masses of searching" (participant 1/1). Flexible ways of searching were deemed useful. Participant 14/1 liked an ability to search by keywords, subject, and author, and participant 3/1 greatly appreciated that images were searchable by caption, owner, date, and location. The ability to save searches online for an extended period of time was also mentioned as a useful feature. Full-text searching of a large document or a corpus was again useful, as well as provision for searching and moving through audio files.

Browsing and an ability to see a broader context of the text was valuable if it could be combined with different access points. Texts grouped in very broad categories, however, were not helpful in retrieval. Provision of browsing periodicals by year allowed the same type of browsing as in a library, but because it did not provide the unique functionality enabled by the electronic medium, a replication of physical arrangements was not perceived to be effective. Participant 6/1 talked about the value of browsing in physical collections and gave an example in which discovery was enabled by browsing a bound volume of different pamphlets, which contextualizes materials. This researcher compared electronic browsing with online shopping because in neither case was it possible to find things in an enjoyable way:

> It's a bit like shopping. If I know exactly what I want to buy, I can buy it on the computer. If I want to go out shopping, I like to browse around the shops and that's part of the enjoyment because I never know what I'm going to see that I like. So, I regard libraries in much the same sort of way. (participant 6/1)

Online collections present their materials in many different ways and some participants found that the general lack of standards was problematic. In some instances, the same collection would use several retrieval systems, analog and electronic, that are not integrated. Participant 2/2 discussed research in an archive that had multiple retrieval systems, where the researcher needed lateral thinking and a background knowledge in digital editing, in addition to archivists' assistance, to use the collection effectively.

Use of technical and library jargon did not mean much to the researchers. Terms that seem simple and straightforward to information professionals had ambiguous meanings to the participants. Terms like "Boolean search" and "keyword search" do not come naturally even to scholars who are immersed in the electronic environment. Names of file formats and some technical terms such as "high resolution" were difficult to remember or confusing.

F. Technical Aspects

Reliable institutional networks and a good computer were identified as important to facilitate access to resources. Participants mostly felt that their networks and equipment were adequate. Participant 8/1 talked about some bottlenecks in resources, such as a limited number of printers, but he was satisfied overall because the technological infrastructure had improved considerably over the years. Some participants noted problems caused by different platforms used by departments in the same institution. Some problems were also created by the mixed use of Macs and PCs within the same university. In addition, technical help was not readily available for specific problems such as display of images and layout of printed pages.

Constant changes in hardware and software and differences between platforms made the researchers feel unsure whether they were aware of what was possible. Some participants referred to the inability to search pdf files and one participant (2/1) was frustrated about working with e-texts in oral form and said, "What would come up in your player ... is just the title of the file. I don't think it has anything else indexed into it. There could, potentially, but my player doesn't show me that." The researcher could not be sure whether the index was available, it was just that her player did not show it.

Design limitations affected the way scholars worked. Screen design made the work tiring after a while. Most researchers found it difficult to read from the screen, and participant 14/1, who was able to read from the screen, did not like that he had to keep clicking the mouse to be able to move from one page to the next. Participant 3/1 talked about difficulties in working with images of maps and moving around the document:

> to get the handwriting, involves zooming in to quite a close level. And then trying to work out where you are on the map. It's a very cumbersome process ... But digitisation and the scale is fantastic. But the process, then, of moving around a very large-scale document, which is what these maps are, in hard copy, it's quite cumbersome and awkward and difficult.

Certain formats seemed to be suited for particular tasks. The participants liked pdf because it looked like print and it was easy to print and cite, but formats such as html were preferred for searching.

Some participants talked about desirable software and services. Participant 16/1 could explore electronic poetry only by watching sections repeatedly because it was very difficult to isolate and analyze parts of the work. A good voice-recognition program was needed, but researchers who talked about that were not able to find adequate software. A technical solution for organizing large personal digital libraries was sorely missed by participant 2/1, and others would have benefited from having an easier way of managing their own e-texts. For example, participant 13/1 had to be careful to establish a system for each project, whereas participant 10/1 maintained very big files to achieve clear organization. Finally, there was a need for software for organizing and managing collaborative work across distances and providing an efficient way of managing the team's digital output.

G. Skills for Working with E-Texts

The main areas of knowledge and skills recognized by the participants were identifying and finding databases, searching efficiently, assessing the accuracy and authenticity of retrieved sources, and using *EndNote*. The participants indicated that other minor aspects of use needed clarification too. None of the participants said that they had been systematically trained in using e-texts and other electronic sources. Some participants referred to a number of available workshops and training sessions. Even participants who attended these sessions or felt confident about their skills thought that there were a number of areas where training was needed. They indicated a need for an overview of different aspects of retrieval and use of e-texts.

Complex skills in working with mixed or multimedia were acquired either because researchers learned them on their own or because they happened to have previous education in dealing with electronic media. According to participant 2/2, good combinations of skills happened accidentally rather than being fostered by formal training. Participant 15/1 explored different ways of working with electronic media and wanted to see a new generation being formally prepared for new types of intellectual and artistic work:

> This is something that I think we can do in an educational context because we can start teaching new media writers, artists, theorists etc., a kind of critical media literacy that engages them in such a way that they learn to improve various stages of development so that they can become, I don't know, better performers, you might say, better performers of writing.

In their discussion of aspects in the electronic environment that aid interactions with e-texts, participants recognized the availability of a range of sources, different representations of the same text (e.g., image and transcription), access to e-texts at any time anywhere, speed, flexible searching and browsing, as well as reliable networks and equipment, as helpful.

VII. Implications for Academic Libraries

Research libraries for years have balanced their role as a campus digital leader with being a book custodian and a patron of traditional scholarship.

Considering the importance of traditional collections for research in the humanities, library support of humanists can be seen as an exemplar of how libraries have to negotiate constantly changing and often opposing demands. By the same token, developments in the humanities research suggest future directions for academic libraries.

Trends indicate that traditional divisions on which information provision had been based are becoming increasingly irrelevant and that libraries will have to continue to work on bringing together previously separate knowledge spheres. The merging boundaries between academic and nonacademic sources will continue and research libraries will have to reconsider how they identify and evaluate information sources they add to their traditional and electronic collections. New communication and social technologies make it increasingly difficult to follow the distinction between information and communication, and therefore, librarians will have to think of innovative ways of bringing the two together within the library as well as aiding information discovery and use anywhere else where research takes place.

Curation of digital outputs and collections is imposing new demands on libraries as custodians. Scholars' current inclination to publish results of their research in digital forms, with blurred distinctions between creative and academic work, will continue and eventually pose significant demands on libraries to support, preserve, and make accessible new formats of academic publications. At the moment, libraries do not have ready answers to questions about preserving multimedia works, especially those of changeable nature.

Scholars' thematic collections and databases require different forms of support, which do not exist at most of today's libraries. Few scholars in the study mentioned a need for assistance from the library in developing their digital collections and databases, but it seems that they would benefit from advice how to work with different electronic formats, digitize materials, and organize and maintain their digital collections.

Some scholars' digital collections are unique and could be useful to other researchers. For example, an extensive textual database, developed by a biographer in the study, contains transcriptions of documents, interviews, and various recordings that need to be preserved and maintained beyond the span of the particular project. Libraries and archives need to develop practices and policies to curate and preserve researchers' collections. They also have to deal with ethical issues involved in handling and making accessible data from research projects, such as the researcher's commitment to the privacy of study participants. Incentives for researchers to give their digital collections to libraries are necessary. Long-term benefits of supporting researchers' collections would be significant for libraries, as well as for scholars as producers and future users of these collections.

Discussions are needed about skills and knowledge in a range of areas where self-directed learning was the most common, although not the most efficient. It is important that university researchers, administrators, and librarians systematically address the development of digital skills. Highly specialized information professionals are needed to work with researchers on selecting and even developing relevant digital tools. In most cases, multidisciplinary teams, including IT staff, are necessary for sophisticated technological applications in research. In such instances, information professionals are in the best position to take on the role of "translator," enabling interdisciplinary communication, particularly between technical staff and humanists.

Because most scholars visit the library less often than in the past, online information services are a promising area for future development. Considering the effectiveness of communication and social technologies, in addition to the increasing reliance on computers and multimedia, library research services would benefit from exploring nonverbal forms of support and collaborative arrangements within the institution and across multiple libraries.

Many researchers look to their university library for advice and guidance when it comes to digital matters, even when they do not welcome digital changes. The digital age has been often compared with the Middle Ages— from "a return to the Dark Ages" and "the potential disappearance of a thousand years of intellectual achievement" (Edmond and Schreibman, 2010, p. 1) to digital refashioning of scriptoria with their intensive scholarly and artistic work on manuscripts. However, in various versions of the Middle Ages metaphor, one key detail is missing—Librarian-Scholar. It is time to refashion the role, which academics in the humanities need and respect the most—the role of a partner on research teams and in intellectual dialogues— the Librarian-iScholar.

References

American Council of Learned Societies (2006). Our Cultural Commonwealth: The Report of the American Council of Learned Societies' Commission on Cyberinfrastructure for Humanities and Social Sciences. Washington, DC.

Andersen, D. L. (1996). *User Driven Technologies: Assessing the Information Needs of History Faculty as a Special User Population*. Unpublished doctoral thesis, State University of New York at Albany, Albany, NY.

Baruchson-Arbib, S., and Bronstein, J. (2007). Humanists as information users in the digital age: The case of Jewish studies scholars in Israel. *Journal of the American Society for Information Science and Technology* **58**(14), 2269–2279.

Bates, M. J. (1989). The design of browsing and berrypicking techniques for the online search interface. *Online Review* **13**(5), 407–424.

Bolter, J. D. (2001). *Writing Space : Computers, Hypertext, and the Remediation of Print*, 2nd ed. Lawrence Erlbaum Associates, Mahwah, NJ.

Brockman, W. S., Neumann, L., Palmer, C. L., and Tidline, T. J. (2001). Scholarly work in the humanities and the evolving information environment (No. 104). Digital Library Foundation, Council on Library and Information Resources, Washington, DC.

Brogan, M. L., and Rentfrow, D. (2005). *A Kaleidoscope of Digital American Literature*. Digital Library Federation, Council on Library and Information Resources, Washington, DC.

Brown, G. J. (2001). Beyond print: Reading digitally. *Library Hi Tech* **19**(4), 390–399.

Brown, C. D. (2002). Straddling the humanities and social sciences: The research process of music scholars. *Library & Information Science Research* **24**(1), 73–94.

Buchanan, G., Cunningham, S. J., Blandford, A., Rimmer, J., and Warwick, C. (2005, September). Information Seeking by Humanities Scholars. *Proceedings of Research and Advanced Technology for Digital Libraries*. Vienna, Austria, 9th European Conference, ECDL.

Byström, K., and Hansen, P. (2005). Conceptual framework for tasks in information studies. *Journal of the American Society for Information Science and Technology* **56**(10), 1050–1061.

Case, D. O. (1991). The collection and use of information by some American historians: A study of motives and methods. *Library Quarterly* **61**(1), 61–82.

Cherry, J. M., and Duff, W. M. (2002). Studying digital library users over time: A follow-up survey of Early Canadiana Online. *Information Research* 7(2). Available at http://informationr.net/ir/7-2/paper123.html.

Chu, C. M. (1999). Literary critics at work and their information needs: A research-phases model. *Library & Information Science Research* **21**(2), 247–273.

Dalton, M. S., and Charnigo, L. (2004). Historians and their information sources. *College & Research Libraries* **65**(5), 400–425.

Davies, C. (1997). Organizational influences on the university electronic library. *Information Processing & Management* **33**(3), 377–392.

de Tiratel, S. R. (2000). Accessing information use by humanists and social scientists: A study at the Universidad de Buenos Aires, Argentina. *The Journal of Academic Librarianship* **26**(5), 346–354.

Digital Library Federation (2002). Dimensions and use of the scholarly information environment: A data set assembled by the Digital Library Federation and Outsell, Inc. Council on Library and Information Resources, Washington, DC.

Duff, W. M., and Cherry, J. M. (2000). Use of historical documents in a digital world: Comparisons with original materials and microfiche. [Research]. *Information Research* 6(1). Available at http://informationr.net/ir/6-1/paper86.html.

Edmond, J., Schreibman, S. (2010, May 14). *European elephants in the Room (Are They the Ones with the Bigger or Smaller Ears?)*. Retrieved from http://cnx.org/content/m34307/1.2/

Education for Change, SIRU University of Brighton, & The Research Partnership (2002). *Researchers' Use of Libraries and Other Information Sources: Current Patterns and Future Trends: Final Report*. Higher Education Funding Council for England (HEFCE), Bristol, England.

Ellis, D. (1993). Modeling the information-seeking patterns of academic researchers: A grounded theory approach. *Library Quarterly* 63(4), 469–486.

Ellis, D., and Oldman, H. (2005). The English literature researcher in the age of the Internet. *Journal of Information Science* 31(1), 29–36.

Flanders, J. (1998). Scholarly research and electronic resources. *WWP Newsletter* 4(2) Available at http://www.brown.edu/project/newsletter/vol04num02/scholarly 042.html.

Foster, A. (2004). A nonlinear model of information-seeking behavior. *Journal of the American Society for Information Science and Technology* 55(3), 228–237.

Gardiner, D., McMenemy, D., and Chowdhury, G. (2006). A snapshot of information use patterns of academics in British universities. *Online Information Review* 30(4), 341–359.

Gilmore, M. B., and Case, D. O. (1992). Historians, books, computers, and the library. *Library Trends* 40(4), 667–686.

Glaser, B. G. (1998). *Doing Grounded Theory: Issues and Discussions*. Sociology Press, Mill Valley, CA.

Hayles, K. N. (2003). Translating media: why we should rethink textuality. *The Yale Journal of Criticism* 16(2), 263–290.

Hillesund, T. (2010). Digital reading spaces: How expert readers handle books, the Web and electronic paper. *First Monday* 15(4–5) Available at http://firstmonday. org/htbin/cgiwrap/bin/ojs/index.php/fm/issue/view/309.

Hockey, S. (2000). *Electronic Texts in the Humanities: Principles and Practice*. Oxford University Press, Oxford, England.

Hockey, S. (2004). The history of humanities computing. In *A Companion to Digital Humanities* (S. Schreibman, R. Siemens and J. Unsworth, eds.). Blackwell, Malden, MA.

Ide, N., and Veronis, J. (eds.) (1995). *Text Encoding Initiative: Background and Context*. Kluwer, Dordecht, Amsterdam, Netherlands.

Kress, G. R., and Van Leeuwen, T. (2001). *Multimodal Discourse: The Modes and Media of Contemporary Communication*. Oxford University Press, London, England; New York.

Kristeva, J. (1980). Word, dialogue, and novel. In *Desire in Language: A Semiotic Approach to Literature and Art* (L. S. Roudiez, ed.), pp. 64–91, Columbia University Press, New York.

Levine-Clark, M. (2007). Electronic books and the humanities: A survey. *Collection Building* 26(1), 7–14.

Liu, Z. (2005). Reading behavior in the digital environment: Changes in reading behavior over the past ten years. *Journal of Documentation* 61(6), 700–712.

Massey-Burzio, V. (1999). The rush to technology: A view from the humanities. *Library Trends* 47(4), 620–639.

McGann, J. (1998). Textual scholarship, textual theory, and the uses of electronic tools: A brief report on current undertakings. *Victorian Studies* 41(4), 609–619.

McKechnie, L., Julien, H., Pecoskie, J. L., and Dixon, C. M. (2006). The presentation of the information user in reports of information behaviour research. *Information Research* 12(1).

Noguchi, S. (2001). *Assessing Users and Uses of Electronic Text: In Case of the Japanese Text Initiative, Japanese Classics Electronic Text on the World Wide Web.* Unpublished doctoral dissertation, University of Pittsburgh, Pittsburth, PA.

Olsen, M. (1993). Signs, symbols and discourses: A new direction for computer-aided literature studies. *Computers and the Humanities* 27(5–6), 309–314.

Palmer, C. L. (2005). Scholarly work and the shaping of digital access. *Journal of the American Society for Information Science and Technology* 56(11), 1140–1153.

Palmer, C. L., and Cragin, M. H. (2008). Scholarship and disciplinary practices. *Annual Review of Information Science and Technology* 42(1), 163–212.

Palmer, C. L., and Neumann, L. J. (2002). The information work of interdisciplinary humanities scholars: Exploration and translation. *Library Quarterly* 72(1), 85–117.

Rastier, F. (1997). Meaning and textuality. (F. Collins and P. Perron, Trans.), University of Toronto Press, Toronto, Canada.

Ricoeur, P. (1991). *A Ricoeur Reader: Reflection and Imagination.* Harvester Wheatsheaf, New York.

Ruhleder, K. (1995). Reconstructing artifacts, reconstructing work: From textual edition to on-line databank. *Science, Technology & Human Values* 20(1), 39–64.

RULOIS (2002). See Education for Change Ltd.

Schonfeld, R. C., and Housewright, R. (2010). *Faculty Survey 2009: Key Strategic Insights for Libraries, Publishers, and Societies.* ITHAKA S+R, New York.

Smith, H. (2004). Cursors and crystal balls: Digital technologies and the futures of writing. *Text: The Journal of the Australian Association of Writing Programs* 8(2).

Stefans, B. (2010). *The Dreamlife of Letters.* Retrieved from http://collection.eliterature.org/1/works/stefans__the_dreamlife_of_letters.html.

Stieg, M. F. (1981). The information of needs of historians. *College & Research Libraries* 38(4), 549–560.

Stone, S. (1982). Humanities scholars: Information needs and uses. *Journal of Documentation* 38(4), 292–313.

Strauss, A. L. (1987). *Qualitative Analysis for Social Scientists.* Cambridge University Press, Cambridge, MA; New York.

Strauss, A., and Corbin, J. (1998a). *Basics of Qualitative Research: Techniques and Procedures for Developing Grounded Theory,* 2nd ed. Sage, Thousand Oaks, CA.

Strauss, A., and Corbin, J. (1998b). Grounded theory methodology: An overview. In *Strategies of Qualitative Inquiry (Handbook of Qualitative Research, Paperback. ed.)* (N. K. Denzin and Y. S. Lincoln, eds.), pp. 158–183, Sage, Thousand Oaks, CA.

Sukovic, S. (2008). Convergent flows: Humanities scholars and their interactions with electronic texts. *Library Quarterly* 78(3), 263–284.

Sukovic, S. (2009). References to e-texts in academic publications. *Journal of Documentation* 65(6), 997–1015.

Summerfield, M., Mandel, C., and Kantor, P. (2000). The potential for scholarly online books: Views from the Columbia University Online Books Evaluation Project. *Publishing Research Quarterly* 16(3), 39–52.

The British Academy (2005). *E-resources for Research in the Humanities and Social Sciences: A British Academy Policy Review.* The British Academy, London, England.

Tibbo, H. R. (2003). Primarily history in America: How U.S. historians search for primary materials at the dawn of the digital age. *The American Archivist* 66(Spring/Summer), 9–50.

Unsworth, J. (2000, May). Scholarly primitives: What methods do humanities researchers have in common, and how might our tools reflect this? *Symposium on Humanities Computing: Formal Methods, Experimental Practice*, King's College, London, England.

Uva, P. A. (1977). *Information-Gathering Habits of Academic Historians: Report of the Pilot Study*. SUNY Upstate Medical Center, Syracuse, NY.

Wiberley, S. E., and Jones, W. G. (2000). Time and technology: A decade-long look at humanists' use of electronic information technology. *College & Research Libraries* 61(5), 421–431.

Wisneski, R. (2005). Investigating the research practices and library needs of contingent, tenure-track, and tenured English faculty. *The Journal of Academic Librarianship* 31(2), 119–133.

Author Index

Subject Index

Noble and less noble traditions
  of education and training in
    Australia, 105
    Australian educational structures,
      emergence of, 108–120
    background, 107–108
    concept of difference, re-assessing,
      120–125
    contemporary LIS education,
      125–126
Nvivo, 140

Objective environment, 14
Online access, 192
Operational Research (OR)
  application to libraries, 7–11
  definition of, 4
  new paradigms in, 13–15
  origins of, 4–6
  traditional paradigm of, 6
  See also Library operational research
    (Library OR)
Organisational/structural capital, 37,
  40–41
  indicative intangible assets for, 39

Pala reservation, 85
Palomar Community College, 87, 91
  library, 92
Paraprofessional, meaning of, 119
Pauma Tribal Library, 84, 86, 91–93, 96
Perseus Digital Library, 182
Phoenix, Joan, 89
Practitioner/modeler interaction,
  15–16, 22
Preparation stage, in research, 169,
  171, 172
Problem structuring methods (PSMs),
  14–15, 22, 23, 24, 25
Projects, e-texts uses in, 137, 170–171,
  180–181, 184
Provision of insights, 11, 22
Public Library Administrators'
  Certificate, 67

Published models, utility of, 13
Puccio, Sandy, 93

Queensland Institute of Technology,
  119
Queuing theory, 7, 9

Registered Training Organisations
  (RTOs), 107–108
Relational capital, 36, 37, 41–42
  indicative intangible assets for, 39
Research process, e-texts in, 168, 188–189
  in humanities, 168–169
  in projects, 185
  in research stages, 171–175
  in study, 169–171
  uses, 175–184
Research projects, uses of, 175
Results stage, 170, 171
Review of Australian Higher Educations, 121
Routine decision support, 8–9
Royal Air Force, defensive successes of, 5
Royal Melbourne Institute of Technology
  (RMIT), 108, 109, 110, 119

San Diego County, 75
  Indians of, 77
  Native American population, 76
  Spanish immigrants in, 78
  success factors in, 94
    history and ongoing saga of, 96–97
    research opportunities, 97
    success levels in, 96
  tribal libraries, 86
    Barona reservation, 87–88
    Barona Tribal Library, 88–90
    history of, 81–86
    Kumeyaay Community College
      Archives Library, 90–91
    Pauma Tribal Library, 91–93
    Santa Ysabel Tribal Library, 93–94
San Diego County Library's (SDCL)
  Outreach Division, 82–83, 85,
    86, 89, 91

San Jose State University (SJSU), 84, 88
Santa Ysabel tribal library, 77, 86,
　93–94, 96
Scholarly primitives, 146
Searching the Internet, 147
Semiotic exchange, 141
SGML (Standard Generalized Markup
　Language), 134
Shipek, Florence, 90, 91
Simulation model, 4, 10
　and inventory control theory, 7
Social environment, 14
Social Responsibilities Round Table, 80
Soft paradigm, 14
Speed, of access and retrieval, 158
Student learning experience and library,
　23–24
Summer Reading Program, 42, 83, 89,
　93
Sycuan Council, 90
Sycuan Education Department, 91
Sycuan Learning Center, 91
Sycuan reservation, 90

Tangible assets, 34, 35–36, 45
Tangible investments, 35
Task Force, formation of, 80
Technical and Further Education
　Colleges (TAFE), 107, 110
TEI (Text Encoding Initiative), 134
Termination Act, 79
Text, 140
Textuality, 140
Tierra Del Sol Census and Needs
　Assessment, 84
Tierra Del Sol project, 97
Tierra Del Sol web site, 87
Townley, Charles, 80
Traditional management courses, focus
　of, 61–62
Traditional OR models, 12, 20–21, 22
Traditional paradigm, 6, 14, 18
Training and Assistance for Indian Library
　Services (TRAILS) project, 81

Training Packages, 111, 124
Transforming Australian Education, 121
*Transforming Australia's Higher
　Education System report*, 125
Tribal College, establishment of, 90
Tribal heritage, preserving, 78–81
Tribal Libraries Project, 84
Tribal library, 83, 94, 95
　definition of, 77
Tribal Library Boot Camp, 85, 97
Tribal Library Census and Needs
　Assessment, 84
Tribal Library Group, 89
21st-century academic library, 13,
　16–18
21st-Century Grant, Laura Bush
　Librarians for, 81

UCLA, 92
U.S. Department of Education's Office
　of Educational Research and
　Improvement, 80–81

Valley Center Branch, of SDCL, 92,
　93
Value-Added Intellectual Coefficient
　(VAIC™), 44
VET training, 124
Victoria's Technical Division, 120
Vignault, Karen, 93, 94
Virtual help desks (VHD), 41
Vocational education (VE) sector, 107,
　111, 114, 116, 120, 121, 122
　versus higher education, 112

Ward, Jennifer, 88, 89, 90
Web surfing, 17, 147–148, 149, 150
White House Pre-Conference, 80
World of library administrators, 52
World Wide Web, 134, 159
Writing and dissemination stage, in
　research, 169–170

Zagarella, Jeremy, 92, 93